Forgotten and Forsaken by God (Lam 5:19–20)

Forgotten and Forsaken by God (Lam 5:19–20)

The Community in Pain in Lamentations and Related Old Testament Texts

LINA RONG

◥PICKWICK *Publications* · Eugene, Oregon

FORGOTTEN AND FORSAKEN BY GOD (LAM 5:19-20)
The Community in Pain in Lamentations and Related Old Testament Texts

Copyright © 2013 Lina Rong. All rights reserved. Except for brief quotations in critical publications or reviews, no part of this book may be reproduced in any manner without prior written permission from the publisher. Write: Permissions, Wipf and Stock Publishers, 199 W. 8th Ave., Suite 3, Eugene, OR 97401.

Pickwick Publications
An Imprint of Wipf and Stock Publishers
199 W. 8th Ave., Suite 3
Eugene, OR 97401

www.wipfandstock.com

ISBN 13: 978-1-62032-590-2

Cataloguing-in-Publication data:

Rong, Lina.

Forgotten and forsaken by God (Lam 5:19–20) : the community in pain in Lamentations and related Old Testament texts / Lina Rong ; with a foreword by Christopher Begg.

xvi + 208 pp. ; 23 cm. Includes bibliographical references.

ISBN 13: 978-1-62032-590-2

1. Bible—O.T.—Lamentations—Criticism, interpretation, etc. 2. Suffering—Religious aspects. I. Begg, Christopher. II. Title.

BS1535.53 R100 2013

When indicated, Scripture comes from the New Revised Standard Version Bible, copyright 1989, Division of Christian Education of the National Council of the Churches of Christ in the United States of America. Used by permission. All rights reserved.

When indicated, Scripture comes from the Revised Standard Version of the Bible, copyright 1952 [2nd edition, 1971] by the Division of Christian Education of the National Council of the Churches of Christ in the United States of America. Used by permission. All rights reserved.

Manufactured in the U.S.A.

This book is dedicated to my beloved mother,
Mrs. Chunling Jin Rong,
who has been diagnosed with lung cancer
while I am preparing this manuscript.
My cries go to God day and night.
May God sustain her and heal her.

Contents

List of Abbreviations | viii
Foreword | xi
Acknowledgments | xiii

1 History of Research and Overview of the Book | 1
2 Acrostic in Lamentations | 29
3 Exegesis of Lamentations | 53
4 Mood Change in Lamentations and Related OT Texts | 113
5 Admission of Guilt in Lamentations and Related OT Laments | 138
6 Significance of Lamentations for Suffering Individuals and Communities | 166
7 Review of Findings and Possibilities for Further Study | 190

Bibliography | 197

Abbreviations

AOTC	Abingdon Old Testament Commentaries
AB	Anchor Bible
ABD	*Anchor Bible Dictionary*. Edited by D. N. Freedman. 6 vols. New York, 1992
ArBib	The Aramaic Bible
ABR	*Australian Biblical Review*
BCOT	Baker Commentary of the Old Testament
BEATAJ	Beiträge zur Erforschung des Alten Testaments und des antiken Judentum
BETL	Bibliotheca ephemeridum theologicarum lovaniensium
Bib	*Biblica*
BibOr	Biblica et Orientalia
BA	*Biblical Archaeologist*
BHQ	*Biblia Hebraica Quinta*
BHS	*Biblica Hebraica Stuttgartensia*
BibInt	*Biblical Interpretation*
BIS	Biblical Interpretation Series
BR	*Biblical Research*
BSac	*Bibliotheca Sacra*
BZ	*Biblische Zeitschrift*
BDB	F. Brown, S. R. Driver, and C. A. Briggs, *A Hebrew and English Lexicon of the Old Testament*. Oxford, 1907
CBQ	*Catholic Biblical Quarterly*
CBQMS	Catholic Biblical Quarterly Monograph Series
CBR	*Currents in Biblical Research*

Abbreviations

DJD	Discoveries in the Judaean Desert
ErIsr	*Eretz Israel*
EvJ	*Evangelical Journal*
FOTL	The Forms of the Old Testament Literature
HAT	Handbuch zum Alten Testament
HTR	*Harvard Theological Review*
HAR	*Hebrew Annual Review*
HALOT	Ludwig Koehler et al. *The Hebrew and Aramaic Lexicon of the Old Testament*. Translated by and edited under the supervision of M. E. J. Richardson. 5 vols. Leiden, 1994–2000
HS	*Hebrew Studies*
HUCA	*Hebrew Union College Annual*
HCOT	Historical Commentary on the Old Testament
HTIBS	Historic Texts and Interpreters in Biblical Scholarship
HBT	*Horizons in Biblical Theology*
HTKAT	Herders Theologischer Kommentar zum Alten Testament
ICC	International Critical Commentary
Int	*Interpretation*
IBS	*Irish Biblical Studies*
IDB	*The Interpreter's Dictionary of the Bible*. Edited by G. A. Buttrick. 4 vols. Nashville, 1962
JAOS	*Journal of the American Oriental Society*
JBL	*Journal of Biblical Literature*
JANES	*Journal of the Ancient Near Eastern Society*
JFSR	*Journal of Feminist Studies in Religion*
JHS	*Journal of Hebrew Scriptures*
JNSL	*Journal of Northwest Semitic Languages*
JR	*Journal of Religion*
JSem	*Journal for Semitics*
JSOT	*Journal for the Study of the Old Testament*
JSOTSup	Journal for the Study of the Old Testament Supplement Series
KAT	Kommentar zum Alten Testament
LHBOTS	Library of Hebrew Bible/Old Testament Studies

Abbreviations

NCBC	New Century Bible Commentary
NIBC	New International Bible Commentary, Old Testament Series
OTE	*Old Testament Essays*
OTG	Old Testament Guides
OTL	The Old Testament Library
OBT	Overtures to Biblical Theology
PSB	*Princeton Seminary Bulletin*
ResQ	*Restoration Quarterly*
RevExp	*Review & Expositor*
RB	*Revue Biblique*
SJOT	*Scandinavian Journal of the Old Testament*
SemeiaSt	Semeia Studies
SBL	Society of Biblical Literature
SBLABib	Society of Biblical Literature Academia Biblica
SBLDS	Society of Biblical Literature Dissertation Series
SBLEJL	Society of Biblical Literature Early Judaism and its Literature
SBLMS	Society of Biblical Literature Monograph Series
SBLSP	Society of Biblical Literature Seminar Papers
SemSt	Society of Biblical Literature Semeia Studies
SBT	Studies in Biblical Theology
SBB	Stuttgarter biblische Beiträige
SubBi	Subsidia biblica
VTG	Vetus Testamentum Graecum
VTSup	Supplements to Vetus Testamentum
TDOT	*Theological Dictionary of the Old Testament,* Edited by G. J. Botterweck and H. Ringgren. Translated by J. T. Willis et al. 15 vols. Grand Rapids, 1974–
TThSt	Trierer Theologische Studien
VT	*Vetus Testamentum*
WMANT	Wissenschaftliche Monographien zum Alten und Neuten Testament
WBC	Word Biblical Commentary
ZAW	*Zeitschrift für die alttestamentliche Wissenschaft*

Foreword

IN THE CHRISTIAN BIBLE, the short book of Lamentations with its five chapters is nestled between two much longer books, i.e. Jeremiah (52 chapters) and Ezekiel (48 chapters). Therefore, Lamentations might well be overlooked by the casual Bible reader. Lamentations is likewise a book to which Christians get only limited liturgical exposure. In Roman Catholicism, e.g., the book was featured above all at the Tenebrae ("Shadows") service of the pre-Vatican II Holy Week liturgies, but that service was largely dropped in the post-conciliar period (although more recently it seems to making something of a comeback). Also until rather recently, scholarship on Lamentations mostly concentrated on rather limited and technical questions, focusing on, e.g., the book's text-critical problems, authorship, unity, and dating.

In the last three decades, however, in the wake of the Holocaust and other well-publicized horrors, interdisciplinary study of the grieving process, and recurrent calls for a greater place for lament in the (Christian) liturgy, Lamentations has become the beneficiary of heightened scholarly attention. In this development, the book has, moreover, been approached from a variety of newer perspectives, synchronic, literary, intra- and intertextual, and psychological. Dr. Lina Rong's work, a revision of her PhD dissertation defended at Catholic University in the spring of 2012 under my direction, both reflects and makes its own contribution to these newer trends in Lamentations scholarship. In particular, Dr. Rong provides here a "final form" study of the book that devotes special attention to the nature and function of the oft-neglected chapter 5, which, unlike the preceding chapters, does not make use of the alphabetic acrostic device and which serves to end the book on a note of renewed uncertainty and questioning after the seeming shift to trust and affirmation in chapter 3. In addition, Dr. Rong's work—in this too reflecting a widespread contemporary scholarly trend—seeks to bring Lamentations into a dialogue with other comparable texts of the Psalter and the Prophetic Corpus, thereby allowing the specificity of its laments to emerge more sharply.

More generally, Dr. Rong also highlights the (as yet underutilized) pastoral and liturgical resource that Lamentations represents, with, e.g., its scriptural warrant for believers' remaining in lament as long as their circumstances require this and resisting the pressure to move on too quickly to praise and confidence. In so doing, Dr. Rong makes discreet reference to the Chinese context from which she comes and to which she is now returning, and Lamentations' particular relevance for that context.

It is a great pleasure for me to write this brief foreword to the published version of Dr. Rong's multi-faceted and well-written dissertation. I wish her God's blessings as she returns to China to undertake the important work of promoting knowledge and appreciation of the Bible among her compatriots.

Professor Christopher Begg, PhD, STD
Catholic University of America
August 2012

Acknowledgments

MY EXPERIENCES AS A doctoral student in the United States have been enriching, fruitful, and unforgettable. I thank all of my professors, friends, and classmates who have been accompanying me during these five years of my studying here.

I am grateful to the Catholic University of America for granting me full tuition scholarships, and to the Maryknoll Society for covering my living expenses and health insurance.

My heartfelt gratitude goes to Fr. Christopher Begg, my dissertation director, a fine scholar, a caring pastor, and an accommodating mentor with a sharp mind and quick wits. He constantly amazes me with his prompt replies, thorough reviews, erudition, and gentleness. My sincere thanks go to Dr. Robert Miller and Dr. David Bosworth, my two readers, for their valuable suggestions and timely reviews. I thank Dr. Miller for providing me various information in a wider academic field and possibilities for further research. I owe a lot to Dr. Bosworth, a lover and researcher of lament literature himself, who generously lent me his article even before its publication and forwarded me important data for my research; a conversation with him always inspires me.

I thank Fr. Frank Matera, for his listening to my struggles, for his concern, encouragement, and support.

I am extremely grateful to Fr. Larry Lewis, MM, the director of the Maryknoll China Project, to Anli Lin Hsu, his executive assistant, to Sr. Janet Carroll, MM, for their constant encouragement, concern, care, and support.

I thank Tom McGuire, who showed great interest in my research from the very beginning, for sharing with me his own struggles in suffering and those of others, and for the inspirations he brings me.

Finally, my thanks go to my religious community and dear Sisters in China, for their unconditional support and prayers; to my beloved parents, who have been continuously journeying with me; to the newest

Acknowledgments

member of our family, my one-year-old nephew, Moses, who has to live in hiding, as the biblical Moses first did, due to the one-child policy in China; to my brother and sister-in-law, who share with me their real-life struggles in choosing life.

1

History of Research and Overview of the Book

INTRODUCTION

LAMENTATIONS IS A UNIQUE and complex book. It is unique since it is a very tiny book in the Hebrew Bible, composed of only 154 verses, (mostly) following a strict alphabetic acrostic format, yet, it deals with the most painful subject matter in Jewish history: the ruin of Judah and the destruction of the temple. Its poignant poetry seems timeless, holding meaning for all suffering people across the ages.[1] Lamentations is also complex. It applies various literary devices, including metaphors, images, play of sounds and words, shifts of voices and personae. It also incorporates a variety of literary genres such as individual and communal laments, lament over a fallen city, and funeral dirge.[2]

As a whole, Lamentations lacks plot and argumentative structure.[3] Its five poems are all responding to a national tragedy, but nowhere does the poet(s) try to tell a story. Neither is there a clear movement from grief to

---

1. Cohen says in his Introduction to the Midrash on Lamentations that the overwhelming catastrophe narrated in Lamentations, which involved the downfall of temple and state, made a profound impression that lingered in the hearts of Jews throughout the succeeding generations. See Freedman and Simon, *Midrash Rabbah* vol. 7, *Deuteronomy; Lamentations*, vii.

2. Westermann, *Lamentations*, 83 notes the unique combination of lament with the dirge in Lamentations, a phenomenon that occurs only here in the Old Testament.

3. A number of scholars have called attention to this feature. See Dobbs-Allsopp, *Lamentations*, 13; Morse, "Lamentations Project," 113–27, here 115.

Forgotten and Forsaken by God (Lam 5:19–20)

hope, as one might find in the lament psalms. Lamentations gazes at the destruction and ruin, digs into it and probes it from various perspectives. The book ends on a very uncertain note, wondering if indeed God has forgotten and forsaken God's people forever.

Scholars have paid much attention to this tiny book in recent years. Their various interests and inquiries range from comparisons between Lamentations and Mesopotamian lament literature, trying to define the main purpose of Lamentations as either conveying a message of hope in suffering or expressing pain, examining the dialogic interaction between Lamentations and prophetic literature, to questions about unity of the book and the connection between structure and content in Lamentations. This chapter will first provide a general picture of the text and versions of Lamentations, then a history of research on the above (and other) issues, and finally lay out the approach this book is going to take.

TEXT AND VERSIONS OF LAMENTATIONS

It has been generally recognized that the Hebrew text of Lamentations is well preserved, and accordingly it is taken as the base text by most commentators.[4] R. B. Salters lists a number of reasons for this general recognition: first, there are not so many places that the Hebrew is unintelligible and where the exegete is driven to despair; second, the alphabetic acrostic pattern is sustained throughout chapters 1–4 while chapter 5 is "alphabetic" in that it consists of 22 lines; and third, the poetic 3+2 rhythm chosen by the poet in chapters 1–4 is maintained for the most part.[5] D. R. Hillers points out that the advantage of the well-preserved MT Lamentations is to some extant balanced by a corresponding disadvantage: the ancient translations offer relatively little help at those places in which the received Hebrew text may be suspected of being corrupt. Under these circumstances, commentators have to rely more on conjectural emendation than might otherwise be necessary.[6]

The Greek translation (LXX) of Lamentations is based on a Hebrew text that must have been identical with the MT.[7] The LXX is on the whole quite literal, "in several passages even extremely slavish," as Albrektson

---

4. For an evaluation and comparison of texts and versions of Lamentations, see Albrektson, *Studies*, 208–13; Hillers, *Lamentations*, 39–48; House, *Song of Songs; Lamentations*, 281–83; Salters, *Lamentations*, 21–26.

5. Salters, *Lamentations*, 22.

6. Hillers, *Lamentations*, 39.

7. I will use the Greek text of Ziegler, *Threni*, 467–94, in this book.

puts it.⁸ The Greek translator does not attempt to render the meaning of the book's Hebrew sentences, but "resorts to an atomistic and mechanical translation of the details of the Hebrew text."⁹ Albrektson holds that while the LXX translation of Lamentations is not a good one, it is nonetheless valuable for textual criticism since "its literal character often allows us to establish with tolerable certainty the underlying Hebrew text."¹⁰

The Old Latin version of Lamentations is clearly a rendering of the Greek, Salters notes, and exists only in fragmentary form.¹¹ The Vulgate usually agrees with the consonantal text of MT, although Jerome's presupposed vocalization is occasionally different and he sometimes forces a christological interpretation upon the text.

The Syriac translation of Lamentations is like the LXX; it is based on a Hebrew text almost identical with the MT of which it is a faithful translation. It has some minor additions and strives for clarity and intelligibility.¹²

The Aramaic version of Lamentations is not a mere translation.¹³ According to É. Levine, "the *targum* has virtually rewritten the book," whose perspective it expands to include the fall of the Second Temple as well.¹⁴ The *targum* emendates, elaborates and paraphrases the original text; it is "part translation, part commentary, part polemical tract, and part inspirational book."¹⁵ It thus is of value not only for textual criticism of Lamentations, but also for understanding ancient Jewish liturgy long after the destruction of 587 BCE.

The Dead Sea Scrolls contain small portions of Lamentations.¹⁶ According to A. Berlin, these scrolls provide ample evidence that Lamentations

---

8. Albrektson, *Studies*, 208.

9. Ibid., 209–10.

10. Ibid., 210.

11. Salters, *Lamentations*, 26.

12. I will use the Ambrosianus edition of the Syriac text, which is printed unchanged in Albrektson, *Studies*, 41–54.

13. I will use the Aramaic text of Sperber, *Bible in Aramaic*, 4A:142–49 (*Targum to Lamentations*).

14. Levine, *Aramaic Version of Lamentations*, 9.

15. House, *Song of Songs; Lamentations*, 283.

16. Four fragments of the book of Lamentations have been found among the Dead Sea Scrolls: 3QLam (3Q3, Baillet et al., *Les "petites grottes" de Qumran*, 1:95) contains fragments of Lam 1:10–12 and 3:53–62; 4QLam (4Q111, Ulrich et al., *Psalms to Chronicles*, 229–37) contains Lam 1:1–17, the beginning of 1:18 and a very small fragment of 2:5; 5QLama (5Q6, Baillet et al., *Les "petites grottes" de Qumran* 1:174–77) contains Lam 4:5–8, 11–16, 19–22; 5:3–13, 16–17, and 5QLamb (5Q7, Baillet et al., *Les "petites grottes" de Qumran*, 1:178–79) comprises Lam 4:17–19.

was regarded as "canonical" in the Qumran community.[17] They also offer clear evidence that Lamentations was used in the community's liturgy, although the occasion for its use remains unclear.[18] At Qumran, Lamentations was not just copied from an old scroll to a new one, as Hillers notes, but rather, "was recited, remembered, commented, used—and changed—by a living community."[19]

RELATIONSHIP BETWEEN LAMENTATIONS AND MESOPOTAMIAN LAMENTS[20]

Scholars have defined three distinct but related types of laments in the Mesopotamian lament literature: the five Sumerian city laments, *eršemma*, and *balag*. The five Sumerian city laments are the Lamentation over the Destruction of Ur, the Lamentations over the Destruction of Sumer and Ur, the Nippur Lament, the Eridu Lament and the Uruk Lament.[21] These are the earliest Mesopotamian laments; the usually accepted *terminus ante quem* for them is 1925 BCE.[22] The *Eršemma* composition and the *balag* lament emerged nearly simultaneously in the Old Babylonian era and were

---

17. Berlin, *Lamentations*, 36–37.

18. House (*Song of Songs; Lamentations*, 303) affirms that Lamentations was almost certainly used in worship from its time of origin and has had a long history of liturgical usage.

19. Hillers (*Lamentations*, 41–48, here 41) treats 4QLam extensively in an excursus.

20. Works comparing Lamentations and Sumerian city laments are the following (in chronological order): McDaniel, "Alleged Sumerian Influence," 198–209; Kramer, "Lamentation over the Destruction of Nippur," 89–93; Gwaltney, "Biblical Book of Lamentations," 191–211; Walton, *Ancient Israelite Literature i*, 135–68; Dobbs-Allsopp, *Weep, O Daughter of Zion*; Lee, *Singers of Lamentations*. Studies of biblical communal laments and ANE lament literature include, e.g., Ferris, *Genre of Communal Lament*; and Bouzard, *We Have Heard with Our Ears, O God*.

21. For a translation of Sumerian city lament texts, see C. J. Gadd, "Second Lamentation for Ur," 59–71; Michalowski, *Lamentation over the Destruction of Sumer and Ur*. Gwaltney ("Biblical Book of Lamentations," 202) lists six common themes underlying these five earliest Mesopotamian laments, even though each one is different in style and structure. The six themes are (1) the destruction of the entire city—everything was destroyed and life ceased; (2) the destruction is a conscious decision of the gods in assembly; (3) the abandonment of the city by the suzerain god, his consort, and their entourage; (4) the laments either specifically mention, or at least presume, restoration of the city or sanctuary; (5) the chief god eventually returns to his city with his entire entourage; this element is indispensable to the plot; (6) and there is a concluding prayer to the chief god.

22. See Gwaltney, "Biblical Book of Lamentations," 195–96; Dobbs-Allsopp, *Weep, O Daughter of Zion*, 13.

used continuously into the Seleucid era. *Eršemma* literally means "wail of the šèm drum" and comprises three kinds of material, according to Dobbs-Allsopp: mythological narratives, grieving over catastrophes, and hymns of praise.[23] Gwaltney says that the *balag*s were "congregational laments," while Dobbs-Allsopp states that "the *balag* consists of three principle elements: praise of the deity; narrative describing the destruction of the land, city, and population and the reactions of the weeping goddess; and entreaties designed to halt the destruction and assuage the god's anger."[24] During the first millennium, *eršemmas* and *balags* became somewhat interchangeable and the two genres coalesced. Every *balag* was provided with a concluding *eršemma*. The *balag* and *eršemma* laments continued to be sung in rituals for various occasions, including the razing of an old building.[25]

No consensus has been reached concerning whether there is Mesopotamian influence upon the book of Lamentations. Dobbs-Allsopp takes a more radical approach to the question than previous scholars and proposes that there existed a native Israelite city lament genre comparable to the Mesopotamian one. Heskett affirms Dobbs-Allsopp's view that the Israelite city-lament genre operated through indigenous forms.[26] A number of other scholars, however, remain unconvinced by Dobbs-Allsopp's proposal.[27] Berlin, e.g., holds that Lamentations contains elements of both the קינה (*qinâ*) and communal lament; it transcends both genres and constitutes a new post-586 type of lament that she names the "Jerusalem lament."[28] Lee regards the labeling of not only the Mesopotamian lamentations over cities but also the book of Lamentations as "city-laments" as not compelling since the book of Lamentations is not just a "city lament;" it is at the same time a "communal dirge" and a "lament prayer."[29] It is neither solely lament nor communal dirge; rather, it "holds the two in tension."[30]

Even though no consensus has been reached in these comparative studies, scholars' findings do situate Lamentations within a larger culture

---

23. Gwaltney, "Biblical Book of Lamentations," 196; and Dobbs-Allsopp, *Weep, O Daughter of Zion*, 14.

24. Gwaltney, "Biblical Book of Lamentations," 198; and Dobbs-Allsopp, *Weep, O Daughter of Zion*, 14.

25. Gwaltney, "Biblical Book of Lamentations," 200.

26. Heskett, *Reading the Book of Isaiah*, 2.

27. Berlin, "Review of Books," 319.

28. Berlin (*Lamentations*, 24–25) explains that a *qinâ* is an outpouring of grief for a loss that has already occurred, with no expectation of reversing that loss, while a communal lament is a plea to prevent a calamity or reverse it.

29. Lee, *Singers of Lamentations*, 39.

30. Ibid., 40.

milieu. Scholars disagree on the reasons behind the similarities and differences between Lamentations and Mesopotamian laments; no one, however, can deny a certain level of similarity and some differences between them. If we forgo preoccupation with the question of direct influence, and focus rather on the textual data, the findings of these comparative studies can help us read Lamentations in a more holistic way.

Similarities between Lamentations and Mesopotamian Laments[31]

First, both treat a common subject matter, i.e. the destruction of cities, and their mood is mournful and somber.[32]

Second, they share some characteristic structural devices and poetic techniques: (1) there is an interchange of speakers involving first, second and third persons accompanied by a change of perspective; (2) both Lamentations and Mesopotamian laments use contrast and reversal: their poets contrast the glorious past with desolate present: the order of things has been reversed, slaves rule, leaders cannot lead, the family is broken down, parents abandon their children and singing is turned into weeping.

Third, the city was destroyed only because its god had abandoned it and the chief god is responsible for its destruction.[33]

Forth, Yhwh in Lamentations fulfills many of the same roles as Enlil in Mesopotamian laments, who, as the divine warrior, goes into battle on the day of his fierce anger.

Fifth, there is a detailed description of destruction, this affecting the capital city and the surrounding areas, roads and buildings, citizens, the economy, and political, social and religious customs. The destruction culminates in the ruin of the temple(s). Lamentations and Mesopotamian laments also share similar images of famine, human slaughter and portrayals of exile.

Finally, personified Jerusalem, daughter Zion in Lamentations, parallels the weeping goddess in Mesopotamian laments.[34]

---

31. The following is a summary of Dobbs-Allsopp and Gwaltney's discussions: see Dobbs-Allsopp, *Weep, O Daughter of Zion*, 30–96; and Gwaltney, "Biblical Book of Lamentations," 207–10.

32. Dobbs-Allsopp (*Weep, O Daughter of Zion*, 31–32) considers these two features highly significant in identifying a city lament genre, despite their more general nature, when they are used in conjunction with other generic features.

33. Lamentations holds onto biblical monotheism: it is Yhwh alone who abandons and destroys the city.

34. For a detailed description of the findings relevant to the weeping goddess in Sumerian lament literature, see Kramer, "Weeping Goddess," 69–80.

Differences between Lamentations and Mesopotamian Laments

First, in Mesopotamian laments, the city goddess is the sufferer who is made to abandon her city by the national gods. In Lamentations, Yhwh is both city and national God, and personified Zion is a sufferer who combines both goddess and city imagery.

Second, in Mesopotamian laments, there is a perceivable movement from abandonment, invasion, and pleas to the gods to gaze upon the ruins, to the restoration and return of the gods. In Lamentations, there is no plot movement of this sort.

Third, the external structure in Lamentations is fundamentally different from that of Mesopotamian laments. Mesopotamian laments have structural rubrics to mark the end of individual songs within a single composition. Such structural rubrics are lacking in Lamentations. Lamentations shapes each of its poems according to the Hebrew alphabet instead.

Fourth, the reasons for destruction are different. The divine act is arbitrary in Mesopotamian laments. No fault is found with the city, its leaders, citizens or its gods. For instance, Enlil explains that Ur's destruction happens simply because Ur had not been given kingship eternally. Hence, Ur's fate is fixed and predestined. The guiltlessness of the city remains a characteristic of Mesopotamian laments. In Lamentations, the divine act is not arbitrary. To a certain degree, God is justified in the decision to destroy since the people have transgressed (Lam 1:5, 8, 18, 20; 4:6), and the prophets and priests (Lam 2:14; 4:13) failed in their responsibility. Israel sinned and Israel has broken its covenant with God.[35]

Fifth, Gwaltney notes that more space is given to humans and their plight in Lamentations than in Mesopotamian laments. The description of suffering is also more poignant and more gruesome in Lamentations.[36]

Sixth, the depiction of the divine is very different in Lamentations. There are no long lists of epithets honoring God in Lamentations as there are in the Mesopotamian laments. The motifs of the god's being aroused from sleep, a deity's heart and liver being pacified and soothed as found in Mesopotamian laments are likewise missing in Lamentations. No direct speech from God is found in Lamentations. The calling upon God to return to his abandoned city, so prominent in Mesopotamian laments, is also absent in Lamentations.

---

35. To say that God's action to destroy in Lamentations is justified is only correct to a certain degree. How the admission of sin functions in Lamentations is a complex issue that should not be considered merely at a superficial level. This question will be dealt in more depth later in the volume.

36. Gwaltney, "Biblical Book of Lamentations," 208.

Forgotten and Forsaken by God (Lam 5:19–20)

Finally and most important, the Mesopotamian laments usually end with restoration of the city and return of the gods. In most cases, these laments functioned in restoration ceremonies of cities and/or temples, such that the return of the gods is an essential condition for the restoration and a sure sign of the reversal of the gods' abandonment of the city. Among the Mesopotamian laments, the Curse of Agade, however, is very different. Instead of looking forward to restoration, it emphasizes the opposite at the end: "Agade is destroyed, Praise Inanna!" The themes of restoration and return of the gods become even more powerful when the opposites are juxtaposed in this way. To use Dobbs-Allsopp's words, the Curse of Agade shows "a nice example of how a poet plays upon the generic expectations of his audience while not actually fulfilling them. In doing so he is able to give a whole different feel to his text."[37] In this respect, Lamentations shares a similarity with the Curse of Agade and differs from other Mesopotamian laments. It does not end in restoration and there is no sign of Yhwh's return to the temple. It rather affirms Yhwh's absence and abandonment at the end: "For if truly you have utterly rejected us and are angry with us beyond measure—" (Lam 5:22).[38] This last line undercuts the thrust of the prayer in Lamentations 5 and gives a different feel to the whole book.

The similarities between Lamentations and Mesopotamian laments show that Lamentations did not arise in a vacuum; it incorporates some common themes and characteristics known from the larger Mesopotamian context. However, the differences highlight that the fact that Jewish writer(s) of Lamentations made his/their own distinctive composition. Lamentations demonstrates how its writer(s) perceives the plight of the people, the destruction of their city, state and temple, and above all, their covenant relationship with God.

OVERALL MESSAGE OF LAMENTATIONS

The interpretation of the book of Lamentations has taken a major turn in recent years. Traditionally, scholars (e.g., N. K. Gottwald, R. Gordis, and D. R. Hillers) have focused on Lam 3:22–33.[39] In these verses, the poet affirms

37. Dobbs-Allsopp, *Weep, O Daughter of Zion*, 93.

38. Translations of Lamentations in this volume are my own; citations of other biblical passages are from NRSV.

39. Gottwald, *Studies*, 91–111; and Gottwald, "Book of Lamentations Reconsidered," 165–73; Gordis, *Song of Songs and Lamentations*, 125–27; Hillers, *Lamentations*, 5–6. Brevard Childs (*Introduction to the Old Testament as Scripture*, 594–95) also holds that Lamentations 3 plays a crucial role in interpreting the whole book. That chapter translates Israel's historically conditioned plight into the language of faith and states

that the חסד "compassion" and רחם "mercy" of Yhwh never cease, and that Yhwh does not afflict willingly or reject forever; thus, it is good to wait for the Lord. Lamentations 3:29 contains the only explicit statement of hope in the book: "Let him put his mouth in the dust, perhaps there is hope." Therefore this passage is considered by the above scholars as the core of Lamentations.

An alternative interpretation has been advanced more recently, i.e., Lamentations is not primarily about the meaning of suffering, but rather is a communal expression of pain by the personified figure Zion (Linafelt, O'Connor).[40] The book's expression of hope is just one voice among a number of other voices from various perspectives.[41] This evolution in scholarly interpretation finds expression in a number of ways.

Message of Hope as One Voice Rather Than the Voice

Lamentations 3 is the central chapter of the book and is written in a triple acrostic with each line of every verse starting with the same Hebrew letter. It conveys a more hopeful message in the midst of the bleak picture depicted in other chapters. The speaker of the chapter is a male, הגבר ראה עני "the man who has seen affliction" (Lam 3:1). Lamentations 3 and the voice of the "suffering man" have received more attention than the other chapters and other voices in the traditional approach.

Gottwald finds an explicit theology of hope in Lamentations. He says that Israel's present "has usually been severe and bitter and thus the ground for grief and lamentation (1:8, 12, 17–18; 2:13, 18–22; 3:19, 43–51; 5:1, 20). But the future holds promise of restoration and therefore provides a basis for hope (3:20–36; 4:22; 5:21)."[42] Gottwald declares that this "theology of hope" centers upon the revealed character of God, which appears mainly in Lam 3:20–36.[43] Gordis holds that the book of Lamentations consists of three concentric sections. He says that Lamentations 3 constitutes the "core" surround-

---

the grounds for hope even though the promises of God to Israel have seemingly come to an end.

40. Linafelt, *Surviving Lamentations*; O'Connor, *Lamentations and the Tears of the World*; Michael B. Moore ("Human Suffering in Lamentations," 535–55) also considers human suffering as the main theme of Lamentations.

41. Thomas ("'I Will Hope in Him,'" 203–21) examines the shape of hope in Lamentations 3; he notes that the hopeful message of Lam 3:25–39 is surrounded by lament, and hope here is not certainty, such that "this shape of hope is not contravened as much as it is coupled with lament."

42. Gottwald, *Studies*, 62.

43. Ibid., 92.

ed by two layers. The inner layer formed by chapters 2 and 4 are dirges on the national catastrophe, while the outer layer constituted by chapters 1 and 5 reflects the indignities of national subjection.[44] Gordis says that Lamentations 3 "expresses a more positive faith in the triumph of righteousness," which is rooted in the conviction that God cannot be the source of evil in the world. The people may hope for restoration if they recognize their sins and repent of their wrong doing.[45] Hillers declares that central to the book of Lamentations is "the expression and strengthening of hope" uttered by the typical sufferer, this "everyman" in chapter 3.[46] This man moves from near despair to confidence that God's mercy is not at an end. From this beginning of hope, the man calls the nation to "penitent waiting for God's mercy."[47]

Iain Provan evaluates previous scholarship on Lamentations and observes that its emphasis on the hopeful nature of the book seems particularly misguided. First of all, chapter 3 as a whole is not hopeful. The reader who reads this chapter through to the end does not receive an impression of great hopefulness; nor does the one who reads the book as a whole, which does not end with Lam 3:21–27, but rather with 5:22. It is doubt, not hope, that Lamentations leaves us with, and to characterize it as a hopeful book is therefore to mislead.[48]

Linafelt points out three perceivable biases in past scholarship's focus on the suffering man in Lamentations 3. First, there is a male bias toward the male figure; the male figure is constructed as "everyone," a model for humanity, while the female figure of Daughter Zion is not. The male figure is likewise assigned the role of theologian while the female figure assumes the role of "victim,"[49] thus "eliding the fact that the man is also presented as victimized and that Zion may be construed as doing theology."[50] Second, there is a Christian bias toward the suffering man based on his perceived similarity to the figure of Christ; the suffering man in Lamentations 3 is seen as foreshadowing the passion of Jesus. Third, there is a broader emphasis on reconciliation with God rather than confrontation; Linafelt points out that this bias is shared by nearly all modern biblical scholars, both male and

---

44. Gordis, *Song of Songs and Lamentations*, 127.
45. Ibid., 139–40.
46. Hillers, *Lamentations*, 5–6.
47. Ibid.
48. Provan, *Lamentations*, 22–23.
49. Mintz, *Ḥurban*, 3, states that the female figure is used to emblemize the experience of victimization while the male figure represents the struggle for theological reconciliation.
50. Linafelt, *Surviving Lamentations*, 6.

female, Jewish and Christian.⁵¹ This third factor emphasizes the interpretive preference for submission and reconciliation with God that finds expression in a dual focus on the theological categories of guilt and hope. God is righteous in his judgment and destruction is due to Israel's sin. There is hope, however, as long as Israel recognizes its guilt and reconciles with God. In such a reading, not much space is given to the expression of pain, neither is extensive attention given to the book's description of destruction nor the accusation of Zion against God. Thus, lament is seen more as the recognition of guilt than an expression of pain. The book's scant and uncertain admission of guilt is emphasized more than its pervasive description of suffering and destruction.

Linafelt takes the figure of Zion as an alternative model and focuses mainly on Lamentations 1 and 2. He compares Lamentations 1 and 2 with survival literature and finds that, contrary to the consensus of biblical scholars, Lamentations is "more about the expression of suffering than the meaning behind it, more about the vicissitudes of survival than the abstraction of sin and guilt, more about protest as a religious posture than capitulation or confession."⁵² For Linafelt, Lamentations 1 and 2 are a mixture of the forms of dirge and lament in which the figure Zion manifests a move away from dirge to lament, from death to life; thus Lamentations evinces the fundamental dynamic of survival literature, which is "the paradox of life in death and death in life."⁵³ As survival literature, Lamentations is more about the articulation of pain than the interpretation of pain. Linafelt acknowledges that the figure Zion never claims innocence, but just as in other survival literature, she neither admonishes nor condemns nor begs for forgiveness, because her attention lies elsewhere. Her desire is to persuade the reader regarding the experience of her survival and to make her concerns the concerns of the reader as well. Zion's primary concern is the survival of her children and the primary one she desires to persuade is God.⁵⁴ Linafelt

51. Ibid., 9.

52. Ibid., 4.

53. Linafelt (*Surviving Lamentations*, 37–38) explains that the genre of lament is like the genre of dirge, in that it arises out of pain and has much to say about death. Yet lament is also unlike dirge; its primary aim is life. Lament looks beyond the situation and death, addressing God and expecting an answer.

54. Linafelt (*Surviving Lamentations*, 47) quotes Terrence Des Pres (*The Survivor*, 44): "with very few exceptions, the testimony of survivors does not concern itself with guilt of any sort. Their books neither admonish nor condemn nor beg forgiveness; not because survivors are drained of their humanity, but because their attention lies wholly elsewhere." While aiming to persuade readers to enter into Zion's experience and make Zion's concerns their own, Lamentations is different from other survival literature regarding whom it is primarily trying to persuade. Modern survival literature tries to persuade those who

thinks that in Zion's rhetoric of persuasion, the survival of Zion's children occupies a privileged and critical role, representing a key to the literary and emotional structure of Lamentations 1 and 2.

K. O'Connor's reading of Lamentations is along the same lines as Linafelt's. She describes the book as "an artistic jewel, a theological enigma, and a courageous act of survival."[55] For O'Connor, Lamentations is poetry of "truth-telling;" by revealing pain, it brings into the open experiences and memories that many try to deny or hide.[56] She analyzes the culture of denial in its personal, social, and political dimensions. She affirms, along with other humanists and social-psychological analysts, that it is the denial of pain and grief that cause alienation, hopelessness, and violence among both the privileged and the deprived. It is by recognizing our own brokenness, pain and despair that we become capable of constructive action.[57] Lamentations is a book that "denies denial" and "gives primacy to suffering voices like no other biblical book."[58]

O'Connor affirms that all voices in Lamentations have to be fully respected. "No voice wins out, unifies or dominates the claims of other voices."[59] All perspectives of the different voices remain together in a "churning, unsettled interaction."[60] Among the voices, the most desired one is the voice of God, but God's voice remains absent throughout the book. O'Connor considers the absence of God's voice an "inspired restraint" since any words from God would overwhelm the human voices; God's words would bring Lamentations to "premature resolution," and the book's capacity to house sorrow would dissipate.[61] What usually happens, however, is that readers and interpreters, both Jewish and Christian alike, cling to the voice of hope uttered by the גבר, "strong man" in Lamentations 3, as if "these few hopeful passages were the only words of the book" even when this voice of hope is tentative and faltering. Meanwhile, the voices of anger and grief, pain and doubt "slide into the interpretative margins, smothered and silenced

---

did not share the experience of suffering it tries to describe. Lamentations does try to persuade readers who did not share the original experience, but as liturgical poetry, the one Lamentations tries desperately to persuade is God.

55. O'Connor, *Lamentations and the Tears of the World*, 1.

56. Ibid., 4.

57. For O'Connor's more detailed analysis of denial—its roots, symptoms and consequences—see ibid., 86–94.

58. Ibid., 94.

59. Ibid., 84.

60. Ibid.

61. Ibid., 85.

by hope."⁶² However, as O'Connor affirms, the brilliance of Lamentations is that it does not speak for God; hence it leaves wounds open to the air, requiring them to be seen and attended to. It prevents readers and interpreters from "sliding prematurely over suffering to happy endings."⁶³

O'Connor also emphasizes that truth about pain and suffering is a precondition for reconciliation.⁶⁴ She says that crushed spirits cannot worship unless worship speaks from their pain. It is by telling the truth that passions are released and compassion is called forth. Lamentations, written as poetry, has the capacity to mirror pain across cultures and ages. Lamentations, by revealing the truth, albeit ugly and disturbing, is immensely comforting; by its invitation to allow tears to flow like a river, Lamentations is able to encompass the tears of the whole world.

Admission of Sin and Guilt As Perfunctory Rather Than Primary

Scholars who emphasize the main message of Lamentations as hope and downplay its expression of pain tend to stress the admission of guilt more than the book itself does. It is undeniable that God is the agent of destruction in Lamentations. If God is just and righteous at the same time, then God's destructive action as punishment must be justified. It is Israel's sin that caused God's anger and Israel's destruction, even though this punishment might seem a bit too severe or harsh. By admitting their sin and submitting to the will of God, Israel can have hope that God's favor will return in the future.⁶⁵ In this reading, suffering becomes manageable and the future depends on admission of guilt and submission to the will of God.

Scholars who see hope as *one* voice among the broader expressions of pain rather than *the* voice of the book do so for the following reasons. First of all, Provan points out that the admission of guilt in the book does not appear wholehearted, and is accompanied by reproach to God for his actions.⁶⁶ Secondly, Dobbs-Allsopp observes that the sin motif in Lamentations is almost perfunctory in nature since the sins spoken of are general ones and are nowhere specified. The orthodox view that Jerusalem's destruction and the people's suffering are Yhwh's punishment for sin may,

---

62. Ibid.
63. Ibid., 86.
64. Ibid., 94.
65. Gottwald (*Studies*, 62) says that the moment of the restoration of Israel's historical life begins when she makes full satisfaction for her guilt; then and only then will the tide of fortune turn in her direction.
66. Provan, *Lamentations*, 23.

in fact, serve as a sort of foil in the book to point out the injustice of the situation, no matter what the cause.[67]

Importance of Lament vs. Devaluation of Lament

Connected with the scholarly emphasis on hope and admission of guilt is a general tendency to devalue lament. Gottwald, e.g., regards the book of Lamentations as far above pathos, being imbued with greater significance than a mere lament.[68] Plöger comments that lamenting, no matter how extensive it might be, has, in contrast to the funeral dirge, no significance of its own.[69] Similarly, Renate Brandscheidt asserts that the real issue of lament is the recognition of guilt and that the people have to have a proper attitude before they can lament before God.[70]

Westermann notes that such devaluation of lament does not directly stem from the interpreters of Lamentations; it is rooted rather in a pre-understanding that it is inappropriate to lament before God.[71] Lament is not considered as prayer. In Christian interpretations of Lamentations, the book's laments are simply not allowed to be laments. They are either "recast as something else or they are devalued for what they are."[72] Linafelt views this devaluation of lament as reflecting a preference for reconciling with God rather than confrontation.[73]

On the other hand, scholars who value the expression of pain in Lamentations also recognize the prayerful nature of the book. C. Mandolfo affirms that Lamentations is among the few biblical texts that speak at length

---

67. Dobbs-Allsopp, *Weep, O Daughter of Zion*, 54–55.

68. Gottwald, *Studies*, 62.

69. Otto Plöger ("Die Klagelieder," 162) says that "in einem Klagelied hat die Klage selbst, mag sie auch noch so ausführlich zu Worte kommen, in Gegensatz zum Leichenlied keine selbständige Bedeutung."

70. Renate Brandscheidt (*Gotteszorn und Menschenleid*, 212) says that "Bevor die Klage angestimmt werden kann, muß dem Volk eines Klar sein: Jahwe hat das Gericht verfügt wegen der Sünden des Volkes."

71. Westermann, *Lamentations*, 81.

72. Westermann (ibid., 82–85) points out six different ways that the devaluation of lament manifests itself in the interpretation of Lamentations: (1) lamentation and accusation are seen as unsuitable forms for the pious; prayer reflects a higher point of view than lament; (2) the language of suffering is seen as secondary to the spiritual or theological mastery of the situation; (3) lament stands totally outside the domain of prayer for some interpreters; (4) lament is actually a confession to God; (5) lament cannot also be reproach or accusation against God; and (6) lament has no value in and of itself; it can only be evaluated positively when something else is added to it.

73. Linafelt, *Surviving Lamentations*, 11–12.

"*to* Yhwh rather than *about* Yhwh."[74] The silence of God in the book does not negate the prayerful nature of the book since Lamentations yearns for God, reaches out toward God, and passionately seeks an intervention from God. O'Connor considers Lamentations a daring prayer of truthfulness, a prayer of and for the wounded world.[75]

DIALOGIC INTERACTION BETWEEN LAMENTATIONS AND PROPHETIC LITERATURE

In his review article of research on Lamentations, C. W. Miller notes that while scholars have paid great attention to the relationship between Lamentations and similar ancient Near Eastern literature, connections between Lamentations and other biblical texts have attracted serious attention only recently.[76]

Connections Between Lamentations and Second Isaiah

Gottwald, following M. Löhr, points out that the affinities between Lamentations and Isaiah 40-66 are numerous and often "strike deeper than mere verbal parallelism;"[77] however, Gottwald thinks that there is a major difference between the two works. In particular, while there has been a scholarly consensus that the original *Sitz im Leben* of Lamentations was a Judean one, the role of Judahites who remained in the land is ignored in Second Isaiah according to Gottwald.[78] In her response to Gottwald,[79] Carol Newsom argues that while it is true that there is little or no explicit reference to the Judahite community in Second Isaiah, Second Isaiah engages the voice of the Judahite community as found in Lamentations dialogically "in terms of reversal," such that is almost "an antiphonal answering" of the lament

---

74. Mandolfo, *Daughter Zion Talks Back*, 67 (italics original).

75. O'Connor, *Lamentations and the Tears of the World*, 124-36. A number of recent scholars have advocated the importance of lament and lament as a true form of prayer; among them are Brueggeman, "Costly Loss of Lament," 57-71; Davidson, *Courage to Doubt*; Balentine, *Prayer in the Hebrew Bible*; Murphy, *Psalms Are Yours* 50-58; Zenger, *A God of Vengeance?*, 87-95.

76. See Miller, "Book of Lamentations in Recent Research," 13.

77. Gottwald, *Studies*, 45; and Löhr, "Der Sprachgebrauch des Buches der Klagelieder," 41-49. Gottwald also provides a list of words and phrases shared by Lamentations and Isaiah 40-66.

78. Gottwald, "Social Class and Ideology in Isaiah 40-55," 43-56.

79. Newsom, "Response," 73-78.

Forgotten and Forsaken by God (Lam 5:19–20)

uttered in the Judahite speech of Lamentations.[80] Patricia T. Willy builds on Newsom's suggestions and studies the strategic engagement with Lamentations in Second Isaiah more exhaustively.[81]

A number of other scholars likewise compare Lamentations and Second Isaiah, though from different angles. Linafelt reads Second Isaiah in terms of the rhetoric of survival and explores how Isaiah 40–55 strives to match the drive for survival so prominent in Lamentations.[82] Jill Middlemas examines the possibility that Second Isaiah wrote Lamentations 3.[83] She analyzes closely the correspondences between the suffering servant in Second Isaiah and the גבר, "strong man" in Lamentations 3. She concludes that the man in Lamentations 3 functions as a response to and a reversal of the overall message of Lamentations. Even if its commonalities with Second Isaiah are insufficient to demonstrate common authorship, Middlemas still believes that Lamentations 3 reflects an exilic setting and that the man is the "personification of EXILED Israel" who, as such complements the figure of personified Zion in Lamentations 1 and 2.[84]

Connections Between Lamentations and the Wider Prophetic Corpus

Employing a Bakhtinian dialogic strategy of reading, Elizabeth Boase and Mandolfo have produced two more extensive works on the dialogic interaction between Lamentations and prophetic literature.[85] Boase identifies a number of shared motifs between Lamentations and prophetic literature, i.e., the personification of Jerusalem as female, the day of Yhwh, and sin and its relation to Yhwh's action against the city. Lamentations transforms these motifs, adapting and subverting them. At times, Lamentations agrees with its prophetic predecessors, but at others, Lamentations challenges the prophetic viewpoint. Thus, Lamentations creates a dialogic tension with prophetic literature. The primary purpose of Lamentations' use of the personification motif is not, e.g., to announce judgment upon the city and/or people as is the case in prophetic literature, but rather "to give voice to the depth and complexity

---

80. Ibid., 76.

81. Willy, "Servant of YHWH and Daughter of Zion," 267–303; Tull, *Remember the Former Things.*

82. Linafelt, *Surviving Lamentations*, 62–79.

83. Middlemas, "Did Second Isaiah Write Lamentations III?," 505–25.

84. Ibid., 523, emphasis original.

85. Boase, *The Fulfillment of Doom?*; and Mandolfo, *Daughter Zion Talks Back.*

of the suffering following the fall of Jerusalem."⁸⁶ The city's personification is more extended and intense in Lamentations than in the prophetic corpus. The city is portrayed as widow, mother, princess, vassal, mourner, menstruant, rape victim, shamed and despised woman, lover or perhaps adulteress—all roles of the one personified Zion. All these roles serve to evoke sympathy and empathy for Zion that are largely absent from prophetic literature. Lamentations also subverts the motif of the day of Yhwh in prophetic literature by emphasizing the pain and suffering of the city throughout Jerusalem's first-person speech. Though the city confesses her sin as the cause of Yhwh's punishment, the absence of detail and the continued stress on suffering undermines the judgment motif. The relationship between sin and punishment in Lamentations is ambiguous. The book presents the orthodox prophetic view that sin was the cause of Yhwh's punishment of the city, but it also voices a contrasting view which questions the deservedness and extent of the suffering. The sense of a balanced correspondence between sin and punishment, so prevalent in prophetic literature, is absent in Lamentations.

Boase emphasizes that by adapting and subverting prophetic motifs, Lamentations enters into dialogue with prophetic literature and creates a dialogic text with them, while meanwhile maintaining a dialogue within itself. Overall, Lamentations functions to express pain and suffering, to lament rather than to judge. In Lamentations, judgment is an act that has already been realized, and the book grieves over the destruction of the city and the suffering of her people.

Mandolfo grounds her study in the dialogic philosophies of Mikhail Bakhtin and Martin Buber; her work is further informed by feminist and postcolonial criticism. She intends to provide an example of "how we might read biblical texts toward the development of a dialogic theology" in order to "highlight the Bible's multiple, conflicting, and complementary voices," and refuses to privilege one point of view.⁸⁷ She first examines the marriage metaphor in Hosea, Jeremiah, and Ezekiel. Since there is no direct discourse by Zion in these prophetic writings, she reads between the lines in order to foster a dialogic encounter that is not explicit in these texts. She reads God's words closely for the story they weave about Zion and searches for Zion's response through these indirect discourses in the prophetic literature. After this, Mandolfo studies Lamentations 1 and 2 and how in these chapters Zion crafts "a counterstory that resists the myopic identity in which God and his prophets have confined her."⁸⁸ She considers Zion's speech in Lamenta-

---

86. Boase, *The Fulfillment of Doom?*, 103.
87. Mandolfo, *Daughter Zion Talks Back*, 26.
88. Ibid., 27.

tions 1 and 2 important since it is mainly spoken from Zion's perspective, a feature which is missing in the prophetic texts. Then she examines God's response in Second Isaiah to Zion's counterstory in Lamentations.

By paying attention to the smothered voices in biblical texts, Mandolfo hopes to "contribute to the dethroning of biblical authority as it is now construed."[89] Zion's counterstory reveals relevant details that dominate master narratives suppress.[90] Mandolfo affirms that biblical God speaks polyphonically, and so she aims to generate a dialogic biblical theology. For her, the divine-human relationship is reciprocal and mutually authorizing; she affirms the importance of human agency in the relationship.[91] Her situating of Zion's voice in relation to the prophetic texts shows how unique and important Zion's perspective in Lamentations 1 and 2 is in fostering such a divine-human dialogue.

UNITY OF AND RELATIONSHIP BETWEEN STRUCTURE AND CONTENT IN LAMENTATIONS

As long as Jeremiah was considered as the author of Lamentations, the unity of the book was not questioned; it was along with challenges to Jeremiah's authorship (first in 1712, by H. von der Hardt) that debates about its unity started.[92] Lamentations obviously lacks plot and argumentative structure; the frequent shifting of voices and the contradicting views expressed in the poems have caused some to question the unity of the book.[93] Elie Assis makes clear that a distinction must be made between the question of single authorship and the literary unity of the book.[94] It is possible that one author wrote five poems and then put them together into one anthology; it is also possible that different authors wrote five poems and an editor shaped them into one literary unit. Assis believes that there is no correlation between the questions of unity of the book and that of its single or multiple authorship.[95]

---

89. Ibid., 5.
90. Ibid., 18.
91. Ibid., 124–25.
92. For a discussion of the book's authorship, see Hillers, *Lamentations*, 10–15; Hunter, *Faces of a Lamenting City*, 44–49.
93. A typical example of proposed multiple authorship is Cornelius Houk, "Multiple Poets in Lamentations," 111–25. He divides the book into different sections written by different poets: 1:1–11, 12–22; 2:1–10, 11–16, 17–19, 20–22; 3:1–24, 25–39, 40–47, 48–66; 4:1–10; 5:1–14, 15–22.
94. Assis, "Unity of the Book of Lamentations," 306.
95. Ibid., 308. Salters ("Unity of Lamentations," 102–10) argues for the unity of the book notwithstanding its different authors. He examines the vocabulary employed in

A determination of single or multiple authorship is not essential for understanding the book, but "the question of its literary unity is a necessity."[96]

Proposed Key Themes in Lamentations

Even though Lamentations lacks plot and argumentative structure, it is possible to read the book thematically. Gottwald determines that Lamentations grapples with the failure of Deuteronomic theology: how could Yhwh's punishment come at a time when the people were so earnest to reform?[97] Albrekson, in his critique of Gottwald, avers that Lamentations has no problem with Deuteronomic theology; rather, it wrestles with Zion theology, since, in contrast to that theology's affirmation of the centrality of Jerusalem and inviolability of Zion, the city fell and the temple was destroyed.[98]

Moore argues that the attempt to define a single interpretative key to Lamentations as Gottwald and Albrektson try to do is "problematic from the very outset."[99] Lamentations is primarily designed to lament the destruction, to articulate anger, guilt, despair, as well as a deeply rooted tenacity to hang on. Various perspectives are held in tension and different themes are interwoven and interlocked in Lamentations. Moore, following H. Wiesmann, focuses more on the book's internal than on its external characteristics.[100] He analyzes the five poems and shows that the primary concern of Lamentations is to portray the horrifying scope of human suffering.

Jill Middlemas identifies four organizing themes that recur throughout Lamentations 1, 2, 4 and 5: the responsibility of Yhwh, the present distress of the lamenter, the exaltation of the enemies and the sinfulness of the people.[101] These four themes stand in conjunction with other concepts featured in Lamentations, such as human suffering, lack of confidence in future hope, the deconstruction of the confession of sin, the vocalization of pain, and the formfulness of grief.

---

its different chapters and concludes that chapter 5 is part of the original work, while chapter 3 is a later addition.

96. Assis, "Unity of the Book of Lamentations," 308.
97. Gottwald, *Studies*, 47–62.
98. Albrektson, *Studies*, 214–39.
99. Moore, "Human Suffering in Lamentations," 535.
100. Wiesmann, *Die Klagelieder*, 5–10.
101. Middlemas (*Troubles of Templeless Judah*, 171–228) considers Lamentations 1, 2, 4 and 5 as Judahite texts and chapter 3 an exilic text. See also Middlemas, *Templeless Age*, 28–51.

Forgotten and Forsaken by God (Lam 5:19-20)

J. Hunter maintains that Lam 1:1-11 depicts the many faces of a lamenting city and the themes of the first 11 verses are not only taken up, but also expanded in the following chapters.[102]

Proposed Patterns in Lamentations

A number of other scholars also read the book as a literary unity and consider Lamentations a well-composed work, one that conveys meaning through its structure. David Dorsey says that even though Lamentations lacks apparent logical arrangement, a closer examination of its macrostructure reveals "a literary architecture that is sophisticated, artistic and emotive."[103] He considers Lamentations "one of the most carefully and thoughtfully arranged compositions in the Hebrew Bible." Homer Heater also sees Lamentations as "the best example in the Bible of a combination of divine inspiration and human artistic ability."[104] Lamentations is a grand achievement of unity between form and content; "rhetoric reflects content, one sees as one savors."[105]

Some scholars have tried to detect more specific unifying patterns in Lamentations. B. Johnson thinks that there is a carefully designed structure in Lamentations, shaping and emphasizing the message of the book.[106] The first four poems employ a similar structure: a "fact half" and an "interpretation half." The two halves correspond to each other and use similar words or expressions. The major themes of these chapters are also similar. Chapter 5 is different. It has the form of a prayer and functions as the conclusion of the book. Johnson suggests that chapter 5 could be seen as the basis from which the rest of the poems were built up.

W. Shea avers that the *qinâ* or lament meter, with 3+2 stress accents, is the more prominent meter in Lamentations.[107] The five clearly delimited chapters of Lamentations constitute a grand *qinâ* scheme of 3+2, three chapters followed by two. The book's *qinâ* scheme is further apparent from the fact that "the first three chapters were written in units that were collected in multiples of three, while the last two chapters were written in units collected

---

102. Hunter, *Faces of a Lamenting City*, 85-134.
103. Dorsey, "Lamentations," 83.
104. Heater, "Structure and Meaning in Lamentations," 304.
105. Grossberg, "Form and Content and Their Correspondence," 47.
106. Johnson, "Form and Message in Lamentations," 72.
107. Shea, "The *qinah* Structure," 103.

in multiples of two."[108] Shea thinks that this structure is a strong argument against the view that Lamentations 5 should be attributed to a later author.[109]

J. Renkema's work is probably the most elaborate attempt to identify an overarching pattern in Lamentations.[110] He identifies a concentric pattern in the book, asking readers not to read ancient Hebrew poetry as one reads modern poetry. Lamentations should be read concentrically rather than linearly. Renkema analyzes each poem according to its concentric structure, including chapter 5; then he lays out the concentric pattern of the whole book.[111] He considers the second and the forth songs as the most strongly connected, though the inclusion formed by the first and fifth song is also strong.[112] His study is filled with lists of words, charts and diagrams.

R. B. Salters evaluates these previous attempts at detecting patterns in Lamentations.[113] He considers Johnson's suggestion forced, since there is no obvious divisions into two halves in Lamentations 2, 3 and 4, as there is in Lamentations 1. Salters calls Shea's ingenious theory "wishful thinking."[114] In particular, Salters points out that the *qinâ* meter, 3+2 "limping" meter that Shea names the lament meter, is not the only meter in Lamentations; the 2+1 meter occurs in Lamentations as well. The 3+2 *qinâ* meter is also employed elsewhere in the Hebrew Bible for nonlament genres. Salters regards Renkema's work as obviously subjective since "he finds things which are not there and he ignores things which are."[115] In particular, Salters notes that Renkema says little about the acrostic pattern in four of the five poems even though "the alphabetic sequence suggests linear rather than concentric structure!"[116]

Salters further observes that Lamentations is a communal lament mixed with dirge-like motifs.[117] Salters's criticism of the previous three scholars' work might be a bit too harsh since they do have a certain value; one however, definitely needs to be mindful of Salters's call to pay attention first to the Hebrew text itself before one stands back and looks for patterns.

---

108. Ibid., 106.
109. Ibid., 107.
110. Renkema, "Literary Structure of Lamentations," 294–396.
111. Ibid., 388.
112. Renkema (ibid., 388–91) lists his conclusions and findings of the book's unifying features.
113. Salters, "Searching for Pattern," 93–104.
114. Ibid., 97.
115. Ibid., 98.
116. Ibid.
117. Ibid., 103.

Another pattern in Lamentations is identified by David Marcus, this involving "non-recurring doublets," i.e., words and phrases that occur only twice in the entire book.[118] Marcus finds that these non-recurring doublets occupy about forty percent of the book and lists 183 of them in an appendix. Marcus believes that this feature is not a coincidence or an unconscious choice of words, but rather a deliberate effort on the part of the author who selected his words very carefully.[119] Marcus thus argues not only for the unity of Lamentations, but also for a single authorship.

Identifying patterns may help us perceive the structure of the book better; in particular, it may enable us to understand the book on a deeper level. However, these efforts should not be allowed to become too elaborate. Any pattern has to be based on the Hebrew text and the primary purpose of studying such patterns is to understand the book better. If it takes more effort to understand explanations of the proposed pattern than the book itself, then the proposed pattern is no longer helpful.

Alphabetic Acrostics in Lamentations

Alphabetic acrostic is one literary feature that dominates the structure of Lamentations. Even though Lamentations 5 is not written as an alphabetic acrostic, it does consist of twenty-two lines corresponding to the twenty-two letters of the Hebrew alphabet. A conclusive view regarding the function of the acrostic in Lamentations has not been attained. Some scholars suggest that the acrostic is secondary, i.e. an editor formed already existing poems into acrostics; the divice functions either to aid memory in oral performance, for aesthetic purposes, or to create a sense of completeness, with regard to both the transgressions Israel had committed and the grief expressed in the poems.[120] Other scholars consider the acrostic not a secondary feature, not an irrelevant, beside-the-point detail but rather intrinsically

---

118. Marcus, "Non-Recurring Doublets in the Book of Lamentations," 177–95.

119. Ibid., 180.

120. The mnemonic function of the acrostic is identified in *Midrash Lamentations Rabbah* (Buber edition; Vilna, 1909—other editions quote this one) chapter 1:1 "Why was the book of Lamentations written in alphabetic acrostic? So that it will be learnt by chanters." *Midrash Rabbah, Lamentations,* 7:87, says, "Why is the book of Lamentations composed as an alphabetical acrostic? . . . because it is written (Dan 9) 'Yea, all Israel have transgressed' . . . which is written from Aleph to Taw. Therefore is this book composed as an alphabetical acrostic, one corresponding to the other." Westermann (*Lamentations,* 99–100) argues that the acrostic is a late stylistic feature used for aesthetic purposes. Renkema ("Meaning of the Parallel Acrostics in Lamentations," 379) holds that the acrostic form corresponds to the completeness of grief expressed in the poems.

connected with the spirit and intention of the book.¹²¹ Dobbs-Allsopp, e.g., argues that the acrostic is "more than fancy window dressing for the poetry's otherwise semantic and propositional content."¹²² These scholars value the alphabetic acrostic in Lamentations as corresponding to the intention of the book. For them, the characteristics of the acrostic as applied in Lamentations carry the message of the book.

Still other attempts have been made to understand the acrostic in Lamentations. Joseph Prouser, e.g., addresses the structure of Lamentations as a whole.¹²³ He compares the structure of Lamentations, six laboriously constructed acrostics of equal extant (Lamentations 1–4) followed by a more relaxed chapter of free verse (Lamentations 5), with the six days of creation followed by one day of rest. Prouser interprets Lamentations from a midrashic point of view and concludes that Lamentations gently insists that the Creator grants all who mourn the ability to foresee a new day, even in the darkest of times.¹²⁴

Philippe Guillaume, reading Lamentations as a whole, considers Lamentations 5 as the seventh acrostic of the book. Guillaume here follows D. N. Freedman, who holds that the omission of the alphabetic device in Lamentations 5 "represents a modification, a slight sophistication, of the original arrangement, and not the other way around."¹²⁵ Guillaume notes that acrostics are often used in conjunction with telestics. *Telestic* refers to reading the last rather than the first letter of each line in sequence; it is the opposite of acrostic.¹²⁶ Guillaume identifies a number of hidden messages in Lamentations 5 that emerge when we attend to its telestics together with its acrostics, e.g., the acrostic-telestic of Lam 5:19–22 generates אלהיך רם מד "your God is exalted greatly." If this is read in connection with the acrostic in Lam 5:1–3, together they articulate the message "Zechariah the prophet [says]: your God is greatly exalted!" Guillaume concludes that "the acrostic-telestic in Lamentations 5 makes a new dawn rise at the end of the book, a wink to the careful reader."¹²⁷

---

121. Gottwald, *Studies*, 30.

122. Dobbs-Allsopp, *Lamentations*, 18.

123. Prouser, "Darkness on the Face of the Deep," 37–42.

124. Ibid., 41.

125. Freedman, "Acrostic Poems in the Hebrew Bible," 415; and Guillaume, "Lamentations 5," 2.

126. Guillaume, "Lamentations 5," 4.

127. Ibid., 5.

Forgotten and Forsaken by God (Lam 5:19–20)

APPROACH OF THIS STUDY

This book will follow the majority scholarly view that the originating *Sitz im Leben* of Lamentations was Judah; it is most likely that Lamentations is a Judahite text written by the less privileged left behind in the land. This book will also posit that the five poems were written not long after the destruction of the temple in 587 BCE, since most commentators date Lamentations after 587 BCE and before the return of the exiles in 539 BCE, or at least prior to the temple's rebuilding in 515 BCE.[128] Lamentations thus offers a unique perspective on how the destruction was perceived in the homeland.

A Holistic Approach to Lamentations

I take Lamentations as a literary unit. I will examine to what extent an intrinsic connection between the acrostic structure and the content of Lamentations exists. The acrostic structure will be thoroughly studied; likewise, its connection with the book's shift of voices and changing perspectives will be carefully examined.

I will give special attention to the much neglected second half of the book, Lamentations 4 and 5, especially the mini-acrostic in Lam 5:19–20 and the ending in Lam 5:21–22, about which I will say a word already at this point.

Importance of Poetic Closure: Lam 5:19–22

B. H. Smith demonstrates how poetic closure is essential for the understanding of a poem.[129] She explores the general dynamics of the relation between structure and closure in poetry and analyzes the failure of poetic closure. I consider Smith's study on poetry in general valuable for our understanding of biblical Lamentations. Borrowing Smith's terms, we may call the ending of Lamentations "disappointing" since it leaves the reader with

---

128. See Middlemas, *Troubles of Templeless Judah*, 181. Joyce ("Sitting Loose to History," 246–78) points out that the meaning of Lamentations is not necessarily tied to the destruction of Jerusalem after the Babylonian invasion. It is possible and meaningful to read it apart from its original historical setting. However, O'Connor ("Book of Lamentations," 1015) rightly points out that if the Babylonian invasion of Judah is not the precise tragedy underlying Lamentations, then it is at least "a central catastrophe in Israel's history" that provides an illuminating backdrop for understanding the fury, grief, and disorientation that Lamentations expresses.

129. Smith, *Poetic Closure.*

History of Research and Overview of the Book

"residual expectations."[130] God remains silent and absent; readers' rightful expectation of God's return to Jerusalem is not fulfilled. Will God respond or will God not? The reader is left wondering, pressing for an answer but finding none.

The ending of Lamentations has long puzzled biblical interpreters. Different scholars have tried to understand it in every possible way, yet, no consensus has been reached.[131] What can be said for sure is that the book has an open ending; it retains its polyphonic nature until the very end, still longing for a response from the silent God. Its despair is immeasurable and it is doubtful if God will ever respond, yet, the book refuses to end just there.

Heater notices that Lam 5:19–20 forms a mini-acrostic:[132]

אתה יהוה לעולם תשב כסאך לדר ודור
למה לנצח תשכחנו תעזבנו לארך ימים

You, O Yhwh, sit forever, your throne is from generation to generation;
Why have you forgotten us completely, why have you forsaken us these many days?

He observes that this mini-acrostic combines two main themes running through the book: "God is sovereign and just, but Zion's suffering is so great." He says this in passing, however, and does not explore further how the two main themes in Lam 5:19–20 are carried through the book as a whole.

Beside the mini-acrostic formed by Lam 5:19–20, the poetic closure in Lamentations (5:19–22) evidences a number of features that makes it indispensable for the understanding of the whole book. First, the second line of this mini-acrostic contains two verbs that rarely occur together, namely, שכח "forget" and עזב "forsake," with Yhwh as the subject only once elsewhere in the MT, i.e., in Isa 49:14: "But Zion said, 'The Lord has forsaken me, my Lord has forgotten me,'" where there is an obvious quotation of Lam 5:20.[133] Second, Yhwh is referred to as "You" here. It is worth noting that the second-person pronoun אתה occurs only three times in the book

---

130. Ibid., 213.

131. Gordis, "Conclusion of the Book of Lamentations," 289–93; Linafelt, "Refusal of a Conclusion" 340–43.

132. Heater, "Structure and Meaning," 310–11.

133. The two verbs also occur together with a subject other than Yhwh in Isa 65:11; Prov 2:17 and Job 9:27. Willey (Tull, *Remember the Former Things*, 189) notes the unique biblical combination of the two verbs with Yhwh as the subject. Sommer (*A Prophet Reads Scripture*, 130) claims that there is no correspondence between Deutero-Isaiah and Lamentations 5; he reasons that Lamentations 5 must be a later addition to the book since Deutero-Isaiah does not seem to know it. However, the correspondence between Lam 5:20 and Isa 49:14 certainly counts as a strong connection between the two texts.

Forgotten and Forsaken by God (Lam 5:19–20)

(Lam 1:21; 3:42 and 5:19), and all three refer to Yhwh. Third, as previously noted, the first letters of the book's last four lines form the word אלהך "your God." Lam 5:19–22 on the one hand affirms the eternal kingship of Yhwh, while on the other hand, it complains about the unbearable hardship caused by Yhwh's forgetfulness and abandonment. Meanwhile, Lamentations undoubtedly refers to Yhwh as "You" and affirms that the ultimate partner and listener of this dialogue is Yhwh. Accordingly, I now turn to some initial considerations on the concept of dialogue in biblical studies.

A Dialogic Interpretation

Bakhtin and Buber's dialogic interpretation has been applied to biblical studies in general and the book of Lamentations in particular.[134] Bakhtin's approach promotes "a dialogic sense of truth," and this truth is polyphonic, personal, dynamic and always open.[135] In a polyphonic text, "the dialogic play of ideas is not merely a function of plot and character but is the motive of the entire work."[136] In such a text, one must not look for plot, but rather read the dialogue and participate in it. Also, one cannot expect closure to a polyphonic text since dialogue is by nature open, "unfinalizable" in Bakhtin's term.[137]

Martin Buber's *Ich und Du*, for its part, insists on establishing genuine dialogue. Such dialogue is first with God, the God "to whom one might cry out in gratitude, despair or agony," "to whom one complains or prays spontaneously."[138] A perfect relationship with this God would leave out nothing, leave nothing behind, would comprehend the whole world in comprehending the You and "to have nothing besides God but to grasp everything in him."[139] This genuine dialogue needs to be established also with people and nature, as well as with a book. Kaufmann says that Buber's idea of reading is

---

134. Bakhtin's revolutionary concept of "dialogism" (polyphony) was first presented by him in 1929 in his *Problems of Dostoevsky's Art*. See Bakhtin, *The Dialogic Imagination*, xxiv.

135. Newsom, "Bakhtin, the Bible, and Dialogic Truth," 291.

136. Ibid., 296.

137. Ibid.

138. Walter Kaufmann notes in his prologue that to translate Buber's *Du* with the formal archaic English "Thou" is to misunderstand Buber. In German, *Du* is a word for lovers and friends; it reflects a spontaneous and unpretentious relationship, which the English "Thou" does not. Hence, it is more fitting to translate Buber's *Du* as "you." See Buber, *I and Thou*, 14.

139. Ibid., 127.

not to treat a book as an object to be put to use, or as an object of experience, but rather as "the voice of You speaking to me, requiring a response."[140]

Previous scholarship has mainly focused on the dialogic interaction between Lamentations and the prophetic literature. In particular, scholars have sought to identify God's response to Zion in Second Isaiah—whether that response is considered adequate or not.[141] I think Lamentations deserves to be studied on its own terms. I will hence first apply the dialogic approach to the book of Lamentations itself and then to its connections with other communal laments in the Hebrew Bible. Lamentations is truly a polyphonic text: the dialogic play of its different voices and perspectives is the motive of the entire book, and Lamentations remains open. How these voices and perspectives interact will be studied in this book. This book will also explore the dialogic interaction between Lamentations and other communal laments. Lamentations occupies a unique place within the communal lament genre since it does not end on a hopeful note and so does not move from lament to praise, this in contrast to the Psalter's overall movement from lament to praise. The uniqueness of Lamentations' ending in lament and the voice of God remaining absent in the book is fully respected in this study. Accordingly, the widely held scholarly view that biblical laments regularly lead into praise will need to be revisited.

Lament as Authentic Prayer

This book considers lament as an authentic and indispensable form of prayer when God is absent and silent. Lament reflects our real-life experiences and highlights the dialogic nature of our faith. Overall, Lamentations is a prayer of truthfulness, whose ultimate dialogue partner is God.

Outline of the Book

This book intends to contribute to Lamentations scholarship by providing a more holistic approach to the book that will show the intrinsic connection between structure and content in Lamentations, and to read the book as a whole from the angle of the mini-acrostic in Lam 5:19–20. It further aims to advance the scholarly conversation on communal lament by looking at the

---

140. Ibid., 19. See also Kepnes, *The Text as Thou*.

141. Mandolfo (*Daughter Zion Talks Back to the Prophets*, 103–19) considers God's response to Zion in Second Isaiah inadequate since God never answers Zion's question in Lamentations, "why have you done this?"; and God tries to divert Zion's attention to other great things he is going to do for her without genuine reconciliation with the past.

Forgotten and Forsaken by God (Lam 5:19–20)

key elements of admission of guilt and mood change. It likewise hopes to raise awareness of mood change in communal lament from praise to lament and the significance of remaining in lament for a suffering community.

After the history of research on Lamentations here in chapter 1, chapter 2 will study the intrinsic connection between the acrostic structure and the content of Lamentations, in light of the mini-acrostic in Lam 5:19–20.

Chapter 3 will exegete Lamentations chapter by chapter, paying attention to the interconnectedness of the poems, the dialogic interaction among the voices, and the significance of the acrostic structure of the first four poems and the lack of such a structure in chapter 5.

Chapter 4 will compare Lamentations with other selected communal laments (e.g., Psalms 12 and 89) in the Hebrew Bible. This chapter will focus on the mood change in communal laments and the question of whether such mood change is invariably from lament to praise or rather also from praise to lament.

Chapter 5 will consider the admission of guilt as voiced in Lamentations and other selected communal laments (e.g., Isa 63:7—64:12; Jer 14:1—15:9; Psalms 79 and 106). In particular, this chapter will study the role of admission of guilt for a suffering community, and its bearing on the community's dealing with its suffering.

Chapter 6 will explore the significance of remaining in lament in Lamentations and related Old Testament texts for suffering individuals and communities and the implications of doing so has for the relationship between the suffering community and God. It will also examine the image of God that the suffering community espouses and the significance of remaining in lament for modern day suffering persons and communities.

Chapter 7 will conclude the dissertation, synthesize findings of the previous chapters, and explore possibilities for further study.

2

Acrostic in Lamentations

INTRODUCTION

LAMENTATIONS IS A LITERARY masterpiece, a perfect unity of form and content. It combines careful composition and profound reflections and emotions. It possesses the power to move and shake the reader; volumes of commentaries and interpretations cannot exhaust its meaning. Lamentations also employs various literary devices. Daniel Grossberg affirms that the book "strikes a balance between the predominance of the whole and the emphasis on the parts with its point of balance somewhere midway on the structural scale."[1] He further states that the complex of the book's interrelated features makes it "hover between the centripetal and centrifugal extremes."[2]

The alphabetic acrostic is the most dominant literary feature of Lamentations and serves to unite its five poems.[3] Even though scholars disagree on its function, it is obvious that the alphabetic acrostic is a unifying and consolidating literary device of the book. The first four poems of Lamentations are written in alphabetic acrostic. Each of the first two poems has twenty two strophes; each strophe is composed (mostly) of three lines with

---

1. Grossberg, *Centripetal and Centrifugal Structures in Biblical Poetry*, 7.

2. Ibid., 83.

3. For a metric pattern analysis of the acrostic form, see Freedman, "Acrostic and Metrics in Hebrew Poetry," 367–92; Freedman, "Acrostic Poems in the Hebrew Bible," 408–31. For a contemporary English translation of Lamentations in acrostic form, see Slavitt, *The Book of Lamentations*, 60–85. For a comparison of biblical and ANE acrostics, see Soll, "Babylonian and Biblical Acrostics," 305–22; Brug, "Biblical Acrostics and Their Relationship to Other Ancient Near Eastern Acrostics," 283–304.

the opening letters of first lines following the sequence of the Hebrew alphabet. The fourth poem exhibits the same feature, with the only difference being that each strophe is formed of only two lines. The third poem has twenty two strophes as well; each strophe is formed of three lines, but the alphabetic acrostic intensifies here since the first letter of each line in every strophe starts with the same letter. The last poem is not written in acrostic, but does have twenty two lines, the same number as the letters of the Hebrew alphabet.

K. M. O'Connor provides a list of the acrostic arrangements in Lamentations as follows (with my modifications of the number of lines in poems 1 and 2):[4]

Poem 1

Acrostic

22 strophes of 3 lines each

(67 lines)

Poem 2

Acrostic

22 strophes of 3 lines each

(67 lines)

Poem 3

Acrostic

22 strophes of 3 lines each

Each line starts with the same letter)

(44 lines)

Poem 4

Acrostic

22 strophes of 2 lines each

(66 lines)

Poem 5

Not acrostic

22 strophes of 1 line each

---

4. O'Connor (*Lamentations and the Tears of the World*, 12) lists 66 lines for poems 1 and 2; however, Lam 1:7 and 2:19 have four lines instead of three, so the two poems each end with a total of 67 lines.

(22 lines)

Even though Lamentations 5 is not an alphabetic acrostic, 5:19-20 forms a mini-acrostic that harks back to the structure of the previous acrostic poems and is connected with the messages of the whole book.

This chapter will first look at the function of the alphabetic acrostic in Lamentations, then its characteristics in the book, including those of the mini-acrostic in Lam 5:19-20, and finally will note connections between the book's different voices and the acrostic structure.

FUNCTION OF THE ACROSTIC IN LAMENTATIONS

Several functions of the acrostic as used in Lamentations have been proposed. It is suggested in *Midrash Lamentations Rabbah* (only in the Buber edition) that the device functions as an aid to memory in oral performance.[5] But this view is problematic since the acrostic form is noticed by the eye, not by the ear. Besides, those reciting from memory would be confused by the interchange of ע and פ that occurs in Lamentations 2, 3, and 4 (see below). In the other alphabetic acrostics that occur in the Hebrew Bible (Psalms 9-10, 25, 34, 37, 111-12, 119, 145; Nah 1:2-8; Prov 31:10-31; Sir 51:13-30), there are often disrupted sequences, inversion of letters or missing letters.[6] These features militate against a mnemonic purpose for the acrostic.[7]

Another function proposed is aesthetic. C. Westermann advocates this function since he considers the acrostic as "a relatively late stylistic feature."[8] Many scholars accept the proposal that the alphabetic acrostic expresses a sense of completeness. The poet(s) treat their subject in an exhaustive manner by employing the complete alphabet which contains everything that can

---

5. *Midrash Lamentations Rabbah* (Buber edition; Vilna, 1909) chapter 1:1 "Why was the book of Lamentations written in alphabetic acrostic? So that it will be learnt by chanters." See Assis, "Alphabetic Acrostic in the Book of Lamentations," 712; Salters, *Lamentations*, 19-20.

6. For an analysis of these other acrostics, see Treves, "Two Acrostic Psalms," 81-90; De Vries, "Acrostic of Nahum" 476-81; Babinowitz, "The Qumran Hebrew Original," 173-84; Watson, *Classical Hebrew Poetry*, 192-200; Spronk, "Acrostics in the Book of Nahum," 209-22; Benun, "Evil and the Disruption of Order," 2-30; Maloney, "Intertextual Links," 11-21; and Renz, "A Perfectly Broken Acrostic in Nahum 1?," 2-26.

7. Soll ("Acrostic," 1:59) holds that it is problematic to consider biblical alphabetic acrostics as mnemonic devices in light of Babylonian acrostics, which no one supposes were written for such purposes.

8. Westermann (*Lamentations*, 99-100) considers the acrostic "a mechanical type of arrangement" that has "no intrinsic connection with content." He thinks it unlikely that the songs in Lamentations were originally composed as acrostics; they acquired this form "only during the course of their transmission."

be said by means of letters.⁹ In Lamentations, the sense of completeness generated by the acrostics would serve to express either the completeness of transgression that Israel had committed or more likely the completeness of grief expressed in the poems.

A number of scholars argue that the acrostic is an intrinsic feature of Lamentations.¹⁰ B. S. Childs holds that the book's form and the function of its various parts in relation to the whole are essential for understanding the book.¹¹ E. Assis makes a strong argument that the acrostic form is the key for interpreting the book as a whole and its literary unity.¹² N. K. Gottwald, F. W. Dobbs-Allsopp and J. Hunter hold that the "external" principle of the acrostic in Lamentations is intended to correspond to the internal spirit and intention of the book.¹³ I follow the view that the alphabetic acrostic is an intrinsic feature of Lamentations, not a late stylistic adaptation.¹⁴ It is a vehicle that contains and constrains the book's emotions and conflicting views. One should not look for a univocal message from Lamentations; rather, within the overarching acrostic structure, various views are expressed and different messages conveyed.

Scholars have proposed various and interconnected ways that the acrostic functions in Lamentations, among which are the following:

First, O'Connor says that acrostic devices are "deeply symbolic."¹⁵ They "contain and control the chaos of unstructured pain" that the survivors experienced.¹⁶ They expose the depth and breadth of unfathomable suffering in contrasting ways.

Second, the acrostic also gives "order and shape to suffering that is otherwise inherently chaotic, formless, and out of control."¹⁷ Dobbs-Allsopp holds that Lamentations's acrostics serve as a literary "container" of the poems. Given the fragmentary character of Lamentations and its lack of

---

9. Johnson, "Form and Message in Lamentations," 60–61.

10. Renkema, "Literary Structure of Lamentations," 295–96; Renkema, "Meaning of the Parallel Acrostics in Lamentations," 379–83.

11. Childs, *Introduction to the Old Testament as Scripture*, 593–94.

12. Assis, "Unity of the Book of Lamentations," 306–29; Assis, "Alphabetic Acrostic in Lamentations," 710–24.

13. Gottwald, *Studies,* 30; Dobbs-Allsopp, *Lamentations* 18; and Hunter, *Faces of a Lamenting City,* 56uHuH.

14. Grossberg ("Form and Content and Their Correspondence," 47) states, "we need to be mindful of many ways that the ancient artists/sages employ particular literary expressions *in the service of* their message" (italics original).

15. O'Connor, *Lamentations and the Tears of the World,* 13.

16. Ibid., 12.

17. Ibid., 13.

plot and form, the acrostic holds the poems together and guides the reader from beginning to end.[18] The acrostic generates coherence for the individual poems and Lamentations as a whole.

Third, Assis believes that the acrostic was employed in order to "create an unparalleled tension between the deep emotional mode and the contemplated structure," and to convey the idea that "Lamentations is a rational reflection on the horrifying situation."[19] Lamentations thus exhibits an intentional tension between the book's constraining form and the unrestrained content, such that the book interacts with the reader on both emotional and rational levels.

Fourth, the acrostic varies in its use throughout Lamentations: the changes in stanza length, the reversed positions of ע and פ in chapters 2, 3, and 4, and the structure of the acrostic in connection with the book's shifting voices and perspectives all give the poetry a "trajectory and a sense of dynamism."[20] Regarding the overall unfolding of the acrostic in Lamentations, J. F. Brug argues that the acrostic builds in intensity until the third poem, then fades away in the forth poem and effectively disappears in the fifth; this movement is designed "to convey the impression that the intensity of the poet's grief has exhausted his poetic powers."[21] Beyond its purely literary functions, the acrostic thus also has semantic and theological meaning.

Fifth, Dobbs-Allsopp suggests that since the alphabet stands as the paradigmatic symbol of culture and civilization, the acrostic, in its forward movement and formal completeness, functions as a means of consolation. It is used as a token and a security, guaranteeing cosmic order in the midst of utter devastation and most dehumanizing suffering.[22]

All these possible functions show that the acrostic is not a late stylistic feature in Lamentations. It corresponds to the intention of the book. The characteristics of the acrostic as used in Lamentations carry the message of the book.

CHARACTERISTICS OF THE ACROSTIC IN LAMENTATIONS

The acrostic poems are carefully laid out in a sequence in Lamentations. The acrostic gives shape to each poem and also to the overall structure of

---

18. Dobbs-Allsopp, *Lamentations*, 18.
19. Assis, "Alphabetic Acrostic in Lamentations," 717.
20. Dobbs-Allsopp, *Lamentations*, 18.
21. Brug, "Biblical Acrostics," 286.
22. Dobbs-Allsopp, *Lamentations*, 18.

the book. We will now look in turn at the concentric structure of the book and its four acrostic poems, the reversal of the letters ע and פ in chapters 2, 3 and 4, the triple acrostic in chapter 3, the absence of acrostic in chapter 5, and the mini-acrostic in 5:19–20.

The Concentric Structure of Lamentations

The book of Lamentations as a whole can be seen as organized according to a concentric structure. The triple acrostic in chapter 3 is at the center of the book. Assis observes that chapter 4 is parallel to 2, and that the two chapters share common vocabulary and themes: e.g., famine (2:11–12, 19–20; 4:1, 4–5, 9–10), God's anger (2:3–4; 4:11), the enemy's rejoicing (2:15; 4:14–15) and the iniquity of Israel (2:14; 4:22). Chapter 5 is parallel to 1, and these two chapters exhibit some common motifs as well: the widowhood of city Zion and mothers (1:1; 5:3), comparison with the past (1:7; 5:21), weeping over desolation (1:16; 5:17–18), the feeling of loss and pain (1:20, 22; 5:15, 17) and the mourning motif (1:4; 5:14–15).[23]

That Lamentations as a book is organized in a concentric structure was first pointed out by R. Gordis, and this observation has been developed by R. Brandscheidt.[24] Brandscheidt presents the structure of the five chapters as follows:

1. Lament—the lament of Zion and judgment doxology
2. Report—enraged judgment of Yhwh and Zion's helplessness
3. Instruction—Attitude of Zion during the time of judgment
4. Report—enraged judgment of Yhwh and Zion's hope
5. Lament—Lament of the nation and despairing questions addressed to Yhwh

I. G. P. Gous agrees with Brandscheidt on the structure of the five chapters, but disagrees with her on the chapters' themes. In addition, Gous sees a further development in the chapters from past to present to future. He thus lays out the structure of Lamentations as follows:[25]

---

23. Assis ("Unity of Lamentations," 313–28) provides a more detailed analysis and lists of the chapters' parallel passages.

24. Gordis, *Song of Songs and Lamentations*, 127; Brandscheidt, *Gotteszorn und Menschenleid*, 231.

25. Gous, "A Survey of Research on the Book of Lamentations," 198. For a more detailed layout of the chiastic structure of the Lamentations, see Dorsey, "Lamentations," 83–90.

1. Past: description of the chaos and prayers for restoration
2. Past: despair as a result of the cancellation of election
3. Present: instruction—hope in Yhwh
4. Future: overcoming despair and new hope
5. Future: description of present despair and prayers for restoration

Gous's labeling of the five chapters gives one the false impression that almost half of the book is about hope and the future, which is hardly the case. It does, however, call attention to a forward movement from chapter to chapter in the book.

B. Morse points out that the beginning and end of the book also form a double *inclusio*.[26] The inner circle of the *inclusio* is constituted by the affirmation of divine sovereignty in Lam 1:5: "the Lord has made (Israel) suffer for the multitude of her transgressions" and 5:19 "but you, O Lord, reign forever; your throne endures to all generations." The outer circle of the *inclusio* is more obvious, i.e. the inclusion of despair formed by 1:1–5a and 5:22, with the loneliness of the city at the book's beginning and anger over abandonment by God at its end.

The Concentric Pattern in the Acrostic Poems

A number of scholars have observed that the four acrostics in Lamentations consist of two halves: the "fact half" and the "interpretation half," which are constructed according to a concentric structure with its turning point at the center (the ל and מ lines).[27] This pattern is pretty clear in chapter 1. The first half (א-כ) describes the pitiful state of city Zion. She is personified throughout and the third person is used except in 1:9c and 11c when she bursts out in a cry to Yhwh. Lam 1:11c also serves as a transition to the second half (ל-ת) where there is a shift from the third to the first person and city Zion becomes the speaker. The first half depicts the calamities Zion has gone through and the afflictions caused by the enemy, culminating in the famine described in v. 11. The second half explains what happened, the calamities now being ascribed to Yhwh acting in response to Israel's iniquities. Verses 11–12 stand at the center of the chapter with a call to the Lord and passersby to see the misery and sorrow inflicted by the Lord's anger upon Zion.

---

26. Morse, "Lamentations Project," 114.
27. Johnson, "Form and Message in Lamentations," 61–70; Renkema, "Literary Structure of Lamentations," 388–91; Heater, "Structure and Meaning in Lamentations," 304–15.

Forgotten and Forsaken by God (Lam 5:19-20)

Johnson observes that the last two verses of the chapter also correspond to its first two but at the same time go a step further.[28] Zion's distress and the lack of a comforter for her are emphasized in these four framework verses. In vv. 1-2, Zion's friends and lovers became her enemies; in vv. 21-22, all her enemies rejoice over her calamities. Since the second half of the chapter reflects the view that the Lord stands behind all that happened, the last two verses end with a wish that the Lord will deal with Zion's enemies as the Lord had dealt with her.

Chapter 2 starts from the center of chapter 1, the anger of the Lord (1:12), which is mentioned twice in 2:1, with the Lord being further identified as an enemy (2:5). The first half of the chapter depicts in vivid language what the Lord has done to his own people. The Lord has humiliated, thrown down, destroyed without mercy, cut down, burned like a flaming fire, killed, poured out his fury, abolished festivals and Sabbath, spurned king and priests, scorned his altar, disowned his sanctuary and laid Zion in ruins.[29] Verses 11-12 stand at the center of the chapter; here, the narrator, who talks in the first person, is exhausted with weeping and there is a heart-wrenching description of starving children dying in their mothers' bosoms. The tone of the narrator in the second part of chapter 2 is different from that in the first; it is gentler and milder, voicing, as it does, a desire to comfort Jerusalem and an encouragement to her to cry out to the Lord. Chapter 2 is not as clearly split in the middle by the letters ל and כ as is the case in chapter 1, but there is no doubt that the two letters are utilized to form the center of the chapter.

It is difficult to divide chapter 3 clearly into two halves. Chapter 3 differs from the first two chapters in its use of the first person singular to articulate the perspective of an afflicted man. It also presents traditional ideas about retribution. The speaker laments in a Jobian way, but unlike Job, he never protests his innocence. A number of scholars propose that here too the middle two letters ל and כ constitute the center of the chapter. Heater points out that in the triple acrostic in Lamentations 3, only the כ ל ט strophes use the same word three times.[30] He argues that the ל and כ verses seem to represent the center of the chapter's message since they affirm that God is good, compassionate and just. Johnson also sees 3:31-36 as the exact center and core of the chapter and as a theological answer to Israel's distress.[31] The

---

28. Johnson, "Form and Message in Lamentations," 63.

29. For an analysis of the metaphors and images used in the first part of Lamentations 2, see Labahn, "Fire from Above," 239-56.

30. Heater, "Structure and Meaning in Lamentations," 309. The three lines in the ל strophe do not feature the exact same words, but ל functions as a preposition in each line.

31. Johnson, "Form and Message in Lamentations," 66. Ulrich Berges ("'Ich bin de Mann, der Elend sah' [Klgl 3, 1],"16) sees a concentric pattern in chapter 3 as well. He

affliction Israel experienced was a punishment, but not a final rejection; rather, the punishment aims at rehabilitation. O'Connor observes that 3:31 is noticeably shorter than any other line in the poem and "the power of this verse stretches backward and forward in the poem."[32] Lam 3:31, "Adonai does not reject forever" makes the theological dilemma of the poet clear: God rejects, but not forever, causes grief, but will show compassion (3:32) and does not willingly cause grief or affliction (3:33). Herein "lies the theological tension residing at the poem's heart."[33] The rest of the poem struggles with the conflict between divine rejection and mercy. Renkema, for his part, compares the corresponding strophes of the chapter (etc. ג//ר, ב//ש, א//ת) and notes that connections between most of them are not strong. He further questions whether the core of the song can be found in its ל and כ strophes.[34]

The acrostic becomes shorter in chapter 4, with only two lines to each verse. Chapter 4, like chapters 1 and 2, is formed of two parts. The first part, from ל to א, describes the devastated condition of Zion. It starts in v. 1 with a reference to dimmed gold and scattered sacred stones which could allude to the sanctuary; it then moves to the children who were as valuable as gold, but who perished like clay in v. 2. The people become as cruel as ostriches due to hunger (4:3), and the punishment of Jerusalem is harsher than that of Sodom (4:6). The first part culminates in v. 10 where the hands of compassionate women are said to have boiled their own children for food. The name of Yhwh appears for the first time in the chapter in v. 11 which dramatically ends the first part with mention of the Lord's giving full vent to his wrath and consuming the foundation of Zion. The chapter's second part starts in v. 12, using ל, with a statement that no one believes this could have happened to Jerusalem. The segment moves on to state that the reason for the calamity is the iniquities of the prophets and priests (v. 13). The leaders

---

lays out the chapter's structure with a division between ל and כ as follows (my translation from German):
1–16 the Central Report: I—He (Yhwh);
  17–20 Statement: You—I—He;
    21–24 Statement of Confidence: I—He—You;
      25–33 Explanation 1: He does not afflict willingly;
      34–39 Explanation 2: He (three questions/three answers);
    40–47 Penitential Song: We—He—You;
    48–51 Lament Song of the Individual: I—Daughter of My People—He;
52–56 Lament with a Plea for the Destruction of Enemies: I—You—Enemies.
This structure seems a bit forced. The corresponding parts are of very unequal length, escpecially the first and last.

32. O'Connor, *Lamentations and the Tears of the World*, 51.

33. Ibid.

34. Renkema, "Literary Structure of Lamentations," 321. The triple acrostic in chapter 3 and its function in the book will be dealt with more fully later.

Forgotten and Forsaken by God (Lam 5:19–20)

of the people were scattered like fugitives (vv. 14–17), and Zion has come to an end (v. 18). The chapter ends with a curse on Edom (v. 21) and the affirmation of the end of exile (v. 22a), along with a reference to punishment for Edom's sins (v. 22b).

The Reversal of the ע and פ Letters

There is a reversal of the letters ע and פ in Lam 2:16–17; 3:46–51; and 4:16–17.

Lam 2:16 פ	Lam 3:46-48 פ	Lam 4:16 פ
פצו עליך פיהם כל־אויביך שרקו ויחרקו־שן אמרו בלענו אך זה היום שקוינהו מצאנו ראינו	פצו עלינו פיהם כל־איבינו פחד ופחת היה לנו השאת והשבר פלגי־מים תרד עיני על־שבר בת־עמי	פני יהוה חלקם לא יוסיף להביטם פני כהנים לא נשאו זקנים לא חננו
All your enemies open their mouth against you; they hiss, they gnash their teeth, they cry: "we have devoured her! Ah, this is the day for which we waited; at last we have seen it!"	All our enemies have opened their mouth against us; panic and pitfall have come upon us, devastation and destruction. My eyes flow with rivers of tears because of the destruction of my people.	The Lord himself has scattered them, he will regard them no more; no honor was shown to the priests, no favor to the elders.
Lam 2:17 ע	Lam 3:49-51 ע	Lam 4:17 ע
עשה יהוה אשר זמם בצע אמרתו אשר צוה מימי־קדם הרס ולא חמל וישמח עליך אויב הרים קרן צריך	עיני נגרה ולא תדמה מאין הפגות עד־ישקיף וירא יהוה משמים עיני עוללה לנפשי מכל בנות עירי	עודינה תכלינה עינינו אל־עזרתנו חמל בצפיתנו צפינו אל־גוי לא יושע
The Lord has done what he purposed, he has carried out his threat, as he ordained long ago, he has thrown down without sparing; he has made the enemy rejoice over you, and exalted the might of your foes.	My eyes will flow without ceasing, without respite, until the Lord from heaven looks down and sees. My eyes torment my soul at the sight of all the daughters of my city.	Our eyes failed, ever watching vainly for help; in our watching, we have watched, for a nation that could not save.

The above three parallel passages are connected with one another and there is a progression in thought as well. In its פ lines, chapter 2 mainly talks about the enemy, those lines in chapter 3 move from the enemy to the destruction the people experienced and the poet's unceasing lament over this, while the פ line in chapter 4 talks about the Lord himself who scattered the people and disregarded the leaders. In its ע lines, chapter 2 says that it is the Lord who carried out what he had proposed and made the enemy rejoice over Israel. The ע lines in chapter 3 continue from v. 48, the last line of the פ section, stating that the poet's eyes are flowing with unceasing tears (also Lam 2:11, 18). The desire that the Lord look and see (Lam 3:50) is a major theme throughout the book (Lam 1:11; 2:20; 5:1). The fate of the young women in the city (Lam 3:51) is also cited in Lam 2:21; 5:11. The ע lines in chapter 4 begin and end with mention of eyes that look in vain for help. Scholars offer various proposals concerning the reversal of the two letters in the above passages.[35] One early proposal was that these represent a mistake either by the copyist or the poet; it is, however, hard to explain why the same mistake happens three times in the same sequence.[36] Another proposal is that the order of the two letters was still not fixed at the time when Lamentations was written down.[37] D. R. Hillers considers this suggestion "sheerly hypothetical and rather improbable" since the consistent sequence is *ayin-pe* in Ugaritic literature, almost a millennium earlier than Lamentations.[38] The most probable explanation is that the interchange serves to catch readers' attention precisely by its irregularity; it is a literary device used by the poet in order to make a point.[39] Heater points out that the פ line in Lam 4:16 differs in content from the פ lines in chapters 2 and 3.[40] He is correct in saying that Lam 4:16 involves a play on the word פני,

---

35. For a discussion of such proposals, see Wiesmann, *Die Klagelieder*, 32–33; and Heater, "Structure and Meaning in Lamentations," 313–15.

36. C. F. Houbigant, B. Kennicott, and J. Jahn attribute the deviation from the correct alphabetic sequence to a copyist's error, while L. Bertholdt thinks that the original poet made a mistake. See the discussion in Heater, "Structure and Meaning in Lamentations," 314.

37. This proposal goes back to H. Grotius; see the discussion in Wiesmann, *Die Klagelieder*, 32.

38. Hillers, *Lamentations*, 29.

39. Renz ("A Perfectly Broken Acrostic in Nahum 1?" 22) studies the "broken acrostic" in Nahum 1 and concludes that the acrostic there serves to convey the concept of order while its irregularities are intended to indicate that divine order is not to be equated with the status quo. It is likely that the irregularities in Lamentations are literary devices as well, just like those in Nahum 1. Benun ("Evil and the Disruption of Order," 2) says that "a deliberate disruption in the alphabetic sequence at precise locations in the text and other more subtle anomalies in an otherwise very structured poem" serve as signposts. Neusner, *Lamentations Rabbah*, 237, offers an explanation only of the reversal of the two letters in chapter 2. He avers that the two letters were reversed because the enemies were saying with their mouth (פה) what they had not seen with their eyes (עין).

40. Heater ("Structural and Meaning in Lamentations," 315) points out that the פ lines in chapters 2 and 3 are almost identical in their speaking of the enemies' opening their mouth against Zion; in the פ lines in chapter 4, it is Yhwh who scattered the elders and priests.

Forgotten and Forsaken by God (Lam 5:19–20)

"face." God's face that gives peace in the priestly benediction in Num 6:26 now destroys God's people and "the faces of the priests are not to be lifted up" (פני כהנים לא נשׂאו, Lam 4:16). Heater also notes that no verse in chapter 4 begins its two component lines with the same word except for v. 16 with its double use of פני at the start of each colon. The favored status of Zion with God is now reversed.[41] Gottwald holds that the most striking structural element of Lamentations is "the recurring theme of reversal" of past and present, of faith and reality,[42] calling this a "dramatic contrast" from the literary and a "tragic reversal" from the theological point of view, which gives Lamentations its "overwhelming emotional effectiveness."[43] I suggest that the interchange of the two letters reflects the book's theme of reversal as well.

The supposition that the reversal of the two letters is a deliberate literary choice by the poet is further strengthened by the position of the two instances of ע in chapter 5. P. Guillaume, who considers Lamentations 5 as the seventh acrostic of the book (see above p. 23), observes that Lam 5:17–18 are "the only consecutive verses that start with identical letters and the initial ע of verse 17 would be the only initial letter in the correct position in the ע-פ sequence had chapter 5 been an alphabetic acrostic"—as are Lamentations 2–4.[44] According to Guillaume, the ע in 5:18 underlines the use of the same letter in 5:17 and serves to demarcate the book's last four lines, Lam 5:19–22, the initial letters of which form the word אלהך, "your God."[45]

Triple Acrostic in Lamentations 3

The triple acrostic in chapter 3 has attracted a lot of attention, not only because of its intensified form, but also due to its content. Chapter 3 differs from Lamentations' other acrostics in a number of ways. First, it does not start with איכה, "how" as do chapters 1, 2 and 4, but rather with הגבר ראה עני אני, "I am the man who has seen affliction." The chapter is thus distinctive as a personal lament with a fourfold repetition of the word גבר, "man" (vv. 1, 27, 35, and 39). Second, there is little reference to the fall of Jerusalem, which is the focus of the other chapters. Thirdly and most noticeably, this chapter contains the only voices of explicit hope in the book (Lam 3:22–33).

As an intensified triple acrostic, Lamentations 3 occupies the poetic center of the book. But the book as a whole also has a forward movement

---

41. Ibid.
42. Gottwald, *Studies*, 52–53.
43. Ibid., 53.
44. Guillaume, "Lamentations 5," 3–4.
45. Ibid., 4. This point will be further elaborated later in the chapter.

and chapter 3's triple acrostic has to be understood in this wider context. Dobbs-Allsopp affirms that "chapter 5 is the thematic climax of Lamentations—not ch. 3, as so often stated."⁴⁶ As previously mentioned in Chapter I, Lamentation 3's message of hope is just one voice among several others and so cannot be taken as the sole message of the whole book. Moreover, the voice of hope expressed in Lam 3:22–33 is fleeting, not being sustained throughout the entire chapter; it appears suddenly, and it is not emphatic enough to override the grim picture depicted in the book's other poems.

Absence of the Acrostic in Lamentations 5

Renkema thinks that the lack of acrostic in Lamentations' last poem is a deliberate decision on the part of the poet who intended it as a closing prayer.⁴⁷ According to him, the strict acrostic form ill fits prayer: "In that state of misery one cannot pray from *A* to *Z* and then stop. To the contrary, praying and shedding of tears must go on, restlessly, day and night, until the Lord in heaven looks down, watches their affliction and renews their days."⁴⁸ Freedman holds that the absence of the alphabetic acrostic in Lamentations 5 "represents a modification, a slight sophistication, of the original arrangement, and not the other way around."⁴⁹ Hunter considers the prayer character of Lamentations 5 very important, with the book as a whole building up to this prayer: "the chapter should probably be seen as the most important within the argument of the poets in favor of the restoration of the city and its people."⁵⁰ Grossberg claims that this "codalike" chapter 5 recapitulates the motifs of the entire book and serves as its concluding prayer. It is part of a "deliberate, compositional design."⁵¹ Lamentations 5 can rightly be considered as the climax of the book

46. Dobbs-Allsopp, "Tragedy, Tradition, and Theology," 41. Assis ("Unity of Lamentations," 311–13) considers Lamentations 3 as the crux of the book, but Lamentations 5 as its climax.

47. Renkema, "Literary Structure of Lamentations," 365.

48. Ibid., 365–66. Renkema also makes the point that the use of the singular אב (literally "father") in Lam 5:3 is strange. It could be understood as collective ("no fathers/leaders") or as an abbreviation of the alphabet: no *aleph*, no *bet*.

49. Freedman, "Acrostic Poems in the Hebrew Bible," 415; and Guillaume, "Lamentations 5," 2.

50. Hunter, *Faces of a Lamenting City*, 61.

51. Grossberg (*Centripetal and Centrifugal Structures*, 101) says: "the possible interpretation of Lamentations as an arbitrary, whimsical conglomeration of styles is disqualified in favor of the view of a deliberate, compositional design." He admits that chapter 5 differs greatly from the previous four chapters; therefore, it reflects an obvious centrifugal movement. But this feature is balanced by compensatory centripetal forces that pick up themes and vocabulary of suffering humanity from the previous chapters.

Forgotten and Forsaken by God (Lam 5:19–20)

due to its character as a prayer uttered by the first person plural voice throughout the chapter, the apparent percentage increase of parallel lines vis-à-vis the previous four chapters, and its genre as a communal lament.[52]

Several scholars approach Lamentations 5 from other perspectives in their reading of Lamentations as a literary unity. Prouser, e.g., reads the book from a midrashic point of view and considers Lamentations 1–4 as reflecting the six days of creation and Lamentations 5 the one day of rest, while Guillaume views Lamentations 5 as the seventh acrostic of the book.[53] Still, both do view Lamentations 5 as the culmination of the book.

Mini-Acrostic in Lam 5:19–20

It is in the context of the importance of chapter 5 for Lamentations as a whole that the mini-acrostic in 5:19–20 is now to be analyzed. The two verses read as follows in Hebrew:

אתה יהוה לעולם תשב כסאך לדו ודור
למה לנצח תשכחנו תעזבנו לארך ימים

"You, O Yhwh, sit forever; your throne is from generation to generation.
Why have you forgotten us for so long, forsaken us these many days?"

As previously noted in chapter I, this mini-acrostic features certain characteristics.[54] First, there is the rare combination of verbs שכח "forget" and עזב "forsake," with Yhwh as subject. Second, Yhwh is referred to as "You" here, the second-person pronoun אתה occurring only three times in the book (Lam 1:21; 3:42 and 5:19), all in reference to Yhwh. Third, the first letters of the four lines of Lam 5:19–22 form the word אלהך, "your God."

It is most probable that the poet carefully chose his words to summarize the teaching of the entire book by using the four letters ה and ל, כ, א to start the component cola in Lam 5:19–20. Lam 5:19, כ to א, firmly articulates the reign of the Lord that endures for all generations. Lamentations never questions the sovereignty of God explicitly and accepts calamity as God's punishment for sins. Yet, the belief that God reigns for all generations offers little comfort in such severe suffering. Lam 5:20, ה to ל, asks the

---

52. Hillers (*Lamentations*, 19–20) notes that 86 percent of the lines in Lamentations 5 contain parallelism, while only 59 percent do in chapters 1–4; see also Parry, *Lamentations*, 17–18.

53. Prouser, "Darkness on the Face of the Deep," 37–42; Guillaume, "Lamentations 5," 2–7.

54. See chapter 1, 25.

desperate question that echoes throughout the whole book: "Why have you forgotten us for so long, forsaken us these many days?"

Renkema states that the final question asked in Lam 5:20 captures the pain of the poet(s) who appeal to God against God.[55] This question far exceeds any attempt to provide an answer in the poems. It also reveals that the attitude of those who had remained faithful to Yhwh is "far removed from one of resignation that might have its basis in the conviction that YHWH was ultimately not responsible for everything that overcame them."[56] Probably the absence of the alphabetic acrostic in chapter 5 overall is intended to highlight the presence of its concluding mini-acrostic in 5:19–20 and to emphasize these two verses. God is unquestionably sovereign and just, but Zion's suffering is too great. The final why question thunders and echoes, refusing to be silenced before an utterly silent God.

The mini-acrostic is also connected with the structure of the book as a whole. First, its splitting of the alphabet at the middle points up the importance of the ל and מ verses in Lamentations 1–4. In Lam 1:11–12, the speaker shifts from the third person to the first, and Zion pleads with Yhwh and the passersby to look and see her sorrow and affliction, especially the hunger of the people. It is clear that Zion's sorrow was inflicted by the Lord. In Lam 2:11–12, the speaker's shift to the first person is accompanied by a changed attitude toward Zion, whose hunger is intensified and whose children die in their mothers' bosoms. In Lam 3:31–36, the positive characteristics of Yhwh are stressed; Yhwh does not reject forever and does not afflict willingly. Lam 3:36, however, is ambiguous with its statement that "Adonai does not see it," which sets up a tension with the rest of the book. Lam 4:11–12 follows after the heart-wrenching picture of compassionate women boiling their own children for food in v. 10. These two verses stress again that it is indeed Yhwh who destroyed Jerusalem, doing so to such a degree that the rest of the world could not believe what had happened.

Second, the mini-acrostic addresses Yhwh as "You." It affirms the dialogic nature of the book as a whole, even though it is Yhwh who forgets and forsakes, and it is Yhwh who remains silent and absent.

Third, the mini-acrostic in Lam 5:19–20 is part of an acrostic-telestic structure found in Lamentations 5.[57] Guillaume points out that vv. 17–18 are the only consecutive verses in this chapter that start with an identical letter, i.e., ע. The ע in v. 17 would be the only letter in the correct position

55. Renkema, "Theodicy in Lamentations?," 428.
56. Ibid.
57. Guillaume ("Lamentations 5," 4) explains that telestics involving reading the last letter of each line in sequence; they are the opposite of acrostics. This paragraph is a summary of Guillaume's article.

Forgotten and Forsaken by God (Lam 5:19–20)

in the ע-פ sequence as in Lamentations 2–4 had chapter 5 been an alphabetic acrostic. The ע in v. 18 serves to demarcate the last four lines of the chapter. The acrostic-telestic of vv. 19–22 reads אלהך רם מאד "your God is exalted greatly" (the א of מאד is in fact missing, but chapter 5—and the whole book—end with the word מאד). Moreover, Guillaume, following A. Rosenfeld, calls attention to a message formed by the first two words of 5:1a יהוה זכר, "Zachariah," and the mesotic (reading the first letters of half verses) of 5:1b–3, which constitutes the word הנביא, "prophet," thus the phrase "Zachariah the prophet."[58] This feature can be set out as follows:

5:1a זכר יהוה מה־היה לנו
5:1b הביט וראה את־חרפתנו
5:2a נחלתנו נהפכה לזרים
5:2b בתינו לנכרים
5:3a יתומים היינו אין אב
5:3b אמתנו כאלמנות

Thus, the acrostic-mesotic-telestic device of the chapter's beginning (Lam 5:1–3) and ending (Lam 5:19–22) features the following sentence: זכר היוה הנביא אלהך רם מד "Zechariah the prophet [says]: your God is greatly exalted" (the name "Zechariah," זכריה is written in full as זכרהיוה here).[59] Lamentations 5 thus contains a hidden alphabetic message.

Overall, Lamentations 5 is a highly sophisticated chapter that is carefully thought out and well planned. The mini-acrostic underlines two main themes running through the book: it affirms the sovereignty of God while it also protests against God, given the people's seemly endless suffering. The mini-acrostic affirms once again the dialogic nature of the book, where it is "to God—You" that the poet(s) pour out their hearts, trying to comprehend and change the current situation through recourse to You—God. The acrostic-mesotic-telestic of Lam 5:1–3 and 19–22 expresses the poet(s)' deeply rooted faith in God, in whom despite everything, their ultimate hope still lies.

---

58. Guillaume, "Lamentations 5," 4; Azriel Rosenfeld, "Aqrostikon be-'ekhah pereq 5," צ.

59. In Jer 26:18, Micah is quoted as announcing the destruction of Jerusalem, "Zion shall be plowed as a field; Jerusalem shall become a heap of ruins," while Zech 8:4 says, "old men and old women shall again sit in the streets of Jerusalem." It is recorded in *Lamentations Rabbah* 5:18 (Neusner, *Lamentations Rabbah*, 352–53) that Rabbi Akiba surprised his companions twice by rejoicing while they were weeping over the destruction of Jerusalem. Akiba rejoiced because he believed that if the above words of Micah had been proved true, then Zechariah's hopeful words will be fulfilled as well. See also Hasan-Rokem, *Web of Life*, 14.

DIFFERENT VOICES AND THE ACROSTIC STRUCTURE

W. Lanahan identifies five speaking voices or *personae* discernible in Lamentations.[60] His work has been very influential and widely cited. He makes clear that different speaking voices do not necessarily imply different authorship. He uses the term *persona* to refer to "the mask or characterization assumed by the poet as the medium through which he perceives and gives expression to his world."[61] The five voices Lanahan identifies are those of the narrator and city Zion that alternate in chapters 1 and 2, the voice of a defeated soldier in chapter 3, the voice of a "bourgeois" in chapter 4 and the voice of the community in chapter 5.[62] In contrast to Lanahan, I regard the main voice in chapter 4 as that of the narrator.[63] Thus, four voices, i.e. the narrator (Lam 1:1–11; 2:1–19; 4:1–16, 21–22), Zion (Lam 1:12–22; 2:20–22), the strong man (Lamentations 3) and the community (Lamentations 5), will be analyzed in this dissertation.

Grossberg further states that the shifts in personae are "abrupt" and usually "occur with no explicit announcement or 'stage direction.'" This feature could have generated "a fragmented kaleidoscopic effect" and destroyed the unity of the book, but it is counterbalanced by the unifying theme of suffering and the acrostic structure.[64]

Voices of the Narrator and City Zion

The interplay of the voices of the narrator and city Zion is very much connected with the acrostic structure of the first two chapters. Chapter 1 starts with the detached voice of a narrator who describes the state of Jerusalem objectively; his voice basically runs through the first half of the chapter from א to כ, with a sudden intrusion of a first person utterance in 9c: ראה יהוה את־עניי כי הגדיל אויב, "See, O Yhwh, my affliction, for the enemy has magnified himself!" Then, the chapter shifts back to the third person perspective. In 11c, the exact center of the chapter, the voice shifts to a passionate appeal by Jerusalem that the Lord look and see. The wording is very similar to 9c: ראה יהוה והביטה כי הייתי זוללה, "See, O Yhwh, and look, how worthless I have become!" The first person voice runs through the second half of

---

60. Lanahan, "Speaking Voice in the Book of Lamentations," 41–49.
61. Ibid., 41.
62. Ibid., 47–48.
63. Provan (*Lamentations*, 109–10) and O'Connor (*Lamentations and the Tears of the World*, 58) both identify the narrator as the main speaker in chapter 4.
64. Grossberg, *Centripetal and Centrifugal Structures*, 88–89.

Forgotten and Forsaken by God (Lam 5:19–20)

the chapter with the exception in v. 17, where the narrator breaks in for a single half-verse: "Zion stretches out her hands but there is no comforter for her" (17a).

The loneliness of the city is immediately highlighted by the narrator in chapter 1: איכה ישבה בדד, "Alas, she sits alone" (v. 1). She has no one to comfort her (אין לה מנחם), and the word "comforter" (מנחם) is repeated six times in the chapter (Lam 1:2, 3, 9, 16, 17, and 21). The narrator compares the present deserted state of the city with her glorious past; the contrast between the two is painfully apparent. The one time princess is now under hard servitude; the roads to Zion that once bustled with traffic now are desolate; the former friends and lovers are now enemies; those who used to honor her now despise her and she has become an object of mockery. She herself is fully responsible for her downfall, which is due to her own transgressions (Lam 1:5, 8).

The pitiful state of Jerusalem intensifies in the second part of the chapter when the city herself becomes the speaker. She admits her transgressions (Lam 1:14, 18, 20, and 22); yet, her unfathomable suffering compels her to call to the Lord and the passersby for attention.

The voice of the narrator dominates chapter 2 from v. 1 to v. 19. He attributes the present state of Jerusalem to the anger of the Lord (Lam 2:1–10). He speaks about himself for the first time in vv. 11–12, and addresses Jerusalem in the second person in vv. 13–19. The chapter's final three verses belong to woman Zion who uses the same imperatives as in chapter 1, "Look, O Lord, and see!" (Lam 1:11; 2:20). A significant change in tone occurs in the middle of chapter 2 (vv. 11–12). The narrator's detachment is replaced by words of compassion; the narrator himself becomes sick because of the suffering of Jerusalem, especially the heart-wrenching picture of mothers watching their own starving children die in their bosoms. O'Connor calls this change "the narrator's conversion."[65] The narrator is so affected by Zion's suffering that he tries to comfort her (Lam 2:13), the very thing Jerusalem desires in chapter 1. The narrator tries to explain to her what caused her downfall and encourages her to cry out to the Lord and to let her tears run down like a torrent without respite (Lam 2:18).[66]

The chapter's final three verses are tied together by more than their common speaker. According to Grossberg, they are also unified by a grim play of words and sound, the related labials of *b*, *p*, and *l* in particular.[67]

---

65. O'Connor, *Lamentations and the Tears of the World*, 35.

66. Miskotte (*When the Gods Are Silent*, 248) beautifully states that tears are the language to God when words fail.

67. Grossberg, *Centripetal and Centrifugal Structures*, 91.

Moreover, Grossberg points out a further link between vv. 19 and 20. There is a sad word association among the threatened lives of the children (עולליך על־נפש, "for the lives of your children," v. 19), the severe act of Yhwh (למי עוללת כה, "to whom you have acted so severely," v. 20), and the cannibalized children (עללי טפחים, "the children they have borne," v. 20). The term for Yhwh's "severe action" and the cannibalized "children" are formed from the same root, i.e. עלל.[68]

The narrator's description of Zion's suffering in chapter 4 focuses on the situation "in the streets," a key word in this poem (חוצות in Lam 4:1, 5, 8, and 14; חוץ in 4:18). There is no prayer to Yhwh, who is referred to in the third person only in this chapter. The narrator's main concern is again the suffering of the children (4:10) and priests and the prophets are said to be responsible for Zion's current state. The first person plural surfaces once in vv. 17–19, but does not appear abruptly here.[69] The chapter ends on a brighter note with its affirmation that Zion's exile will be ended and Edom's sins punished (4:22).

Voice of the Strong Man

The גבר "strong man" in Lamentations 3 utilizes the personal lament genre. He affirms from the very beginning that he has been afflicted by the Lord. In the first part of the chapter, he describes in general terms and metaphorical language how Yhwh (third person "he") afflicted him (first person "me"), this alternating with occasional outcries of pain using the first person voice "I" (vv. 14, 17–20). Lam 3:21, one third into the chapter, serves as a turning point; the man claims "this I call to mind, therefore I have hope." Lam 3:22–33 contains the only explicit statement of hope in the book, and this unexpected affirmation of hope is grounded in God's own faithful character. In Lam 3:40–47, the voice shifts to the first person plural and God is addressed in the second person. The genre changes into a communal lament. Lam 3:48 serves as another turning point, with the voice shifting back to the first person singular, and the genre reverting to individual lament. As Grossberg puts it, Lamentations 3 "closes with the same form with which it opened."[70] The chapter has come full circle.

Lanahan agrees that "the dominate image throughout the chapter has been that of encirclement;" the speaker who has been trapped in the drowning-pit, surrounded by his enemies, can escape "neither by prayer nor by

68. Ibid.
69. Ibid., 93.
70. Ibid.

the subterfuge of self-exoneration."[71] O'Connor thinks that the strong man is theologically confused.[72] Cooper too holds that the poet of Lamentations 3 is not a theologian, but a wretched and confused human being trying to cope with an impossible situation.[73] Assis, however, disagrees with Cooper since the poet is able to express well-structured thoughts in well-planned poetry, and is thus not "confused;" rather, his theology is complex and profound.[74] Nevertheless, it seems legitimate to assert that the hope expressed here is "vague" and is encompassed by the suffering all around it.[75] The book as a whole is ambivalent about hope for the future.[76] The strong man's voice has to be heard within the book as a whole. It offers *one* perspective, not *the* perspective.

Voice of the Community: Refusing Closure

Lamentations 5 uses the first person plural and its genre is closest to that of a communal lament. The collective perspective is highlighted by the recurrence of the first person plural suffix נו. Grossberg points out that this suffix occurs thirty-four times in the chapter; he further states that it serves as a *Leitmotif* that ties together the poem's distinct lines which lack an acrostic bond and also functions as a sort of rhyme which provides additional cohesiveness.[77]

The chapter starts with an appeal for Yhwh to "remember" and to "look and see." In so doing, it recalls the motifs of previous chapters: in Lam 2:1, the Lord has not remembered his footstool on the day of his hot anger, while in Lam 1:11 and 2:20, Zion asks Yhwh to "look and see." Then the chapter moves on to describe the miserable situation in the land, picking up motifs of the entire book and recapitulating the picture of the "suffering community" described in previous chapters.[78] Finally, the chapter and the book end on a poignant note in vv. 19–22. The call to God that echoes throughout the book

71. Lanahan, "Speaking Voice in the Book of Lamentations," 46.
72. O'Connor, *Lamentations and the Tears of the World*, 52.
73. Cooper, "Message of Lamentations," 18.
74. Assis, "Alphabetic Acrostic in Lamentations," 717.
75. Lanahan, "Speaking Voice, in the Book of Lamentations," 47.
76. Some look at this ambivalence about hope from a psychological perspective; see Joyce, "Lamentations and the Grief Process," 304–20; Reimer, "Good Grief?," 542–59.
77. Grossberg, *Centripetal and Centrifugal Structures*, 93–94.
78. Johnson ("Form and Message in Lamentations," 72) suggests that chapter 5 is the oldest part of the book since motifs of the entire book are to be found in this chapter. Moore ("Human Suffering in Lamentations," 552) thinks that chapter 5 is carefully laced with references to the human groupings evoked in previous chapters. He lists eleven such groupings.

remains unanswered and the voice of God is still absent at the end. This fact is the origin of the Jewish custom whereby any public reading of Lamentations repeats v. 21 after v. 22 in order not to end the reading on a negative note.[79]

Scholars have emphasized the importance of the book's last verse 5:22 for the understanding of the whole book.[80] The wording of the verse is rather simple כי אם־מאס מאסתנו קצפת עלינו עד־מאד; however, there is a problem with the rendering of its first phrase, כי אם.

The Old Greek and Syriac do not have an equivalent to אם, which they probably deleted in order to make sense of a difficult verse. However, the Hebrew is to be preferred as the more difficult reading.[81] Various proposed renderings of the phrase כי אם are as follows:[82]

First, the translation of JPSV in 1917 inserts a negative into the text: "Thou canst not have utterly rejected us, and be exceedingly wroth against us!" But this lacks textual support and the NJPSV drops it.[83]

Second, RSV translates the verse as a question: "Or hast thou utterly rejected us? Art thou exceedingly angry with us?" Westermann adopts this reading since, he holds, it best captures the sense the sentence carries in context, but admits that it is not a "strictly literal rendering" given that there is no textual evidence in the Hebrew Bible for taking כי אם as introducing a question.[84]

Third, both NRSV and NIV translate the phrase as "unless." כי אם in Lam 5:22 is cited under the heading "unless, except" in BDB.[85] Here, the phrase is taken as the equivalent of a negative, one which usually follows after a negative statement, an oath, or a question. BDB thus renders it as "unless thou have utterly rejected us, (and) art very wroth with us." The problem with this reading is that כי אם does not follow a negative statement in Lam 5:22.

Forth, Hillers translates the phrase as an adversative "but instead," following the Vulgate, Luther, and the King James Version. But adversatives usually follow a negative, which is not the case in Lam 5:22, though Hillers

---

79. See the translation of Lam 5:21–22 in *The Jewish Study Bible*, 1602.

80. See Linafelt, "Refusal of a Conclusion," 340; Gordis, "Conclusion of the Book of Lamentations (5:22)," 289.

81. Hillers, *Lamentations*, 160.

82. For this part, I rely heavily on Linafelt, "Refusal of a Conclusion," 340–43; Gordis, "Conclusion of Lamentations," 289–93.

83. See Gordis, "Conclusion of Lamentations," 340.

84. Westermann, *Lamentations*, 211. The phrase כי אם occurs 156 times in the Hebrew Bible, but nowhere introduces a question.

85. BDB, 474.

argues that occasionally כי אם is used as an adversative, even when there is no explicit negative in the preceding context.[86]

Fifth, Gordis renders כי אם as "even if, although" and takes the verbs (קצפת and מאסתנו) in Lam 5:22 as pluperfects. He thus translates Lam 5:20–22 as "Why do you neglect us eternally, forsake us for so long? Turn us to yourself, O Lord, and we shall return; renew our days as of old, even though you had despised us greatly and were very angry with us."[87] Westermann rejects this reading for two reasons: the verbs of Lam 5:22 cannot be taken as pluperfects since the wrath of God is still a reality; and the understanding of "even though" as a connective is questionable.[88]

Finally, I. W. Provan rightly observes that "it is clear the poem does not have a confident ending," whichever way כי אם is rendered.[89] I think the best proposal is that of Linafelt. He takes Lam 5:22 as "a protasis without an apodosis," an *if* conditional clause with the *then* clause left unstated. It is inappropriate to take Lam 5:22 as a complete conditional sentence since the second colon is not the consequence of the first, but rather a restatement of it. Rendering the verse as an incomplete conditional clause best captures the sense of Lamentations as a whole, i.e. refusal to conclude without a response from Yhwh. The ending of Lamentations is indeed "a willful nonending."[90] This deliberate nonending takes the message of Lamentations a step further. On the one hand, Lamentations as a book is complete; there is nothing left unsaid. Lamentations is effective literature; Zion gains sympathy from the narrator (Lam 2:13), and the book involves the reader emotionally, psychologically and intellectually. Yet, on the other hand, the book's very success depends on its failure.[91] The suffering is still too great and God is still silent! The book refuses to accept reality as it is, and holds out for a different future. "For if truly you have rejected us, raging bitterly against us—" (5:22).

---

86. Hillers (*Lamentations*, 160–61) notes uses of the phrase in this way in 2 Sam 13:33 and Num 24:22.

87. Gordis, "Conclusion of Lamentations," 291–93.

88. Westermann, *Lamentations*, 218.

89. Provan, *Lamentations*, 134.

90. Linafelt, "Refusal of a Conclusion," 343; and Linafelt, "Surviving Lamentations (One More Time)," 57–59. Neusner (*Israel after Calamity*, 8) notes that in Lam 5:22 ("For if truly you have rejected us, raging bitterly against us—"), divine rejection is mentioned before God's anger. Rejection is not the book's last word—the last word is anger. Neusner further states that if there is rejection, there is no hope, but if there is anger, there is hope, because someone who is angry may be appeased in the end.

91. See Landy, "Lamentations," in *The Literary Guide to the Bible*, 329.

Absence of God's Voice

God remains silent throughout Lamentations; thus, Dobbs-Allsopp calls Lamentations a tragedy.[92] As previously noted in Chapter I (see above p. 7), the big difference between Lamentations and the Mesopotamian city laments is that Lamentations lacks the return of the gods motif which usually gives a happy ending to Mesopotamian city laments.[93] Lamentations contains a short prayer for the restoration of Jerusalem, comparable to what one finds in Mesopotamian laments (Lam 5:21), but it does not speak of Yhwh's return at all. On the contrary, it ends on a note of abandonment (Lam 5:22). Lamentations is framed by a "thematic *inclusio* involving the divine abandonment theme alone."[94] From the opening depiction of the lonely city as a widow, to the afflicted "strong man" in chapter 3, to the unanswered communal prayer in chapter 5, what finally remains in the book is "a gaping hole."[95]

The absence of God is experienced the more acutely given the disproportionate divine punishment of sin. Sin is acknowledged, but in the face of such a degree of suffering, especially the situation of innocent children dying of hunger that occupies the middle of chapters 1, 2 and 4, the punishment appears excessive. Lamentations protests against the injustice of destruction and the severity of the people's suffering. Dobbs-Allsopp rightly observes that if there is any hope in Lamentations, it lies in the book's eloquent protest.[96]

CONCLUSION

Lamentations is indeed a literary unity of structure and content. It is a coherent and well-planned book. This unity could be expressed in the vivid image proposed by Jill Middlemas, who describes Lamentations as a "violent storm in the shape of a whirlwind."[97] She sees the shape of the book as a cyclone with the restful eye in the center surrounded by chaotic images of unabated violence, destruction, disease, hunger, despair and human suffering on a grand scale.[98] She proposes that its chiastic structure gives the book the shape of a whirlwind. The only message of hope in Lam 3:22-39 represents the restful eye in the center with howling and churning winds

---

92. Dobbs-Allsopp, "Tragedy, Tradition, and Theology," 29–60.
93. Dobbs-Allsopp, *Weep, O Daughter of Zion*, 90–96.
94. Dobbs-Allsopp, "Tragedy, Tradition, and Theology," 33.
95. Linafelt, "Margins of Lamentations," 227.
96. Dobbs-Allsopp, *Weep, O Daughter of Zion*, 94.
97. Middlemas, "Violent Storm in Lamentations," 81.
98. Ibid., 84.

Forgotten and Forsaken by God (Lam 5:19–20)

surrounding it, while the overall structure of the book is one of despair. Like a whirlwind, the book moves around, yet, remains directionless. With the disappearance of the acrostic in chapter 5, the book stops without an ending. The book as a whole refuses to accept reality as it is and demands a response from a silent God.

The mini-acrostic in Lam 5:19–20 underlines this tension and provides the interpretative key for the previous acrostics. Lamentations 3:22–39 does offer words of hope; however, I would suggest that hope in Lamentations is rooted in its insisting that God assume the role of dialogue partner, *You*. Even though God has forgotten and forsaken, Israel still puts its future in the hands of this God. Israel demands that its current situation not be its final one; change has to come, from the side of God.

In light of the intrinsic connection between the acrostic structure and the content of Lamentations, chapter 3 of this book will exegete Lamentations chapter by chapter. The exegesis of Lamentations will be structured according to the shifts of voices in the chapters and the interactions of these voices will be fully analyzed.

3

Exegesis of Lamentations

INTRODUCTION

The overwhelming pain and horror the Judean community experienced in the aftermath of the destruction of Jerusalem finds expression in the different voices featured in Lamentations. These voices interact and form an ongoing dialogue in Lamentations. As previously pointed out in chapter 2, the shifts among the voices are connected with the overall acrostic structure of the book. In my exegesis of Lamentations in this chapter, I will carefully study how these voices interact.

This chapter will first lay out the structure of Lamentations, based on the change of voices within it, and then exegete the book chapter by chapter. The exegesis will include a translation of the MT with textual-critical and translational notes, as well as focused, rather limited comments on the given passage. My comments are far from exhaustive. I will focus on key words and motifs of the passage, and study the unique perspective each voice expresses in its articulation of pain that persona experiences, and then the interactions among the voices over the course of the ongoing dialogue that is Lamentations.

STRUCTURE OF LAMENTATIONS

Lamentations 1: No Comforter for Zion
    1:1–11 Narrator's Description of Zion's Devastation
    1:12–22 Zion's Self-description
Lamentations 2: The Anger of Yhwh

Forgotten and Forsaken by God (Lam 5:19-20)

2:1-10	The Destructive Acts of Yhwh in Anger
2:11-19	The Narrator's Response to Zion's Suffering
2:20-22	Direct Appeal of Zion to Yhwh
Lamentations 3:	A Man of Constant Sorrow
3:1-18	Afflictions the Man Experienced
3:19-39	Hope Expressed but Not Sustained
3:40-47	Call to Communal Confession and Divine Responsibility
3:48-66	Description of Personal Misery
Lamentations 4:	Unlimited Suffering
4:1-10	Everything Grows Dim
4:11-16	Reasons Attempted for Yhwh's Actions
4:17-20	Dashed Hopes of the Community
4:21-22	Revenge and Hope
Lamentations 5:	Communal Lament Prayer
5:1-18	Complaint of a Community
5:19-22	Refusal of a Conclusion

EXEGESIS OF LAMENTATIONS

Lamentations 1: No Comforter for Zion

Translation of MT With Textual Critical and Translational Notes

א 1:1[1] Alas, she sits alone,[2] the city once full of people!
She has become like a widow, she who was once mistress among the nations.[3]
A princess among the provinces, she is now in forced labor.

1. The LXX has an opening preface: καὶ ἐγένετο μετὰ τὸ αἰχμαλωτισθῆναι τὸν Ισραηλ καὶ Ιερουσαλημ ἐρημωθῆναι ἐκάθισεν Ιερεμιας κλαίων καὶ ἐθρήνησεν τὸν θρῆνον τοῦτον ἐπὶ Ιερουσαλημ καὶ εἶπεν, "And it happened after Israel had been taken captive and Jerusalem had been laid waste, Jeremiah sat weeping and lamented this lament over Jerusalem, saying—" See Ziegler, *Threni*, 467. The Vg contains a nearly identical opening. The claim of Jeremianic authorship of Lamentations originated with this preface. It is clearly a later addition. Hillers (*Lamentations*, 64) notes that the style of the preface is Hebraic rather than Greek. It was either translated from a Hebraic *Vorlage* or represents a Hebraizing Greek composition.

2. The word בדד ranges its meaning from the quarantine of a leper (Lev 13:46) to an isolated splendor (Deut 33:28). Hillers (*Lamentations*, 64) points out that the combination of a verb and the noun בדד is used elsewhere (Deut 33:28; Jer 49:31) to express the security of isolation. The phrase ישבה בדד in Lam 1:1a is ironic, and can only be interpreted in connection with 1:1b where the city is like a widow, in the sense that it "sits alone."

3. The word רבתי occurs twice in this verse. I follow Schramm ("Poetic Patterning

ב 1:2 She weeps bitterly in the night, with tears on her cheeks.
There is none to comfort her, among all her lovers.
All her friends betrayed her, they have become her enemies.

ג 1:3 Judah has gone into exile, from[4] suffering and much servitude.[5]
She dwells among the nations, she finds no rest.
All her pursuers have overtaken her, in the mist of distress.[6]

---

in Biblical Hebrew," 180), who translates the two occurrences differently since their grammatical constructions are different. The phrase רַבָּתִי עָם in 1a forms a construct chain, hence my translation "full of people." The phrase רַבָּתִי בַמְּדִינוֹת in 1b is composed of a noun followed by a preposition, where רַבָּתִי is synonymous with שָׂרָתִי in 1c, thus my translation "mistress among the nations." See the same renderings in Berlin, *Lamentations*, 45; Salters, *Lamentations*, 36–37.

4. The preposition מִן in 1:3 is difficult to translate. Salters (*Lamentations*, 42–43) counts eleven MT occurrences of the phrase גלה מן apart from this passage (1 Sam 4:21, 22; 2 Kgs 17:23; 25:21; Isa 5:13; Jer 52:27; Ezek 12:3; Hos 10:5; Amos 7:11, 17; Mic 1:16); ten of them are local with the meaning "from" while only the one in Isa 5:13 is causal, meaning "because of." In the history of interpretation of Lam 1:3, the translation "because of" has gained support (KJV, RSV, and Gottwald, *Studies*, 7). Gordis (*Song of Songs and Lamentations*, 153–54) takes *mem* as the "*Mem* of condition" such that the phrase means "Judah is in exile, in a state of poverty and oppression," but the biblical passages he lists in support of this interpretation (Hos 9:11, 12; Ps 22:11; and Job 3:11) are not convincing. Some contemporary scholars take the preposition in a temporal sense "after," i.e., Judah has gone from a bad to a worse state, from being a vassal of Babylon to exile (Hillers, *Lamentations*, 66; Berlin, *Lamentations*, 45). Salters tries to combine the ideas of "movement from" and "reason for," with a temporal sense: Judah is fleeing the country, going into a worse state, "out of the frying pan into the fire," such that the understanding of מִן as local ("from") seems the most appropriate one. I follow Salters here.

5. For MT Lam 1:3a, LXX has μετῳκίσθη ἡ Ιουδαία ἀπὸ ταπεινώσεως αὐτῆς καὶ ἀπὸ πλήθους δουλείας αὐτῆς, "Judah was deported from/because of her humiliation and from/because of the multitude of her slavery." The הִיא in MT Lam 1:3b has no equivalent in LXX, which adds αὐτῆς twice in 1:3a. Albrektson (*Studies*, 57) regards the LXX translation here as "unexpected" in view of LXX's general literalness. He further suggests that the αὐτῆς of 1:3a is a corruption of an original αὐτή = הִיא in 1:3b.

6. הַמְּצָרִים here is the only occurrence of the plural form of the noun מֵצַר "strait, distress" in the MT, and the only case where the noun is construed with the preposition בֵּין in the Hebrew Bible. The LXX has ἀνὰ μέσον τῶν θλιβόντων, "among the oppressors"; it seems to have taken the rare noun מֵצַר (which occurs three times in the Hebrew Bible, the other two occurrences being Pss 116:3 and 118:5) as a participle of צרר.

Forgotten and Forsaken by God (Lam 5:19–20)

ד 1:4 The roads to Zion are in mourning, no one comes to the festivals.
All her gates are desolate, her priests groan.
Her virgins[7] grieve,[8] she herself is bitter.

ה 1:5 Her foes have become the master, her enemies prosper.[9]
For Yhwh has made her suffer, upon the multitude of her transgressions.
Her little ones went away as captives[10] before the enemy.

---

7. MT בתולת refers to young, still unmarried girls; it is understood in the sense of "young women" here by most commentators; see Renkema, *Lamentations*, 119; Hillers, *Lamentations*, 61; Berlin, *Lamentations*, 41.

8. I take the form נוגות as the Niphal participle of יגה here, with the meaning "to be grieved," following the majority of commentators (see Hillers, *Lamentations*, 67; Berlin, *Lamentations*, 45; and Salters, *Lamentations*, 47). The LXX has ἀγόμεναι, "being led." It seems that the Greek translator understood the form as deriving from the root נהג, "to lead"; according to Salters (ibid.) "either the *Vorlage* read נהוגת or MT was taken as an apocopated form of נהוגת." Vg reads *squalidus*, which could mean either "dirty" or "mourning."

9. The root of שלו here is שלה, which means "to prosper" or "be at ease." The intended meaning is probably "to prosper" since the LXX has εὐθηνοῦσαν, which means "they thrived, prospered."

10. Berlin (*Lamentations*, 46) points out that the phrase הלך בשבי ("to go into captivity") usually has the preposition ב before שבי, as in Amos 9:4; Isa 46:2; Jer 20:6; etc. Since ב is absent here, שבי is best taken as "an adverbial accusative," thus my translation "went away as captives." See Waltke and O'Connor, *An Introduction to Biblical Hebrew Syntax*, 169–77.

Exegesis of Lamentations

ו 1:6 It went out[11] from daughter Zion,[12] all her majesty.
Her leaders have become like stags,[13] they find no pasture.
They fled without strength before the pursuer.

ז 1:7[14] Jerusalem remembers,[15] in the days of her affliction and wandering,
all her precious things that were from the days of old.
When her people fell into the hand of the enemy, there was no one

---

11. The Greek tradition of the translation of ויצא is divided. The Old Greek and LXX have ἐξῄθη, "was taken away," while the Hexaplaric and the Lucianic read ἐξῆλθεν, "went out." Albrektson (*Studies*, 59) considers ἐξῄθη a scribal error for ἐξῆλθεν, which rendering is closer to the Hebrew.

12. A lot of ink has been spilled over the phrase בת־ציון and how it should be translated. Stinespring ("No Daughter of Zion, 133–41) understands the term as appositional genitive that should be translated "daughter Zion." A number of scholars affirm Stinespring's interpretation; e.g., Berlin, *Lamentations*, 11–12; Mandolfo, *Daughter Zion Talks Back*, 12–54; Maier, *Daughter Zion, Mother Zion*, 1–5. Floyd ("Welcome Back, Daughter of Zion," 484–504), however, rejects Stinespring's interpretation and prefers to translate "daughter of Zion; Floyd argues that the expression is a personification not of the city as such but of its inhabitants: she is a single figure who collectively represents the daughters of Zion, and the entire citizenry by extension. The debate is ongoing. J. Andrew Dearman ("Daughter Zion and Her Place in God's Household," 144–59) persuasively argues that the term is better understood as "daughter Zion"; Dearman holds that the term does refer to the city: the connotation of the city as "daughter" is located within the larger metaphor of Yhwh's household wherein the city has other roles (e.g., mother, widow, spouse). I thus opt to translate the term as "daughter Zion."

13. It is better to translate שריה as "her leaders" rather than "princes" since שר often denotes a leader or ruler in the Hebrew Bible; see the discussion in Salters, *Lamentations*, 53–54; Wilkins, *The Book of Lamentations and the Social World*, 22. Xuan Huong Thi Pham (*Mourning and the Hebrew Bible*, 44) prefers to read כְּאֵילִים as "like rams" rather than MT כְּאַיָּלִים "like stags," following LXX (κριοί) and Vg (*arietes*); אַיִל (ram) is also a title for leaders elsewhere (see, e.g., Exod 15:15; 2 Kgs 24:15; Ezek 17:13). I opt to follow the MT vocalization here.

14. This is the only four-line verse in the chapter. O'Connor (*Lamentations and the Tears of the World*, 19) notes that the additional line could be the result of scribal glossing, different textual versions, or an instance of poetic variation. Scholars' proposals to eliminate one line in v. 7 have not led to a consensus. See the detailed discussion in Salters, *Lamentations*, 55–56. Gordis (*Song of Songs and Lamentations*, 154) and Freedman ("Acrostic and Metrics in Hebrew Poetry," 378–92) defend the MT's four-line verse in light of its rhythm and vocabulary. I retain MT's four lines here.

15. 4QLam attests numerous variants throughout this verse. It begins with a direct appeal to Yhwh זכורה יהוה, "remember, O Lord," instead of MT's statement about Jerusalem. Hillers (*Lamentations*, 69) judges 4QLam a badly corrupt text that "is not even a good starting point for correcting the MT." Salters (*Lamentations*, 54) affirms that MT is to be preferred here and notes that "4QLam differs from MT to such an extent that many scholars are loath to adopt its variants."

Forgotten and Forsaken by God (Lam 5:19-20)

to help her.
The enemies saw, they mocked at her collapse.[16]

ח 1:8 Jerusalem sinned grievously, so she has become filthy.[17]
All who honored her despise her, for they saw her pudenda.[18]
Even[19] she herself groans and turns away.

ט 1:9 Her uncleanness was on her skirts, she gave no thought of her future.
She came down astoundingly;[20] there is no comforter for her.
See, O Yhwh, my affliction, for the enemy has triumphed!

---

16. The Hebrew word משבתה is a *hapax legomenon*; it may well be related to the verb שבת, "to stop, cease." 4QLam has משביה, "her ruins."

17. The Hebrew word נידה is another *hapax legomenon*, which is often taken as a variant form of נדה, "a filthy rag." 4QLam, LXX, Vg, and the Targum translate it as "restless, a wanderer," probably from the root נוד, "to move back and forth." Hillers (*Lamentations*, 70) understands the word as "object of head nodding" and translates the colon as "people shake their heads at her." However, this proposed meaning is not well-founded; Albrektson (*Studies*, 63–64) argues that the word "head" would probably be required to convey the meaning of "head nodding"; see, e.g., Ps 44:15: תשימנו משל בגוים מנוד־ראש בלאמים, "you have made us a proverbial saying among the nations, a shaking of the head among the peoples." Provan (*Lamentations*, 44), followed by Salters, argues that the meaning "uncleanness" accords well with both the immediate and wider context, and this is the meaning I adopt in my translation.

18. The word ערוה is usually translated as "nakedness," but literally means "pudenda, genitals" in Hebrew (e.g., Gen 9:22–23; Exod 28;42; Ezek 16:35–39). Salters (*Lamentations*, 61) points out that the image is of a woman whose genitals have been seen and so is utterly disgraced. This line reinforces the previous statement that Zion has become filthy.

19. McDaniel ("Philological Studies in Lamentations, I," 31), followed by Hillers (*Lamentations*, 70–71), prefers to interpret גם as "aloud" based on a homonym *gm* found in Ugaritic. However, it is better to take גם in its usual sense, either as an intensifying particle or as introducing the further statement that "even" Zion herself joins her enemies in despising herself. See Salters, *Lamentations*, 61–62; O'Connor, *Lamentations and the Tears of the World*, 19.

20. פלאים usually functions as a noun. Salters (*Lamentations*, 63) points out that this is the only place in the Hebrew Bible where it may function rather as an adverbial accusative. LXX takes the verb ותרד as a Hiphil and פלאים as its object, thus καὶ κατεβίβασεν ὑπέρογκα, "and she has lowered her haughty tones." Symmachus takes the verb in the phrase ותרד פלאים as ותורד, and translates καὶ κατήχθη, "and she was cast down." I follow the MT.

Exegesis of Lamentations

ו 1:10 The enemy stretched out his hand upon all her precious things.[21]
She has seen the nations entering her sanctuary,[22]
whom you forbade to enter into your assembly.

כ 1:11 All her people groan, searching for bread.
They gave their precious things[23] for food, to keep them alive.
See, O Yhwh, and look, how worthless[24] I have become!

ל 1:12 Is it nothing to you,[25] all you who pass by? Look and see
If there is any pain like my pain, which was severely dealt out to me,[26]
which Yhwh afflicted on the day of his fierce anger.

---

21. A number of scholars rightly hold that the allusion to Zion's enemies stretching out their hands to take away all her "precious things" includes connotations of rape. See Mintz, "Rhetoric of Lamentations and the Representation of Catastrophe," 3–5; Mintz, Ḥurban, 25; Kaiser, "Poet as 'Female Impersonator,'" 175; Guest, "Hiding behind the Naked Women in Lamentations," 413–48; Dobbs-Allsopp and Linafelt, "Rape of Zion in Thr 1,10," 77–81.

22. LXX (γάρ) and Vg (quia) render כי in MT as conjunctive, but there is no causal connection between the first and second lines; accordingly, I opt to leave כי untranslated here. See also Hillers, Lamentations, 62; Salters, A Crticial and Exegetical Commentary on Lamentations, 66.

23. Ketib מהמודיהם, Qere מחמדיהם. The Qere form is the same word that appears in v. 10 and is most likely the correct reading here in v. 11 as well.

24. 4QLam has זולל (masculine participle) instead of MT זוללה (feminine participle). Schäfer (Biblia Hebraica Quinta 18 Megilloth, 116*) suggests that the first-person singular has been incorrectly interpreted as the I of the poet instead of that of personified Zion in 4QLam.

25. The ל with which this verse begins is slightly smaller than normal in the MT. Albrektson (Studies, 67) thinks this as an indication that the Massoretes were uncertain about the text. However, ancient translators seem to have read the consonants of the MT, confirmed directly by LXX, Symmachus, Syriac and which one indirectly by Vg and the Targum. Three main suggestions have been proposed in the history of interpretation regarding how to understand MT's phrase לוא אליכם: (1) to emend it to read לכו לכם, "come, all you" (NAB; Hillers, Lamentations, 71; Salters, Lamentations, 34). However, Renkema (Lamentations, 153) points out that the above imperative usually means "go" rather than "come." (2) To take לוא as a variant of the exclamatory לְי "O," as a way of attracting attention (Renkema, Lamentations, 153–54). (3) To understand לוא as a negative; the colon is then interpreted in two different ways: (a) "may this fate not come to you" (Berlin, Lamentations, 43; Parry, Lamentations 38); (b) "is it nothing to you, all you who pass by" (KJV, RSV, NRSV, NAS, Gottwald, Studies, 8; Gordis, Song of Songs and Lamentations, 157; and Provan, Lamentations, 48). Gordis holds that the interjection "is it nothing to you" serves as "an anacrusis, a phrase outside the meter pattern, and thus serving for greater emphasis." This is the interpretation of most commentators, and I too adopt it.

26. The root עלל means "to glean, to vex." It is uncommon in the Hebrew Bible, but occurs five times in Lamentations (1:12; 2:20; 2:22 [bis] and 3:51). The usage in 1:12 is

Forgotten and Forsaken by God (Lam 5:19–20)

מ 1:13 From on high, he sent fire into my bones, and he brought it down.[27]
He spread a net on my feet, he brought me backwards.
He has left me desolate, faint all day long.

נ 1:14 Tied on is the yoke of my transgressions,[28] by his hand they are fastened together.
They weigh on my neck, sapping my strength.
Adonai[29] handed me over to those whom I cannot withstand.

ס 1:15 Adonai cast aside all my mighty men in the midst of me.
He proclaimed a time against me to crush my young men.
Adonai has trodden as in a wine press the virgin daughter of Judah.

ע 1:16[30] For these things I weep, my eyes, my eyes[31] flow with water.
For far from me is a comforter, who revives my spirits.
My children are desolate, for the enemy has prevailed.

---

the only occurrence of the passive Poal form, while the active Poel occurs in the other four instances.

27. The MT vocalizes וַיִּרְדֶּנָּה as from the root רדה "to rule, to dominate" with a 3rd-person f. s. suffix; MT's rendering is difficult because Jerusalem appears in the 1st person in this verse. LXX translates κατήγαγεν as though the root were ירד and takes ירדנה as a Hiphil form with a 3rd-person f. s. suffix; here Yhwh is the subject and fire is the object, the sense being "from on high he sent fire, into my bones he made it descend." The LXX rendering preserves the syntax of the verse better than MT's vocalization here, and so I adopt its reading.

28. The first word, נשקד in v. 14 is a *hapx legomenon* and is difficult to translate since its root שקד does not appear to exist in other Semitic languages (Salters, *Lamentations*, 78). LXX has ἐγρηγορήθη, the Lucianic version ἐγρηγόρησεν (followed by Vg); both derive the root from שקד "to watch," whence the translations "he has kept watch over my sins" of NAB and "watch is kept over my steps" of Hillers (*Lamentations*, 62). The Targum in the version of Alexander Sperber (*The Bible in Aramaic* 4A:143, *Targum to Lamentations*) reads איתקיד נוד "the fire ... has been lit;" in the version of Étan Levine (*The Aramaic Version of Lamentations*, 100), it reads אתקיד ניד מרודי בידה, "the yoke has become heavy." I follow most scholars here who read the word in light of its context and render the phrase as "my transgressions are bound into a yoke" (KJV, RSV, NRSV, NAS, Provan, *Lamentations*, 51; O'Connor, *Lamentations and the Tears of the World*, 24).

29. The divine name אדני appears here for the first time in Lamentations; this form is used fourteen times in the book, while יהוה occurs thirty-two times. The import of the shift from יהוה to אדני in the book is not clear.

30. 4QLam reverses the order of vv. 16–17 in MT. Schäfer (*BHQ*, 118*) notes that it is hardly possible to decide which sequence is the original one.

31. Hillers (*Lamentations*, 75) regards the two occurrences of עיני in 1:14 as a clear case of dittography and opts to read only one עיני, following 4QLam, LXX, Syriac and Vg. However, a number of scholars prefer to retain MT as the *lectio difficilior* and one that generates a greater poignancy; so Gordis, *Song of Songs and Lamentations*, 159;

Exegesis of Lamentations

פ 1:17 Zion spreads out her hands, but there is no comforter for her.
Concerning Jacob, Yhwh commanded his neighbors to be his enemies.[32]
Jerusalem has become a filthy thing among them.

צ 1:18 Yhwh is in the right,[33] for I have rebelled against his word.
Listen now, all peoples,[34] and see my pain.
My young women and men have gone into captivity.

ק 1:19 I called to my lovers but they deceived me.
My priests and elders perished in the city,
while they seek food to revive themselves.[35]

Renkema, *Lamentations*, 172; Provan, *Lamentations*, 52; Berlin, *Lamentations*, 44; House, *Song of Songs; Lamentations*, 336; Schäfer, *Biblia Hebraica Quinta 18 Megilloth*, 119*; and Salters, *Lamentations*, 84–85.

32. The phrase צוה יהוה ליעקב סביביו צריו is difficult, and the versions struggle with it. LXX reads ἐνετείλατο κύριος τῷ Ιακωβ κύκλῳ αὐτοῦ οἱ θλίβοντες αὐτόν, "the Lord has commanded regarding Jacob; his oppressors are round about him." 4QLam has צפה instead of MT's צוה and reads the phrase as "The Lord kept watch on Jacob; his enemies have surrounded him." Schäfer (*BHQ*, 119*) holds that 4QLam represents the original Hebrew text. Salters (*Lamentations*, 88–89) points out that the difficulty of MT lies in the idea that Yhwh, the covenant God, is the commander-in-chief of the enemies all around Jacob: "Concerning Jacob, Yhwh commanded his neighbors to be his enemies." The MT reading is, however, possible and might be judged the *lectio difficilior*; see the translations in RSV; NRSV; NAB; NAS; Provan, *Lamentations*, 52–53; Renkema, *Lamentations*, 177–78; and Salters, *Lamentations*, 87–89, which all follow MT, as do I.

33. Salters (*Lamentations*, 90) points out that the term צדיק here derives from a legal context (cf. Jer 12:1), and conveys the idea that Yhwh is justified in what he has done, thus my rendering "the Lord is right." Translating it as "the Lord is righteous" (KJV, NAS, NIV) loses this legal nuance.

34. Ketib כל־עמים, Qere כל־העמים. Ketib is to be preferred since it is used more in poetry.

35. The third line in MT is followed exactly by Vg and Targum. LXX adds οὐχ εὗρον, "they found none." Most scholars prefer MT and consider the plus in LXX an elucidation of the difficult MT. The two verbs in MT's third line are the perfect בקשׁ followed by the imperfect וישׁיבו with the conjunction *waw* being used to express purpose. See Hillers, *Lamentations*, 76–77; Joüon, *Grammar of Biblical Hebrew*, 355.

Forgotten and Forsaken by God (Lam 5:19–20)

ר 1:20 See, O Yhwh, for I am in distress; my stomach churns.
My heart is turned within me, for I have been very rebellious.[36]
Outdoors sword bereaves, indoors death.[37]

שׁ 1:21 They have heard[38] that I was groaning, there is no comforter for me.
All my enemies heard of my trouble, they are glad that you have done it.
Bring on the day you have proclaimed, and let them be as I am.

ת 1:22 Let all their evil come before you, and deal severely with them,
as you have dealt severely with me, for all my transgressions.
For my groans are many and my heart faint.

---

36. LXX has παραπικραίνουσα παρεπίκρανα, "it is terribly bitter for me" for MT's מרי מריתי, deriving the root from מרר "bitter" rather than MT's מרה "to rebel"; the Vg and Syriac follow LXX. Seow ("Textual Note on Lamentations 1:20," 416–19) and Berges (*Klagelieder:* 121–22) prefer to read the root as מרר, which would be congruent with the thought pattern and poetic structure here. Berlin (*Lamentations*, 47) follows Seow, but notes that the root מרה occurs in 1:18 where it clearly means "to rebel." The majority of scholars follow MT, which I adopt.

37. The phrase בבית כמות is difficult to translate, and many find MT's כ here problematic. LXX reverses the word order of MT and renders ὥσπερ θάνατος ἐν οἴκῳ, "as death at home." Vg has *et domi mors similis est*, "and it is like death at home." Hillers (*Lamentations*, 77) compares Lam 1:20 with Ezek 7:15 and Jer 14:18, and on that basis renders "outside the sword killed my children, inside, it was famine," which seems to stretch the text too far. Schäfer (*Biblia Hebraica Quinta 18 Megilloth*, 119*) thinks that the easiest solution is to translate MT as it stands, i.e., "in the house it is as death" (so Gottwald, *Studies*, 9). Gordis (*Song of Songs and Lamentations*, 159) takes the כ as asseverative, i.e., as an emphatic particle, and translates "without, the sword bereaves; within, there was death." Berlin (*Lamentations*, 47) finds Gordis's interpretation the best; she considers the usual translation "like death," i.e., something less than death but similar to it—e.g., great suffering, weakens the force of the phrase. Berlin renders the phrase accordingly as "outside the sword bereaved, inside—death." I follow Gordis and Berlin here.

38. MT's שמעו is a perfect form and is followed by Vg. LXX has the imperative plural ἀκούσατε δή, "listen now," but it is unclear to whom this is addressed; Syriac has the imperative singular addressed to Yhwh. Salters (*Lamentations*, 101) argues that LXX and Syriac represent a more original reading; MT's plural form in the first line is a corruption under the influence of שמעו in the second line; the imperative "hear" in v. 21 follows the imperative "see, O Lord" in v. 20, the address to Yhwh, which begins in v. 20 is sustained in v. 21: "Hear how I groan." Albrektson (*Studies*, 83), however, strongly argues for the retention of MT; he thinks that its repetition of שמעו in v. 21 may even reflect a conscious poetic style, with the indefinite subject "they" in the first line being spelled out in the second line, "all my enemies." Berges (*Klagelieder*, 122) agrees with Albrektson and retains the MT. MT is preferable here.

Comments

Lamentations 1 is perhaps "the most striking" of the book's five chapters.[39] It also provides an overview of themes that appear throughout the book.[40] The chapter is clearly divided into two parts and gives its two speakers equal coverage. Salters states that the two parts "are skillfully dovetailed, forming a unity of composition," and are "like two interlocking fists—distinct yet inextricably bound together."[41] Hillers affirms that there is in the chapter a "definite psychological progress" from an external, objective third person view to an internal, subjective first person view.[42] The key phrase in the chapter is "there is no comforter" for Zion (1:2, 7, 9, 16, 17, 21), which appears on the lips of both the narrator and daughter Zion herself. Another rather striking feature in the chapter is the personification of Zion, which according to Berlin, is developed more effectively in Lamentations 1 than are its antecedents in Mesopotamian and successors in Greek literature.[43] K. L. Nguyen studies the personification of Jerusalem as a woman in more detail; she affirms that the Hebrew poets had no need of foreign tradition to conceptualize the city as female since the word "city" in Hebrew is grammatically feminine.[44]

THE PERSONIFICATION OF ZION[45]

Many scholars emphasize the significance of the personification of Zion in Lamentations.[46] The Zion figure speaks mainly in chapters 1–2 and is viewed by a number of scholars as the most prominent and compelling

---

39. Salters (*Lamentations*, 30) suggests that Lamentations 1 was placed at the beginning of the book because it is the most striking of the five poems.

40. Wilkins, *Lamentations and the Social World*, 9. Hunter (*Faces of a Lamenting City*, 88) holds that Lam 1:1–11 lays out the key elements of the whole book, which are then reiterated in various ways throughout the rest of Lamentations.

41. Salters, *Lamentations*, 30.

42. Hillers, *Lamentations*, 79.

43. Berlin, *Lamentations*, 47.

44. Nguyen, "Lady Zion and the Man," 75.

45. In Lamentations, בת־ציון, "daughter of Zion" occurs eight times (1:6; 2:1, 4, 8. 10, 13, 18; 4:22), בתולה בת־ציון, "virgin daughter of Zion" once (2:13), בת־עמי, "daughter of my people" five times (2:11; 3:48; 4:3, 6, 10), בת־יהודה, "daughter of Judah" twice (1:15; 2:2), בתולה בת־יהודה, "virgin daughter of Judah" once (1:15), בת־ירושלם, "daughter of Jerusalem" twice (2:13, 15), and בת־אדום, "daughter of Edom" twice (4:21, 22).

46. Heim, "Personification of Jerusalem," 129–69; Dobbs-Allsopp, *Lamentations*, 50–53; Labahn, "Metaphor and Intertexuality," 49–67; Maier, *Daughter Zion, Mother Zion*, 151–53; Kaiser, "Poet as 'Female Impersonator,'" 174–81.

figure in the book.[47] Among scholarly suggestions concerning the function of the personification of Zion in Lamentations, the following may be noted: First, according to Dobbs-Allsopp, the personified city in Lamentations functions analogously to the sorrowful, tender, and compassionate weeping goddess in Mesopotamian laments.[48] The personified city encompasses various female roles: the daughter, the mother, the unmarried woman, the widow, the rape victim, and the menstruant—thereby enabling her to lament over her own loss and that of her people. In the same line, Heim holds that the personified city expresses both individual and corporate pain at the same time.[49] Nguyen goes a step further and views the city as a mourning virgin who laments her own premature tragic death like the daughter of Jephthah (Judg 11:39-40), hereby engaging the audience effectively and becoming the collective voice of the survivors.[50]

Second, personified Zion is described as "mistress of the nations, a princess among the provinces" (Lam 1:1), i.e. a woman "infused with the aura of divinity and royalty, thus a woman whose testimony cannot be lightly dismissed."[51] As such, she not only draws readers to her side, but also confronts God, the agent of her and her people's destruction. According to O'Connor, Zion's is the most passionate voice of resistance in Lamentations.[52]

Third, the personified city is a powerful literary device that enables the poet(s) to portray suffering in its "humanity and concreteness."[53] Dobbs-Allsopp says that it is one thing to look at a city in ruins, even one's own city, and quite another to imagine a city as a person who has suffered enormously. A ruined city can be rebuilt, but the scars of a person's radical suffering can never be removed.[54] Zion experiences radical suffering with "personal immediacy" and embraces all her people's suffering in her own.[55]

---

47. Linafelt, *Surviving Lamentations*, 20–35; Mandolfo, *Daughter Zion Talks Back*, 67–102.

48. Dobbs-Allsopp, *Lamentations*, 50–51.

49. Heim, "Personification of Jerusalem," 130.

50. Nguyen, "Lady Zion and the Man," 72–98.

51. Dobbs-Allsopp, *Lamentations*, 51.

52. O'Connor, *Lamentations and the Tears of the World*, 14.

53. Dobbs-Allsopp, *Lamentations*, 51; Heim ("Personification of Jerusalem," 129–30) views the personification of Jerusalem as the most important literary device in the book of Lamentations.

54. Dobbs-Allsopp, *Lamentations*, 51.

55. Farley (*Tragic Vision and Divine Compassion*, 56) affirms that "radical suffering" is concrete and contextual. It arises out of the particularity of a situation and is experienced through personal immediacy.

Lam 1:1–11: The Narrator's Description of Zion's Devastation

The narrator's account of Zion's plight starts with a typical exclamation of the funeral dirge: איכה, "how." This opening word catches readers' attention, serves as a bitter declaration that death has occurred, and may also imply an interrogation: "how could this happen to beloved Zion?," as N. Seidman proposes.[56] The reaction of the narrator who approaches Zion is bewilderment and shock: how different she has become! As he comes near, even though it is night, he sees her tears running down her cheeks (1:2a).[57]

The narrator speaks throughout vv. 1–9b without being interrupted. This part features a series of tragic reversals: once full of people, now Zion sits alone; once a mistress and princess, now she is a widow engaged in forced labor (1:1);[58] all her friends and lovers have turned into enemies (1:2);[59] Judah has fared worse than ever, going from servitude into exile (1:3); her roads, which once bustled with traffic, are now in mourning and no pilgrims come to her gates any longer (1:4); her priests, virgins and leaders are all grief filled (1:4, 6); her children have gone off as captives (1:5); her precious things have been taken away (1:7), gone is her honor (1:8b). Zion's grief is unfathomable. To make things worse, she herself has caused

---

56. Seidman ("Burning the Book of Lamentations," 283) further proposes that the opening איכה be pronounced with "a catch in the throat" to convey the breath-blocking shock of the catastrophe. O'Connor (*Lamentations and the Tears of the World*, 19–20) states: "Tragedy threatens to overcome speech, sobs interfere with words and trauma pounds back expression as the book's voices hover in tension between life-denying silence and the life-giving urge to speak."

57. Each chapter in Lamentations 1–4 begins with the theme of darkness. The setting of chapter 1 is at night (1:2); chapter 2 starts with the statement that Adonai beclouded Zion in his anger (2:1a); in chapter 3, God leads the male speaker in darkness without light (3:2); chapter 4 begins with gold turning dim (4:1).

58. Widows, along with orphans and foreigners, ranked at the bottom of Israelite society. They lacked security, were vulnerable, and had an uncertain future. The image of Zion as a widow has caused some discussion in light of traditional biblical imagery of God as the husband of Israel; see Salters, *Lamentations*, 36. The imagery does not necessarily imply the death of Zion's husband, but more likely that the husband is far away and not concerned about her fate. Lamentations not only depicts Zion's sitting alone; it also represents her facing the death of her children, and as someone who cannot hope for further children. Bergant (*Lamentations* 28–29) holds that the metaphor here most probably indicates the vulnerable status of the woman rather than absence through death of her husband.

59. Thompson ("Israel's 'Lovers,'" 475–81) explains that in the Old Testament the term "lover" usually has political connotations (e.g., Hos 8:9; Jer 2:25–36; Ezek 16:26–39; 23:5, 9). Who these lovers were is not explicitly stated in Lam 1:2, but they are evidently former allies of some kind.

her suffering through transgression (1:5) and sin (1:8);[60] she becomes filthy. In the narrator's eyes, her suffering is God's just punishment for sin. She has no comforter (1:2, 4, 9), no helper (1:7); the God who once loved her has deserted her. She cries at night (1:2), groans (1:8), and is utterly ashamed.

Zion interrupts the narrator in 1:9c and speaks very briefly for the first time: "See, O Yhwh, my affliction, for the enemy has triumphed!" O'Connor points out that Zion speaks directly to God here; she does not beg for relief, vindication or restoration; she does not ask for the return of her children; she only asks that God see her pain and note the triumph of the enemy.[61] When the narrator resumes his speech in v. 10, as though picking up on Zion's interjection, he also acknowledges the enemies' success and Zion's distress in seeing the nations enter the sanctuary. Now, it is not only Zion who groans (1:8); all her people groan and search for food (1:11a and b). Zion speaks again in v. 11c and her speech continues in the second part of the chapter; the verb "to look" is added here to her interjection in 1:9c: "see, O Lord, and look." Zion has been convinced by the narrator that she is filthy and unclean (1:8, 9) and wants God to see her worthlessness. Lam 1:11c thus serves as a transition to the second part of the chapter.

Lam 1:12–22: Zion's Self-Description

God continues to be Zion's focus in her self-description in 1:12–22, where the name Yhwh appears four times (1:12, 17, 18, 20), while Adonai is used three times (1:14, 15 [bis]), in contrast to the only occurrence of Yhwh in 1:5c in the narrator's words in the chapter's first part. Zion has twice called upon God to see and look (1:9c, 11c), but God did not respond. In v. 12, Zion calls on those passing by to look at and see (the two verbs are reversed here) her pain, with which Yhwh afflicted her (1:12c). Zion affirms the narrator's words in 1:5 that it was Yhwh who afflicted her and caused her pain, and adds "on the day of his fierce anger" (1:12c). In Zion's speech, God is the subject of a series of activities: he sends fire from above and brings the fire down through her bones (1:13a); he spreads a net for her feet and turns

---

60. The word פשע "transgression" is plural in Lam 1:5 and refers to rebellion(s) in the political realm. Zion's culpability is clear here; she has rebelled against God many times. The word פשע occurs four times in Lamentations (1:5, 14, 22; 3:42); the three instances in chapter 1 are all plurals. For a detailed explanation of the word, see H. Seebass, פשע, *TDOT* 12:133–51. The word חטא in Lam 1:8 alludes to Zion's failure in her covenant responsibilities. The Hebrew expression חטא חטאה "she sinned grievously" denotes the seriousness of her sin. For a detailed analysis of the word, see Koch, חטא, *TDOT* 4:309–19.

61. O'Connor, *Lamentations and the Tears of the World*, 22.

her back (1:13b); he fastens her transgressions into a yoke on her neck (1:14) and breaks her young people (1:15). In response, she weeps; her weeping is endless, as if only weeping could relieve her pain (1:16a). She weeps not because of her lost status, but because it is Yhwh who acted against her, and because her children are desolate and there is no future for her.

The narrator interrupts Zion suddenly in Lam 1:17. He observes that though Zion spreads out her hand as a gesture meant to get someone to see her, still there is no comforter for her. The narrator agrees with Zion that it is Yhwh who acted against her and commanded her neighbors to be her enemies. Zion has become indeed נדה "a filthy thing" (see also 1:8), literally "menstruation and ritual impurity" (see Lev 12:2, 5; 15:19–33), among those enemies. No one would touch a thing like that; it makes Zion's shame "vivid, graphic, and repulsive."[62]

Zion resumes her speech in v. 18. O'Connor points out that like a woman in an abusive relationship, Zion agrees that Yhwh is in the right in his treatment of her because she rebelled against his word (1:18a).[63] Thereafter, she immediately calls again for all peoples to listen and see her pain (1:18b), and her focus reverts to her young people who have gone into captivity (1:18c). Zion admits that she had called upon her lovers and they deceived her. Her situation is desperate; priests and elders perish due to hunger (1:19). She again appeals to Yhwh to see (1:20a), God must see and look and act on her behalf—that is the only solution to her current desperate situation. Zion ends her speech with a plea for Yhwh to punish her enemies. Zion admits her own guilt, but she knows that her triumphant enemies are not innocent either. Zion calls upon God to deal with her enemies according to their evil (1:22a). The final colon of v. 22 is very short: "my groans are many and my heart faint," an understatement of Zion's miserable situation.

One recurring word captures the totality of Zion's suffering in Lamentations 1 is כל. It is repeated sixteen times (1:2 [*bis*], 3, 4, 6, 7, 8, 10, 11, 12, 13, 15, 18, 21, 22 [*bis*]).[64] *All* her lovers and friends deserted her; *all* her enemies rejoice at her fall; she lost *all* her precious things and honor; she suffers *all* the time; and she asks *all* passersby and peoples to see her pain.

To sum up, the narrator in Lamentations 1 believes that Zion's desperate situation is God's just punishment for her transgressions and sins. For him, Zion deserves no comforter since she had many lovers and they all deserted her. The narrator notes Zion's suffering is shocking and total; his attitude toward Zion is sympathetic but reserved; he observes and describes

---

62. Ibid., 27.
63. Ibid.
64. The word כל is used thirty-one times in all in Lamentations.

Forgotten and Forsaken by God (Lam 5:19–20)

her situation; his tone is cool and he remains at a distance. Zion does not respond to the narrator, but talks to God directly throughout her speech. She admits her guilt and recognizes that God is in the right, but pleads with God to see and pay attention to her pain. She longs for someone to see her pain and rescue her from her torment. Her focus is on her present situation and her concern is for her suffering people, especially her children who have gone into captivity. Utter shame and despair dominate her speech. She receives no response from God. Her suffering continues and she laments nonstop.

Lamentations 2: The Anger of Yhwh

Translation of MT With Textual Critical and Translational Notes

א 2:1 How Adonai beclouds[65] daughter Zion in his anger.
He has thrown down, from heaven to earth, the splendor of Israel.[66]
He had no regard[67] for his footstool[68] on the day of his anger.

65 The word יעיב is a *hapax legomenon* and its meaning is unclear. It can be understood in different ways: (1) the term is related to the Arabic word *'yb* "to blame, revile," thus the translation "the Lord has treated . . . with contempt" (see NAB); Hillers (*Lamentations*, 96) holds that this interpretation fits the context very well; (2) a verbal form from the word תועבה, "abomination," so the translation "the Lord has made Zion loathsome"; see Berlin, *Lamentations*, 66; and (3) a denominative from the noun עב "cloud," thus the word יעיב is a Hiphil form which means "to becloud," the LXX, Vg, and the Syriac understand it this way. Albrektson (*Studies*, 85–86) favors the meaning "to becloud" because it sets up a contrast with the idea that a cloud represents God's merciful presence (Exod 19:9; 1 Kgs 8:10). Salters (*Lamentations*, 113) further states that the word might appear to convey the benign protection of God, but the associated phrase "in his anger" suddenly turns the picture in the opposite direction. The meaning "to becloud" is taken over by RSV, NJB, NEB, NIV, Provan, *Lamentations*, 59; it is also the meaning I adopt here.

66. The word "Israel" appears three times in Lamentations, all of them in this chapter (2:1, 3 and 5).

67. The phrase לא־זכר literally means "he did not remember," but Salters (*A Crticial and Exegetical Commentary on Lamentations*, 114) points out that to translate thus is "to miss some of the import of the words" since it does not refer to a lapse in memory on God's part but rather to an active "ignoring." Even though quite a number of translations have "he did not remember" (RSV, NRSV, NAS, NEB, NIV), I render the phrase as "he had no regard" here to bring out the nuance of the Hebrew phrase; see also Hillers, *Lamentations*, 93.

68. Albrektson (*Studies*, 8) holds that "his footstool" refers to the ark of the covenant here; he cites Pss 99:5; 132:7; and 1 Chr 28:2 in support of this claim. Hillers (*Lamentations*, 97) thinks on the basis of Jer 3:16 that the ark was destroyed much earlier than 587 BCE. Renkema (*Lamentations*, 221) points out, however, that it is hard to imagine that the ark disappeared before the destruction of the temple. Whatever the

Exegesis of Lamentations

ב 2:2 Adonai swallowed up,[69] without pity,[70] all the dwellings of Jacob.
In his wrath, he threw down the strongholds of daughter Judah.
He brought down to the ground in dishonor the kingdom[71] and its rulers.

ג 2:3 He cut down in fierce anger all the might of Israel.[72]
He has withdrawn his right hand in the face of the enemy.
And he blazed in Jacob like a flaming fire, consuming all around.[73]

ד 2:4 He bent his bow like an enemy, with his right hand in place.[74]
Like a foe, he killed all who delighted the eye.[75]
In the tent of daughter Zion, he poured out his fury like fire.

---

case, although the ark may have been originally thought of as Yhwh's "footstool," the image was most likely expanded to refer to the temple as well as Jerusalem as a whole.

69. It is worth noting that the word בלע, "to swallow up" occurs five times in Lamentations, all in chapter 2 (2:2, 5 [*bis*], 8, 16).

70. LXX follows MT Ketib לא, Vg, Syriac and Targum rather MT Qere ולא. Schäfer (*Biblia Hebraica Quinta 18 Megilloth*, 119*) considers the Ketib as the *lectio difficilior*, and thus the preferred reading.

71. LXX renders βασιλέα αὐτῆς, "her king" for MT ממלכה, "the kingdom." The LXX reading might indicate a different Hebrew *Vorlage* which read מלכה. Hillers (*Lamentations*, 97) supposes that the original Hebrew read חלל מלכה, thus he translates 2:2c as "He brought down to earth, he profaned her king and princes." I retain MT ממלכה "the kingdom."

72. The Hebrew כל קרן ישראל literally means "every horn of Israel." קרן occurs seventy-two times in the Hebrew Bible, often as a metaphor to represent might and strength; see, e.g., 1 Sam 2:1; Deut 33:17; Ps 18:3; 75:5.

73. LXX has κατέφαγεν πάντα τὰ κύκλῳ, "it consumed everything all around" for MT סביב אכלה; Schäfer (*Biblia Hebraica Quinta 18 Megilloth*, 120*) supposes that LXX reads the last three consonants of אכלה twice, this resulting in its rendering of a Hebrew אכלה כל הסביב. I follow the MT reading here.

74. The syntax of נצב ימינו כצר is difficult. There are a number of problems. First, if כצר is taken as part of the first line, it becomes rather long while the second line is too short; so BHS (but not *Biblia Hebraica Quinta 18 Megilloth*) moves the word to the second line. However, one should not put too much weight on metrical considerations since the two parts of the first line constitute a nice parallel "he has bent his bow like an enemy, his right hand is set like a foe." If, however, we keep כצר in the first line, a second problem arises, i.e. ימין is feminine while the subject of נצב is masculine; accordingly, LXX, Syriac, and Vg take Yhwh as the subject and ימין as the object. The problem with taking ימין as the object of נצב is that נצב is not a finite verb, but rather a Niphal participle according to the MT vocalization נִצָּב. There is no simple solution here. I follow the division of lines in BHS and consider ימין as the subject of נצב since it has been argued that ימין can be construed as masculine in light of Exod 15:6. For a more detailed explanation, see Salters, *Lamentations*, 123–25.

75. The word מחמד is used five times in Lamentations, the other four occurrences all being in chapter 1 (1:7, 10, 11 [*bis*]). The phrase מחמד עין appears also in 1 Kgs 20:6;

Forgotten and Forsaken by God (Lam 5:19-20)

ה 2:5 Adonai has become an enemy; he has destroyed Israel.
He destroyed all her mansions, laid in ruins her strongholds,[76]
And multiplied in daughter Judah mourning and lamentation.[77]

ו 2:6 He has broken down his booth as in a garden,[78] he has destroyed his meeting place;[79]
Yhwh has erased the memory[80] of festival and Sabbath in Zion,
and in his fierce indignation has spurned king and priest.

Ezek 24:16, 21 and 25, where it refers to precious things or people. The phrase most probably refers to people here since it is the object of הרג, "to kill."

76. The divergent possessive forms used with ארמנתיה, "her mansions" and מבצריו, "his strongholds" are perplexing. Schäfer (*BHQ*, 120*) strongly holds that the 3rd person feminine pronoun must not be altered here since it is the *lectio difficilior*; it may refer to Jerusalem, the "mansions" of which are its palaces and big houses. LXX faithfully retains the different MT possessive forms: τὰς βάρεις αὐτῆς διέφθειρεν τὰ ὀχυρώματα αὐτοῦ, "*her* mansions and *his* strongholds." Provan (*Lamentations*, 64) explains that the feminine pronoun may be due to the influence of the daughter Zion notion, the mansions being those of Zion and the strongholds those of Israel. Since rendering "her . . . his" would be infelicitous in English, as Salters (*Lamentations*, 128) points out, I utilize two "her"s here.

77. The combination of the two nouns תאניה ואניה occurs only here and in Isa 29:2. Both words come from the same root, i.e. אנה, "to mourn, lament." LXX has ταπεινουμένην καὶ τεταπεινωμένην, "the afflicted and the humbled"; it seems to have taken the root as ענה rather than אנה; so also Vg, *humiliatum et humiliatam*, "the afflicted man and woman." I render the phrase as "mourning and lamentation."

78. The Old Greek has καὶ διεπέτασεν, "and he scattered" for MT ויחמס, "and he destroyed." According to Schäfer (*BHQ*, 120*), the verb διεπέτασεν is usually regarded as a corruption of an original διέσπασεν "he torn down," which would correspond with the ἐξέσπασεν in Lucianic version. Salters (*Lamentations*, 130) considers the verb "to scatter" in the Old Greek to be out of place in a list of actions by Yhwh which are markedly violent, and for this reason alone, the Greek reading is suspect. LXX has ὡς ἄμπελον "like a vine" for the Hebrew כגן "like a garden"; it may be based on a Hebrew *Vorlage* that read כגפן. Albrektson (*Lamentations*, 95) holds that the MT is clear and intelligible as it stands, and translates 2:6a as "he has broken down his booth as in a garden," an elliptical, poetic way of saying "he has broken down his booth as easily as one shatters a booth in a garden."

79. The word מועד occurs twice in 2:6. Most scholars assign two meanings to the word, even though a writer would hardly mean different things with the same term in most contexts. See Salters, *Lamentations*, 132; Berlin, *Lamentations*, 66. I follow them and render "meeting place" in the first and "appointed time" in the second line.

80. MT שכח in the Piel form means "to cause to forget." Salters (*Lamentations*, 132–33) points out that this is the only MT occurrence of the Piel of this verb. God's demolishing of the temple caused the celebration of festivals and Sabbath to lapse. The poet is accusing God of being the cause of the present void in festal observance.

Exegesis of Lamentations

ז 2:7 Adonai scorned his altar, disowned his sanctuary.
He handed over to the enemy[81] the walls of her mansions.
They raised a clamor in the house of Yhwh as on a day of festival.

ח 2:8 Yhwh determined[82] to lay in ruins the wall of daughter Zion.
He stretched the line; he did not withhold his hand from destroying.
He caused rampart and wall to lament; they languish together.

ט 2:9 Her gates have sunk into the ground; he has ruined and broken her bars;[83]
Her king and princes are among the nations; guidance is no more,
and her prophets obtain no vision from Yhwh.

י 2:10 In silence[84] they sit on the ground, the elders of daughter Zion.
They put dust on their heads, they wear sackcloth.
They bow their heads to the ground, the maidens of Jerusalem.

---

81. The word סגר in the Qal means "to shut," but the Hiphil signifies "to deliver," and together with ביד has the sense "to hand over." LXX has συνέτριψεν, "he broke," probably based on a misunderstanding of the phrase ביד as meaning "by the hand of" instead of "into the hand of"; see Albrektson, *Lamentations*, 99–100.

82. LXX reads καὶ ἐπέστρεψεν, "and he turned," probably reflecting a Hebrew חשיב or וישב. I prefer to read the MT.

83. MT reads two verbs here, אבד ושבר, "he has ruined and broken;" LXX and the other ancient versions testify to two verbs as well. Gordis (*Song of Songs and Lamentations*, 162) considers the phrase אבד ושבר בריחיה "not only metrically too long but ... logically contradictory or redundant." He does not, however, regard the second verb as a gloss on the first; rather, "the two verbs are a conflate, representing variants of manuscripts which were both preserved in a very early state of Proto-masoretic activity." Hillers (*Lamentations*, 99–100) opts to read only one verb, "he destroyed their bars." Salters (*Lamentations*, 140–41; Salters, "Text of Lam. II 9A," 273–76) argues that the text reads awkwardly and is corrupt; he emends the phrase to אבדו בריחיה, "her bars vanished" (along with her gates). Salters considers this proposed reading to be smoother in every way. Although emendation of the text makes for a better reading, a number of translations retain the MT (RSV, NRSV, NAB, NAS), as do I.

84. The root of the word ידמו is דמם, which has two meanings: "to be or grow dumb, silent, still" or "to moan, to wail." Some have adopted the meaning "to moan, to wail" here on the ground that silence has no place in a mourning ceremony, see McDaniel, "Philological Studies in Lamentations I," 39; Berlin, *Lamentations*, 63. Others prefer the meaning "to be silent," pointing out that silence in fact does have a place in ancient Israelite mourning, see, e.g., Job 2:11–13; Ezra 9:3–4. In Job 2:11–13, after the three friends raised their voice in mourning with Job, they sit quietly: "They sat with him on the ground seven days and seven nights, and no one spoke a word to him, for they saw that his suffering was very great." It is likely that the sense "to be silent" in Lam 2:10 has a better claim; see the discussion in Lohfink, "Enthielten die im Alten Testament," 276; Salters, *Lamentations*, 143–44. Pham (*Mourning*, 29–31) also affirms that silence was part of the Israelite mourning rite: "the initial loud weeping and wailing, accompanied

Forgotten and Forsaken by God (Lam 5:19-20)

כ 2:11[85] Worn out from weeping are my eyes;[86] within I am in torment.
My bile[87] is poured out on the ground for the destruction of my people;
while infants and babes faint in the city squares.

ל 2:12 They cry to[88] their mothers, "Where is food and drink?"[89]
As they faint like the wounded in the city squares,
as their lives slipped away[90] in their mothers' bosoms.

מ 2:13 How can I uphold you,[91] with what can I compare you, O daughter Jerusalem?

---

by visible ritual gestures such as tearing clothes, strewing dirt on the head, gashing the body, and so on, was usually followed by a period of stunned silence." Thus I translate "in silence."

85. The identity of the first-person speaker here is not specified. Some identify the speaker with daughter Zion, see Renkema, *Lamentations*, 268. Most scholars, however, hold that it is still the narrator speaking here since Zion is clearly referred to as the third person in 2:13; see Provan, *Lamentations*, 70; O'Connor, *Lamentations and the Tears of the World*, 36–37; Salters, *Lamentations*, 146.

86. The Hebrew כלו בדמעות עיני literally means "my eyes are at an end on account of tears"; this could mean crying has worn his eyes out, which meaning I adopt here, or that his eyes are blinded with tears; see Renkema, *Lamentations*, 268; NEB, NAS.

87. LXX has ἡ δόξα μου, "my glory" for כבדי, as does the Syriac. MT "my bile," כבדי is preferable since different body parts ("eyes" and "inner organs" in 2:11a) are referred to in this verse.

88. Salters (*Lamentations*, 149) points out that the imperfect יאמרו implies frequency: "they keep saying."

89. Literally, דגן ויין "grain and wine." Renkema (*Lamentations*, 273–74) and Salters (*Lamentations*, 149) point out that this is the only occurrence of this combination in the Old Testament; the usual expression is לחם ויין "bread and wine." Scholars have difficulty making sense of the statement that little children are asking for wine. Gottwald (*Studies in the Book of Lamentations*, 11) reads the phrase as דגן ואין, and translates 2:12a as "To their mothers they say, 'where is bread?'—but there is none," as does Pham (*Mourning*, 132). Berlin (*Lamentations*, 72) holds that the children are asking for remnants of stored-up food since both grain and wine can be stored for long periods. The phrase thus points to the fact that the city has no provisions left. I follow most scholars' opinion that the children are simply asking for food and drink of some sort.

90. The phrase בהשתפך נפשם literally means "pouring out one's soul." Provan (*Lamentations*, 71–72) notes that the combination שפך and נפש does not necessarily imply death: it may indicate that a person is experiencing extreme distress as in Job 30:16 and perhaps communicating this distress to another as in 1 Sam 1:15; Ps 42:5. The reference here could suggest that the children are crying with hunger in their mothers' arms. But quite a number of scholars hold that it does imply the death of the children here since children are the most vulnerable in extreme famine. I agree with this view; see NRS, NAB, NAS; Dobbs-Allsopp, *Lamentations*, 94–95; O'Connor, *Lamentations and the Tears of the World*, 37.

91. The phrase מה־אעידך in MT is basically confirmed by all ancient versions, but its

> To what can I liken you, that I may comfort you, O virgin daughter Zion?
> For as vast as the sea is your devastation, who can heal you?

ג 2:14 Your prophets have seen for you false and deceptive visions.[92]
They did not reveal your iniquity so as to change your fortunes.[93]
They showed you false oracles and deceptions.

ס 2:15[94] All who pass by the way clap their hands at you.
They hiss and wag their heads at daughter Jerusalem.
"Is this the city that was called the perfection of beauty, the joy of all the earth?"[95]

---

understanding has caused much debate. Schäfer (*BHQ*, 122*) considers the phrase not as a textual problem, but rather as a question of interpretation. There are a number of possibilities: (1) to take אעידך as a Hiphil form from the root עוד, "to witness," so "what can I testify to/for you?"; thus NRSV interprets the phrase as "what can I say for you?" (2) Albrektson (*Lamentations*, 108) holds that מה־אעידך is synonymous with מה־אדמה־לך, and the original meaning of the Hiphil עוד is "repeat," which most probably means "repeat = produce yet another case of, name a parallel to" here. (3) To emend the phrase to מה אערוך and to take אעידך as from the root ערך, "to liken, compare." The problem with this proposal is that the letter *Kaph* becomes part of the root, while the second-person suffix is lost. (4) Gordis (*Song of Songs and Lamentations*, 164) holds that "the key to the understanding of the passage lies in recognizing the chiasmus of the four verbs: the first and fourth (אעידך and אנחמך) are parallel to each other, as are the second and the third (אדמה and אשוה)." He thinks that the root of אעידך means "to strengthen, fortify," which occurs in the Polel in Ps 146:9 and in the Hithpael in Ps 20:9. He interprets the phrase as "how can I strengthen you?" Similarly, Gottwald (*Studies in the Book of Lamentations*, 11) renders "how shall I uphold you?" Berlin (*Lamentations*, 64) reads "how can I affirm you?" I am inclined to follow this line of interpretation; see translation above.

92. The Hebrew phrase נביאיך חזו לך שוא ותפל literally means "your prophets have seen visions for you, emptiness and whitewash."

93. Ketib שביתך, Qere שבותך. Although the phrase השיב שבות usually means "to bring back the captivity," that is certainly not the meaning intended here. The same expression is used in Jer 31:23; 32:44; and Job 42:10 in the sense of "restoring to the former state." Salters (*Lamentations*, 156–57) points out that the precise meaning of להשיב שבותך depends on the context. If the phrase refers to the prophets' failing to expose the sins of the people in the midst of calamity, then the meaning may be "to restore you to your former state"; see Provan, *Lamentations*, 74; Berlin, *Lamentations*, 64. However, at present the prophets are not receiving visions (2:9); hence, the phrase most likely refers to preexilic prophets who failed in their duty to expose the people's sin so as to "change their fortunes."

94. Scholars recognize that the nature of passersby reaction is hard to determine—is it one of amazement or derision?—since their gestures and words are both ambivalent. Berlin (*Lamentations*, 74) holds that it could be either positive or hostile; both understandings are possible, and readers are not required to choose one over the other.

95. The final line of this verse is unusually long. *BHS* suggests deleting שיאמרו or משוש לכל־הארץ; Gordis (*Song of Songs and Lamentations*, 165) opts to delete the prosaic שיאמרו. Schäfer (*BHQ*, 123*), however, reasons that since there is no textual evidence for

Forgotten and Forsaken by God (Lam 5:19-20)

ע 2:16 All your enemies open their mouths against you;
They hiss, they gnash their teeth, they cry: "We have devoured her!
Surely this is the day for which we waited, we have reached it,[96] we have seen it!"

פ 2:17 Yhwh did what he planned to do, he carried out his threat[97] that he ordained long ago, he demolished without pity.
He made the enemy rejoice over you, and exalted the might of your foes.

צ 2:18 Cry your heart out to Adonai! O wall of daughter Zion![98]
Let tears stream down like a torrent, day and night!
Give yourself no respite, your eyes no rest!

---

a shorter text, such emendations seem arbitrary. I retain the MT reading here.

96. Quite a number of interpreters translate the MT מצאנו literally as "we have found it"; see Gordis, *Song of Songs and Lamentations*, 137; Berlin, *Lamentations*, 64; O'Connor, *Lamentations and the Tears of the World*, 36; Parry, *Lamentations*, 69. I follow Salters (*Lamentations*, 163), who holds the word here has a sense similar to its occurrences in Gen 26:12; Num 31:50; Judg 5:30; i.e., "we have achieved."

97. The phrase בצע אמרתו is unique in the Old Testament. The Qal of בצע usually means "to cut, sever," the Piel form usually signifies "to finish." All the versions testify to the meaning "to fulfill" here. The Vg, Syriac, and Targum follow the MT; LXX has συνετέλεσεν ῥήματα αὐτοῦ, "he accomplished his words"; the plural form ῥήματα attested in LXX indicates that it reads the plural אמרתיו, "his words" instead of the singular אמרתו attested in MT. Renkema (*Lamentations*, 301) notes that Lam 2:17 constitutes "an explicit recognition of a distinct prophetic voice. The words of former prophets, who were once despised and oppressed, have been proven right in contrast to the words of Lady Jerusalem's prophets."

98. MT reads צעק לבם אל־אדני חומת בת־ציון, "their heart cried out to the Lord, wall of Daughter Zion," which is hardly intelligible. Schäfer (*BHQ*, 123*), however, holds that since MT is confirmed by all the ancient versions, any emendation seems highly questionable; Berlin (*Lamentations*, 65) follows the MT. Most scholars opt to read צעקי (feminine imperative) instead of צעק (Qal perfect), and לבך instead of לבם, thus "cry your heart to the Lord, O Wall of Daughter Zion." This reading seems convincing to me for two reasons: (1) the rendering fits the context well since a series of feminine imperatives follows this colon; and (2) since the Masoretes have placed an *athnah* under the word אדני, it seems that they took the following phrase חומת בת־ציון as a vocative. The word "wall" is understood in several ways as well: (1) the actual city wall, which represents the people of Judah; (2) Hillers (*Lamentations*, 101) suggests reading נחמת, a Niphal feminine participle of נחם instead of חומת; and renders "Cry from the heart to the Lord, O remorseful Zion!" (3) Gottwald (*Studies*, 12) understands "wall" to be a metaphor for Yhwh who acts as a protective wall, with reference to Zech 2:9; hence חומת בת־ציון functions as an apposition to אדני. Renkema (*Lamentations*, 311) and Pham (*Mourning*, 141) follow Gottwald here. It is more likely though that "wall" functions as *pars pro toto* for "Zion" here.

Exegesis of Lamentations

ק 2:19 Arise, cry out in the night, at the beginning of the watches![99]
Pour out your heart[100] like water before the presence of the Lord!
Raise your hands toward him for the lives of your little children,
collapsing from starvation at every street corner.

ר 2:20 See, O Yhwh, and look! To whom have you done this?
Should women eat their offspring, the children they have borne?[101]
Should priest and prophet be killed in the sanctuary of Adonai?

ש 2:21 The young and the old are lying on the ground in the streets.
My young women and my young men have fallen by the sword;
On the day of your anger, you killed, you slaughtered without mercy.

ת 2:22 You summoned, as if for a day of festival, my attackers[102] round about.
And on the day of Yhwh's anger, no one escaped or survived.
Those whom I bore and reared my enemy has destroyed.

---

99. The phrase לראש אשמרות can be understood in at least two different ways: the beginning of the watches, i.e., the beginning of the night (Gottwald, *Studies*, 12) or the beginning of every watch, i.e., all night long (Hillers, *Lamentations*, 95; Berlin, *Lamentations*, 75).

100. The combination of the imperative שפך "pour out" and לב/לבב occurs only here and in Ps 62:9.

101. The Hebrew word טפחים is a *hapax legomenon* and difficult to translate. The Old Greek renders the phrase עללי טפחים as ἐπιφυλλίδα ἐποίησεν μάγειρος φονευθήσονται νήπια θηλάζοντα μαστούς, "the butcher has made a gleaning, infants sucking the breasts shall be killed." Shäfer (*BHQ*, 124*) calls this rendering "obviously a double translation," based on several misunderstandings: (1) ἐπιφυλλίδα ἐποίησεν is an equivalent to the Hebrew verb עלל, "to glean" that occurs in Lam 1:22; 3:51; the Greek translator erroneously regarded עללי as a form of the verb עלל. (2) μάγειρος is based on LXX's misreading of טבח "butcher," as טפח "to care for." (3) φονευθήσονται is LXX's second effort to render טפחים, this time taking the root as טבח, "to kill." I agree with Hillers (*Lamentations*, 102) that the phrase עללי טפחים is connected with child-rearing since such a reference fits the context, thus my rendering "the children they have borne."

102. The word מגורי is difficult to interpret; its root גור has three possible meanings: (1) "to sojourn, to stay;" (2) "to provoke, to attack;" (3) "to be afraid;" see BDB, 157–59; HALOT, 184–85. Both BDB and HALOT assign Lam 2:22 the meaning "to be afraid," and this is the most common interpretation. Hillers (*Lamentations*, 102) rejects this meaning and argues that to have "terrors" summoned to a festival would constitute a metaphor not typical of Hebrew poetry. He follows McDaniel ("Philological Studies in Lamentations I," 42–44) and translates the term as "attackers" which fits the context better. Berlin (*Lamentations*, 66) and Salters (*Lamentations*, 182–83) think along the same lines. I too prefer "attackers" here.

Forgotten and Forsaken by God (Lam 5:19–20)

Comments

The most stunning feature of Lamentations 2 is its *Leitmotif*: the wrath of Yhwh. The word אַף, "anger" is repeated six times in the chapter (2:1 [*bis*], 3, 6, 21, 22), specifically, the phrases חֲרוֹן־אַף "hotness of anger" occurs once (2:3) and זַעַם אַף "fierce indignation" once as well (2:6). The nouns עֶבְרָה "fury" (2:2) and חֵמָה "rage" (2:4) are also both used once. Mention of the "day of Yhwh's wrath" starts and ends the chapter, בְּיוֹם אַפּוֹ in v. 1 and בְּיוֹם אַף־יהוה in v. 22, this forming an inclusion that contains and gives meaning to everything so enclosed. Westermann points out that there is hardly any other place in the whole of the Old Testament that talks so much about the wrath of God.[103]

Lamentations 2 is connected to chapter 1 in a number of ways. First, many of the rhetorical devices employed in chapter 1 are applied in the second poem as well, e.g., the personification of Jerusalem (the term בַּת־צִיּוֹן is used in 2:1, 4, 8, 10, 13, 18), the divine agency and warrior motifs (e.g., 2:4), the depiction of human suffering and destruction of buildings (2:1–9a), etc. Second, the "wrath of Yhwh" motif in Lamentations 2 also occupies the center of chapter 1 (1:12). O'Connor observes that Lamentations 2 needs chapter 1 to provide a context since chapter 2 begins in the middle of things and bursts open like an angry storm; "Daughter Zion's desperate situation in chapter 1 provides reasons for the accelerating fury in chapter 2."[104] Third, the two chapters both open with the dirge-like אֵיכָה and share the same speakers, namely, the narrator and Daughter Zion. On the other hand, the tone in chapter 2 is different from chapter 1; the shame and despair that are pervasive in chapter 1 now give way to anger: God is angry with Israel and we can also sense that the poet is angry with God.[105]

The narrator is the more dominant speaker in Lamentations 2; his words run though the bulk of the chapter, vv. 1–19, while Zion speaks only in the last three verses, vv. 20–22. The narrator refers to Zion first in the third person in vv. 1–10, then in the second person in vv. 11–19. Pham points out that Lam 2:1–10 is clearly delimited by the inclusion of בַּת־צִיּוֹן (vv. 1a, 10a) and אֶרֶץ (vv. 1b, 10 ac).[106] Zion could also be the speaker in 2:11, but since the narrator

---

103. Westermann, *Lamentations*, 189. Bergant (*Lamentations*, 56) observes that Lamentations 2 exhibits a very interesting literary feature: "a word or group of words appearing in one verse is repeated in the next, a second word or group connecting this second verse with the third, and so on, yielding a well-constructed literary unit." E.g., verses 1 and 2 both include the word "Lord;" verses 2 and 3 both have "Jacob," a reference to fire links vv. 3 and 4, and a reference to the enemy joins vv. 4 and 5.

104. O'Connor, *Lamentations and the Tears of the World*, 30.

105. Berlin, *Lamentations*, 67.

106. Pham, *Mourning*, 113.

speaks in the same way in v. 13 and v. 11 is imbedded in the narrator's larger speech, I consider the narrator to be the speaker in 2:11 as well.

2:1–10: The Destructive Acts of Yhwh in Anger

Lamentations 2 starts from the heart of the problem, the anger of Yhwh. The narrator's focus shifts from Zion's shame and sinfulness in Lam 1:1–11 to God's cruelty in 2:1–10. It is not clear what causes this abrupt shift—it is only clear that the narrator resumes his speech in 2:1–19, following Zion's speech in 1:12–22.[107] The narrator now agrees with Zion that Yhwh is indeed the ultimate cause of her pain and grief; Yhwh brought her ruin on the "day of his wrath" (1:12c; 2:1c, 21c, 22b).

Lam 2:1 articulates from the very beginning the relevant ideas which will subsequently be illustrated in more detail in the continuation of the chapter: Yhwh is very angry with Zion (2:1ac) and initiated a movement from heaven to earth, fulfilling judgment (2:1b); as a consequence, Zion is no longer regarded as Yhwh's footstool (2:1c). In what follows, various metaphors are employed to describe Yhwh's destructive actions: Yhwh cut down Israel's horn, i.e. might (2:3), withdrew his right hand and burned like a consuming fire. Labahn considers fire (1:13, 2:3, 2:4, 4:11) as Yhwh's most powerful destroying instrument in the chapter.[108] O'Connor calls it "God's weapon to obliterate a world."[109] Harsh verbs appear alongside these images: Yhwh swallowed up (בלע Piel vv. 2a, 5a, 5b, 8b), threw down (הרס Qal vv. 2b, 17b), brought down to the ground (נגע Hiphil v. 2c), cut off (גדע Qal v. 3a), burned (בער Qal v. 3c), poured out his wrath like fire (שפך Qal v. 4c), destroyed Israel's strongholds (שחת Piel vv. 5b, 6a, Hiphil 8a), erased the memory of festivals and Sabbath (שכח Piel v. 6b), spurned king and priests (נאץ Qal v. 6c), rejected his altar (זנח Qal v. 7a) and spurned his sanctuary (נאר Qal v. 7a), caused Zion's wall to lament (אבל Hiphil v. 8c), sank her gates (טבע Qal v. 9a), destroyed (אבד Piel v. 9a) and shattered (שבר Piel v. 9a) her bars.[110] Yhwh, moreover, did all this "without pity" (חמל לא vv. 2, 17, 21). As Dobbs-Allsopp puts it, "the intensity and mercilessness of God's assault is chillingly communicated through verbal repetition

---

107. O'Connor, *Lamentations and the Tears of the World*, 34.
108. Labahn, "Fire from Above," 244–45.
109. O'Connor, "Book of Lamentations," 1038.
110. Among the twenty-one verbs listed above, nine are in the Piel form while three are Hiphils.

Forgotten and Forsaken by God (Lam 5:19-20)

alone": even the most casual reader can sense and feel the savagery of God's attacks.[111]

The narrator presses on. Yhwh acts "like an enemy" (כאויב and כצר in v. 4), and indeed, Yhwh has "become an enemy" (כאויב in v. 5). Lam 2:4-5 is the only place where the forms כאויב and כצר occur in the Hebrew Bible. The narrator dares to describe Yhwh in such terms. Gordis and Berlin regard the *Kaph* in כאויב and כצר of v. 4 as a preposition, but suggest that the *Kaph* in כצר of v. 5 is asseverative, this entailing that "the Lord has indeed become the enemy."[112] Dobbs-Allsopp considers the *Kaph* in כצר of v. 5 a later theological addition since the Syriac lacks it.[113] Renkema rejects the suggestion that the *Kaph* in Lam 2:5 is asseverative and argues that the text is better understood as the result of a certain hesitancy on the poet's part to actually call Yhwh "the enemy," given the unusual character of that comparison.[114] He states "if Adonai were the enemy in the absolute sense of the word then there would be no more point in turning to him for help."[115] Renkema further affirms that the depiction of the situation in Lam 2:5 also contains "an unexpressed positive element," i.e. Yhwh alone can bring the calamity to an end and restore Israel's fortunes.[116] Renkema's reservations are understandable. However, to render the phrase in Lam 2:5 as "Adonai has become an enemy" does not entail that Adonai is an enemy "in the absolute sense"; rather, the term "enemy" serves as a metaphor to express Zion's acute pain in the face of God's destructive power. The metaphor's "is"—God is an enemy, has to be kept in tension with the metaphor's "is not"—God's being an enemy only describes God at a certain time, not God in all times and in all respects.

Several things could be said about Lam 2:1-10 by way of summary. First, Zion's destruction is a matter of God's deliberate plan (2:8); moreover, God's anger appears one-dimensional in this poem; Zion's sins are not mentioned here, neither is there reference to God's felt pain or being wronged; the narrator's charges are against God alone.[117] Second, the divine destruction concerns (only) buildings, strongholds, walls and the Temple; personified Zion continues to survive even after the destruction of the city. Third, God erased the memory of sacred time and rejected his altar and

---

111. Dobbs-Allsopp, *Lamentations*, 82.

112. Gordis, *Song of Songs and Lamentations*, 135 and 162; Berlin, *Lamentations*, 62 and 66.

113. Dobbs-Allsopp, *Lamentations*, 83.

114. Renkema, *Lamentations*, 229.

115. Ibid.

116. Ibid. Salters (*Lamentations*, 122) affirms Renkema's opinion.

117. O'Connor, *Lamentations and the Tears of the World*, 34; Dobbs-Allsopp, *Lamentations*, 81.

sanctuary (2:6–7); hence, he is apparently disinterested in sacred places and institutions; with all these gone, the poet struggles to lead Israel back to faith in a person, not a place.[118]

LAM 2:11–19: THE NARRATOR'S RESPONSE TO ZION'S SUFFERING

Lam 2:11–19 evidence a shift in the narrator's words: he identifies with suffering Zion and laments over her ruin (2:11a); his bile is poured out (שׁפך) because of the destruction of his people (2:11b). The narrator is no longer an observer as in 1:1–11—he now identifies with suffering Zion. Linafelt thinks that it is the fate of the children pouring out (שׁפך) their lives in their mothers' arms (2:12) that finally moves the narrator to address Zion for the first time in 2:13.[119] He urges Zion to pour out (שׁפך) her heart like water before the Lord (2:19), in sharp contrast to God's own pouring out (שׁפך) fury against Zion (2:4). O'Connor calls this shift the narrator's conversion.[120] The narrator encounters Zion as a "you" here and addresses her with a series of rhetorical questions: "How can I uphold you? With what can I compare you? To what can I liken you, that I may comfort you?" (2:13ab). These questions express the incompatibility of Zion's suffering and the desire of the narrator to comfort Zion, the very thing she longs for in Lamentations 1. Immediately thereafter, the narrator acknowledges, "for as vast as the sea is your devastation, who can heal you?" (2:13c); the narrator feels his inadequacy: Zion's suffering is too great and the only one who can heal her is God. Nevertheless, the narrator still tries; in his effort to do so, he calls Zion "virgin." O'Connor wonders what significance this address holds: has he forgotten Zion's own admission that she has many lovers (1:19)? Does the address suggest that she may be innocent after all? Is God's punishment so overwhelming that Zion's guilt is insignificant in comparison with it? Whatever lies behind the use of the term here, it is undoubtedly a term of endearment and respect used by the narrator in an effort to comfort Zion.[121]

The narrator no longer blames Zion and instead explains to her the reasons for her downfall. Her prophets failed in their responsibility to mediate between God and the people, they did not expose her iniquities (2:14);

---

118. Provan, *Lamentations*, 21; Dobbs-Allsopp, *Lamentations*, 89; Bergant, *Lamentations*, 66.

119. Linafelt, *Surviving Lamentations*, 56–57; he further states that Zion's children become "summary" figures for the totality of the city's losses.

120. O'Connor, *Lamentations and the Tears of the World*, 35.

121. Ibid., 38–39.

their seeing false and empty visions is mentioned twice in the verse. If the prophets have done their job, Zion's fate would surely be different! The passersby mock her, clap their hands and wag their heads at her (2:15) instead of seeing her pain, the thing Zion has pleaded with them to do (1:12). Still worse are Zion's enemies, who opened their mouth to swallow her up and longed to see her downfall (2:16). Worst of all, it is God who planned all that happened, threw Zion down without pity and raised up her enemies (2:17). The reversed order of ע and פ in 2:16-17 calls attention to these two verses. The narrator then employs a series of imperatives, pleading with Zion to take action, to cry out, to bring down tears, to pour out her heart like water, to lift up her hand for the lives of her children (2:18-19). The narrator now encourages Zion to make a scene, to rouse God, to plead her case.

2:20–22: Direct Appeal of Zion to Yhwh

The narrator's plea for Zion to take action is effective. Zion addresses God directly in 2:20-22 as she had in chapter 1 (vv. 9c, 11c-22). Her tone is, as the narrator's in 2:1-19, accusatory and reprimanding. She asks Yhwh to see and pay attention (2:20a), the same plea she made in 1:9c and 11c. Her focus is once again on her starving children who occupy the very center of the chapter (2:11-12). Her questions are shocking: should women eat their own children? Should priest and prophet be killed in the sanctuary? Of course not! The mention of cannibalism might be real or more likely an exaggeration of the gruesome situation; whatever the case, the image is extremely effective. Berlin points out that v. 21 utilizes the idea of cannibalism in a manner that goes beyond the conventional; the word טבח "slaughter" in 2:21c is used of butchering an animal in preparation for a meal (e.g., 1 Sam 25:11), but here it is people that are being slaughtered. There is also a wordplay between טבח "slaughter" (2:21c) and טפחים "those cared for" (2:20b). Berlin further claims that "God who slaughters his people is no less a cannibal than the mothers who eat their children."[122] God remains silent throughout Lamentations 2, just as in the first chapter. The second chapter ends with despair, but despair fueled by anger rather than sadness.

To sum up, the narrator focuses on God's destructive actions performed out of anger in Lam 2:1-19. His charge is against God, not Zion as in 1:1-11. His attitude toward Zion changes as well; his voice is passionate, he identifies with her, he talks to her, tries to comfort her, to explain to her what has happened, and encourages her to take action by bringing her case before God. The narrator realizes that the catastrophe is not due to Zion

---

122. Berlin, *Lamentations*, 76.

alone—the prophets failed, and so has God. It is God who magnified the enemies, and is responsible for the desperate hunger and death of Zion's children. Zion's speech in chapter 2 is only three verses long (vv. 20–22), much shorter than the one in chapter 1 (vv. 12–22), but the situation she describes is still worse: mothers eat their own children; prophets and priests die in the sanctuary; no one escaped alive on the day of Yhwh's wrath.

Lamentations 3: A Man of Constant Sorrow

Translation of MT With Textual Critical and Translational Notes

א 3:1 I am the man who has seen affliction[123] under the rod of his wrath.

3:2 He led and guided me into darkness, not light.[124]

3:3 Surely[125] against me he has turned, he has turned his hand, all day long.

ב 3:4 He has worn away my flesh and my skin, he has broken my bones.

3:5 he besieged and encircled me with bitterness and hardship.[126]

3:6 he has made me sit in darkness like those long dead.

---

123. LXX has ὁ βλέπων πτωχείαν, "he who sees poverty" for MT's ראה עני. The Hebrew word עני may mean both "affliction" and "poverty"; "affliction" seems the better option here.

124. MT's חשך ולא אור is a bit ambiguous: it could mean "into darkness and not into light" or "into darkness without light." LXX keeps the ambiguity by translating εἰς σκότος καὶ οὐ φῶς, "into darkness and not light." I choose "into darkness, not light" since it sets a contrast between the experience of the man that Yhwh led into darkness and the usual expectations that Yhwh leads people into light (e.g., Isa 9:1–2; 42:16; Pss 43:3; 56:13; 89:16; Neh 9:12, 19).

125. The particle אך has the meanings "surely/indeed" and "alone/only." Some interpreters adopt the meaning "only," i.e. the man has been singled out for ill treatment; e.g., NRSV, NAB; Berlin, *Lamentations*, 77. I translate it rather as "surely": God's punishment is directed toward him, but does not necessarily exclude others.

126. LXX translates MT ראש ותלאה as κεφαλήν μου καὶ ἐμόχθησεν, "my head and it became exhausted." It is clear that LXX understood ראש as "head" and as the object of ויקף "and he encircled." Albrektson (*Studies*, 131) observes that μου in LXX may be an almost necessary addition in Greek and as such probably does not presuppose a suffix in the Hebrew *Vorlage*. LXX takes ותלאה as a verb in the 3rd person feminine imperfect, probably with "head" as its subject; the problem with this is that ראש is masculine. The word ראש here, however, certainly does not refer to "head"; rather it means a "bitter and poisonous plant" (see, e.g., Deut 29:17; 32:32–33; Jer 9:14; 23:15; Hos 10:4; Amos 6:12).

Forgotten and Forsaken by God (Lam 5:19-20)

נ 3:7 He has walled me in so that I cannot get out; he has made my chain heavy.

3:8 Also when I cry out for help, he shuts out my prayer.[127]

3:9 he has blocked my ways with hewn stones,[128] he has distorted my paths.

ד 3:10 He is a lurking bear for me, a lion in hiding.

3:11 He led me off my way[129] and tore me apart;[130] he made me desolate.

3:12 he bent his bow and set me as a target for his arrows.

ה 3:13 He shot into my innards the shafts of his quiver.[131]

3:14 I have become a joke of all my people,[132] the object of their taunt-songs all day long.

---

127. The Hebrew word שתם is a *hapax legomenon*. Most interpreters understand it as a variant spelling of סתם, which means "to shut, obstruct," the meaning I adopt here.

128. It is worth noting that v. 9 begins with the same word as does v. 7. LXX has ἐνέφραξε, "he fenced in" for MT's בגזית "with hewn stones." Schäfer (*BHQ*, 125*) considers the Greek phrase ἐνέφραξε τρίβους μου, "he fenced in my paths" as a paraphrastic rendering of בגזית נתיבתי... גדר; Albrektson (*Lamentations*, 133) views the Greek as an inner corruption of an original ἐν φράξει, "with fences" = בגזית.

129. LXX has κατεδίωξεν, "he pursued closely" for MT דרכי, "my ways." It is likely that the LXX rendering is derived from the Aramaic דרך "to overtake." Schäfer (*BHQ*, 125*) reasons that the Greek translator probably misunderstood the syntax of the Hebrew where דרכי functions as the object of סורר, taking דרכי rather as a verb.

130. MT ויפשחני is a *hapax legomenon* and has always puzzled translators. The Old Greek has καὶ κατέπαυσέ(ν) με, "and he put an end to me." Ziegler's edition reads καὶ κατέσπασέ(ν) με, "and he pulled me down." Schäfer (*BHQ*, 125*) points out that Ziegler's reading is only found as a correction in one manuscript from the thirteenth or fourteenth century while most Greek manuscripts read καὶ κατέπαυσέ(ν) με, "and he put an end to me" as in the Old Greek, which, Schäfer suggests, renders the real meaning of the Hebrew word. Aquila reads καὶ ἐχώλανέ με, "and he has made me lame." Vg has *et confregit me*, "and he has broken me"; while both Syriac and the Targum have "he has torn me to pieces." I opt for "he tore me apart" since this accords with the meaning "he put an end to me," as witnessed by the Old Greek.

131. MT's בני אשפתו literally means "sons of his quiver," a poetic expression for arrows; Salters (*Lamentations*, 209) notes that this is the only occurrence of the phrase, though the arrow is described figuratively as בֶּן קֶשֶׁת, "son of a bow" in Job 41:20.

132. LXX, Vg, and the Targum follow MT's עמי, "my people." It is difficult to understand why the poet's own people would taunt him; therefore, a number of interpreters read עמים "all peoples/nations" (see NAB; Salters, *Lamentations*, 189). The MT, it should be noted, however, registers a Sebir, i.e. סבר עמים וקר עמי. Gordis (*Song of Songs and Lamentations*, 177) notes that the purpose of the Sebir is to warn the scribe against a suggested reading that might appear attractive; in this instance, the Sebir warns against

Exegesis of Lamentations

3:15 He has filled me with bitterness, sated me with wormwood.

ו 3:16 He ground my teeth on gravel,[133] crushed me down into the dust.[134]

3:17 My soul is rejected from peace; I have forgotten goodness.

3:18 And I said, "Vanished are my future and my hope from Yhwh."[135]

ז 3:19 To remember[136] my affliction and restless wandering[137] is wormwood and bitterness.

3:20 My soul remembers continually and bows down within me.[138]

---

the reading עמים. Thus I opt to follow the MT's "my people."

133. MT ויגרס is the Hiphil of גרס, which BDB (176) lists under the word גרש, "to crush," rendering the colon as "he has crushed my teeth with gravel," a figurative way of speaking about divine chastisement. HALOT (1660) has "make someone's teeth grind." LXX reads καὶ ἐξέβαλεν, "and he cast out," Aquila καὶ ἐξετίναξεν, "and he shook away"; both take the root as גרש. Symmachus combines both these readings. The image seems to be of Yhwh's breaking and knocking out the man's teeth with stones, thus my translation "he ground my teeth on gravel."

134. MT הכפישני is a *hapax legomenon*. Gordis (*Song of Songs and Lamentations*, 177) takes the root כפש as a variant of כבש, which has the meaning "to subdue/trample." Salters (*Lamentations*, 215) understands the image as a continuation of v. 15, where Yhwh, acting like a prison guard, provides the speaker with bitter herbs, crushes his teeth, and presses him into the dust.

135. The Hebrew word נצח could mean "eminence, endurance, perpetuity." Quite a number of interpreters, however, render it as "glory" (NRSV) or "eminence" (O'Connor, *Lamentations and the Tears of the World*, 46). Salters (*Lamentations*, 218) argues that the context rules out the meaning "glory" since the poet is at rock-bottom in every respect and his glory is long gone. Hillers (*Lamentations*, 116) takes the phrase נצחי ותוחלתי, "my enduring and my hope" as a hendiadys meaning "my lasting hope." Gordis (*Song of Songs and Lamentations*, 178), however, points out that the proposed hendiadys would require the reverse order of the two words. Anderson (נצח, *TDOT* 9: 529–33) holds that the term always refers to the future, never to the past. Salters (*Lamentations*, 218) and Berlin (*Lamentations*, 82) translate the word נצח as "future," as do I.

136. MT זְכָר can be either an imperative or infinitive. Aquila, Vg, Syriac and the Targum interpret it as an imperative. LXX has ἐμνήσθην, "I have remembered," probably a free rendering of the MT. If the form is imperative, the poet is asking God to remember his suffering; if infinitive, the poet himself is remembering his own affliction. Scholars are divided. Berlin (*Lamentations*, 78 and 82) takes it as imperative and renders the colon as "Remember my misery and trouble—wormwood and bitterness." Schäfer (*BHQ*, 125*) prefers the infinitive. O'Connor (*Lamentations and the Tears of the World*, 47) and Hillers (*Lamentations*, 114) also opt for infinitive since it makes more sense in view of v. 20, which seems to continue the thought of v. 19. I too take it as an infinitive.

137. LXX has καὶ ἐκ διωγμοῦ μου, "and from my persecution" for MT ומרודי, "and my restless wandering." The word מרוד occurs in Lam 1:7 as well. I prefer the MT.

138. MT Qere וְתָשׁוּחַ is from the root שחח or שוח, which means "to bow down." Hillers (*Lamentations*, 114–15) and Berlin (*Lamentations*, 82–83) choose to give it the more

Forgotten and Forsaken by God (Lam 5:19-20)

3:21 This I call to mind; therefore, I have hope:

ח 3:22[139] The steadfast love of Yhwh is not used up,[140] his mercies never come to an end.

3:23 They are new every morning; great is your faithfulness.

3:24 "Yhwh is my portion," says my soul, "therefore I will hope in him."

ט 3:25[141] Good is Yhwh to those who wait for him, to the soul that seeks him.

3:26 Good it is to wait quietly[142] for the salvation of Yhwh.

3:27 Good it is for a man to bear the yoke in his youth,

י 3:28 That he sits alone in silence when he lays it upon him,[143]

---

extended meaning "feel despondent" on the basis of the parallel passages Pss 42:6-7; 43:5. I opt for the literal meaning, "to bow down."

139. LXX lacks an equivalent to vv. 22-24, the entire ח lines of the MT, which is uncharacteristic for its translation. Albrektson (*Lamentations*, 145) avers that these lines have fallen out through homoioteleuton since 24b is identical with 21b.

140. MT תמנו, "we ended" is awkward. A number of scholars, though, do support the MT. See Albrektson, *Lamentations*, 145; Renkema, *Lamentations*, 385. Provan (*Lamentations*, 93) tries to smooth matters out and suggests reading with what proceeds rather than what follows; he thus translates vv. 21-23a as "But this I call to mind, and therefore have hope: the steadfast love of the LORD! For we are not consumed because his mercies never come to an end: they are new every morning." Berlin (*Lamentations*, 83) holds that Provan's translation accords with the grammar but goes against the syntax. I follow most scholars who alter תמנו to תמו and take Yhwh's "kindness" as the subject, thus my rendering "the steadfast love of Yhwh is not used up." The two כי's in this verse are asseverative, rather than casual; see McDaniel, "Philological Studies II," 212; Hillers, *Lamentations*, 115; Salters, *Lamentations*, 225.

141. The same Hebrew word טוב begins each line of the stanza, a feature I attempt to capture in my translation.

142. MT's טוב ויחיל ודומם is problematic, and scholars have offered various emendations of the text. Salters (*Lamentations*, 231-32) holds that the form after טוב must be verbal, probably the 3rd person masculine singular Hiphil form יחיל from the root יחל "to wait for," with the word נפש in v. 25 as the subject. I adopt Salters's suggestion here.

143. The word נטל occurs only five times in the Hebrew Bible; the other four instances are 2 Sam 24:12; Prov 27:3; Isa 40:15; and 63:9. There are three ways to understand it: (1) Hillers (*Lamentations*, 116) suggests that the meaning here is "heavy" since the related noun in Prov 27:3 means "weight," with the subject "yoke" mentioned in v. 27; he renders "when it is heavy on him." (2) LXX translates the verb as ἦρεν, "he carried upon"; Salters (*Lamentations*, 233) points out that the LXX translator used the same word to translate נשא in 3:27 where the subject is גבר; it follows that the subject was the same here in the eyes of the LXX translator: it is the man who carries the yoke. (3) Salters, following Westermann (*Lamentations*, 162), Renkema (*Lamentations*, 400), Berlin (*Lamentations*, 79), and O'Connor (*Lamentations and the Tears of the World*,

Exegesis of Lamentations

    3:29 That he puts his mouth in the dust; perhaps there is hope,

    3:30 That he gives his cheek to the smiter; he is filled with insult.

כ 3:31[144] For Adonai will not reject forever.[145]

    3:32 For he causes grief, but he has mercy according to the abundance of his steadfast love.

    3:33 For he does not afflict willingly nor grieve the children of humans.

ל 3:34 To crush[146] under his feet all the prisoners of the land,

    3:35 To turn aside the right of a man before the face of the most High,

    3:36 To subvert a human in his cause; Adonai does not see.[147]

---

49) takes the subject as "Yhwh" and the object as the "yoke"; he understands the verb נטל to mean "to lay upon, impose" as in 2 Sam 24:12. In Lam 3:28 then, it is Yhwh who laid the yoke upon the man; the second part of the verse then provides a reason for the advice that the man sit alone in silence in the first part, i.e. because the yoke is a divine imposition. I opt for the third interpretation as well.

144. Each line of the stanza begins with כי.

145. This line is unusually short. Hillers (*Lamentations*, 116) believes that something has been omitted in the course of the line's transmission, but that "it is impossible to supply the deficiency with anything approaching certainty or probability." Renkema (*Lamentations*, 406), however, holds that the shortness of the line is original; he considers any proposed reconstruction of the sentence to be "guess work and . . ., in fact, unnecessary"; moreover, the textual tradition offers no alternative indications. O'Connor (*Lamentations and the Tears of the World*, 49) affirms that the very shortness of the line emphasizes it.

146. The three lines 3:34–36 all start with ל + infinitive construct. Hillers (*Lamentations*, 116) points out that infinitive constructs do not constitute sentences in Hebrew and must depend on some finite verb. Most commentators consider the above infinitives as objects of "Adonai does not see" in v. 36. Hillers, however, argues that the word order is odd on this reading and that ראה is not normally followed by an infinitive with ל; accordingly, he holds that the infinitives depend on the verbs in v. 33, i.e. Adonai is not willing to cause affliction or grief. His rendering of 3:33–36 thus runs: "Because he does not deliberately torment men, or afflict them by crushing under foot all the prisoners of the earth, by denying a man justice before the Most High, by twisting a man's case without the Lord seeing." However, I think it better to take vv. 34–36 as a unit and interpret the infinitives as objects of "Adonai does not see."

147. MT אדני לא ראה can be interpreted either as an interjection "does Adonai not see?" or as a statement "Adonai does not see." I think reading the phrase as a statement is better since it expresses the poet's acute realization of being deserted by God and of the injustice all around him. Renkema (*Lamentations*, 415–18), as well, strongly argues that it should be read as a statement. He thinks that ראה here has to be understood in the context of the entire book, where it is used with Yhwh as the subject in 1:9c, 11c, 20; 2:20; 3:30, 59; 5:1. Renkema (Ibid., 417–18) further holds that "this frequently repeated and urgent appeal to Yhwh to look down and see his people's affliction implies, in fact,

Forgotten and Forsaken by God (Lam 5:19–20)

מ 3:37 Who can speak and it happens, if Adonai does not command?[148]

3:38 Is it not from the mouth of the Most High that good and bad come?

3:39 What living human will complain, a man of his punishment?[149]

נ 3:40 Let us test and examine our ways, and let us return to Yhwh.

3:41 Let us lift up our hearts along with[150] our hands to El in the heavens.

3:42 We have transgressed and rebelled,[151] you have not forgiven.

---

that he has not done so up to the present moment." The man's faith-filled expectations expressed in 3:21–33 "stand in sharp contrast to the affliction which continues to prevail all around him." Dobbs-Allsopp (*Lamentations*, 121–22) likewise affirms that אדני לא ראה in v. 36 should be read as a statement; the claim that God "does not see" serves to highlight all the places in Lamentations where God is requested to "see" the destruction. Claims and counterclaims are given equal linguistic weight in Lamentations, and there is no explicit attempt to resolve the contradictions in the book.

148. There is no particle corresponding to "if" between "it happens" and "Adonai" in the Hebrew. I follow Berlin (*Lamentations*, 83) and O'Connor (*Lamentations and the Tears of the World*, 52) and supply "if" here to make the sentence more intelligible.

149. Ketib חטאו, Qere חטאיו; Ketib is preferable. The literal meaning of the Hebrew is "What should a living person complain, a man over his sin?" I think the underlying idea is: why should anyone complain about the consequences of sin (i.e. punishment) thus my rendering "a man of his punishment."

150. The phrase אֶל־כַּפָּיִם in MT is difficult to interpret. Gordis (*Song of Songs and Lamentations*, 185) suggests emending the MT's vocalization to read אַל "not" instead of אֶל "to"; he translates the verse as "let us lift up our hearts, and not our hands, to God in heaven"; so Gottwald (*Lamentations*, 14). Hillers (*Lamentations*, 117) holds that אל is used in place of על, "with, along with" here. Albrektson (*Studies*, 154–55), on the other hand, holds that it is not necessary to emend the Hebrew text; the word אל can mean "in addition to"; see e.g., Lev 18:18 ואשה אל־אחתה לא תקח, "and you shall not take a woman as wife in addition to her sister." See also BDB, 40, no. 5; Schäfer, *BHQ*, 128*; Salters, *Lamentations*, 249–50. I agree that emendation of the MT is unnecessary and that the verse is alluding to praying with a sincere heart, "along with" (rather than "instead of") lifted up hands.

151. Schäfer (*BHQ*, 128*) points out that the Old Greek reading ἡμαρτήσαμεν ἠσεβήσαμεν, "we sinned, we rebelled" is found in the great majority of the Greek manuscripts as the equivalent for MT's פשענו ומרינו נחנו; Ziegler, however, has ἡμαρτήσαμεν ἠσεβήσαμεν καὶ παρεπικράναμεν, "we sinned, we rebelled, and we have provoked." Albrektson (*Studies in the Text and Theology of Lamentations*, 155) presumes Ziegler's reasoning for reading thus to be as follows: ἀσβέω is never found in LXX for מרה but often for פשע, thus ἠσεβήσαμεν is probably a rendering for פשענו, while παρεπικράναμεν stands for מרינו; accordingly, ἡμαρτήσαμεν must reflect נחנו, which was misread as חטאנו. Nevertheless, Ziegler's reading does not point to a different *Vorlage*; I follow the MT here.

ס 3:43 You have covered us[152] in anger and pursued us, you killed without pity.

3:44 you have covered yourself with a cloud so that prayers cannot pass through.

3:45 Filth and rubbish[153] you have made us among the peoples.

ע 3:46 They opened their mouths against us, all of our enemies;

3:47 Panic and pitfall have come upon us, devastation and destruction.

3:48 My eyes run with streams of tears because of the destruction of my people.

פ 3:49 My eyes will flow without ceasing, without respite,

3:50 until Yhwh looks down from heaven and sees.

3:51 My eyes cause me pain more than all the daughters of my city.[154]

---

152. Hillers (*Lamentations*, 117) holds that the verb סכתה is probably not reflexive since the Qal form is always transitive elsewhere (Exod 25:20; 37:9; 40:3; 1 Kgs 8:7; 1 Chr 28:18; Ps 140:8). Hence, not "you covered yourself," but rather "you covered us"; the object pronoun in ותרדפנו does double duty, encompassing both verbs; one finds the same rendering in O'Connor, *Lamentations and the Tears of the World*, 53; Salters, *Lamentations*, 190 and 252–53.

153. The two forms סחי ומאוס in MT are unique. The meaning of מאוס is not in doubt, its verbal form מאס "to reject" appears in Lam 5:22 as well, while the noun here in Lam 3:45 means "refuse." The word סחי is a *hapax legomenon*. Schäfer (*BHQ*, 128*) points out that none of the ancient versions, with the exception of Symmachus, gives a precise rendering of the word. Salters (*Lamentations*, 255) suggests that the form may be related to the verb סחה, which occurs only at Ezek 26:4, and where it seems to mean "scrape off, clear away" (see also BDB, 695). Thus my translation here: "filth and rubbish."

154. This verse in the MT is very difficult. The literal meaning of the Hebrew is, "my eyes have afflicted my soul more than all the daughters of my city." Hillers (*Lamentations*, 118) holds that the MT is corrupt here, and yields no acceptable sense; he reconstructs the sentence and translates the verse as "the affliction done to me, has consumed my eyes." Gordis (*Song of Songs and Lamentations*, 185), however, affirms that the MT remains preferable to all the proposed emendations even though it is extremely difficult. The function of מן is difficult to determine; it could be causative, i.e. the poet is grieved because of the fate/plight of the young women in his city; cf. NRSV "My eyes cause me grief at the fate of all the young women in my city"; NAB "My eyes torment my soul at the sight of all the daughters of my city"; and NAS "My eyes bring pain to my soul because of all the daughters of my city." The מן could also be comparative. Salters (*Lamentations*, 261–62) points out that the phrase "daughters of my city" is only found here in the Hebrew Bible; it is very possible that these "daughters" are the "professional mourners," especially in a context that speaks of eyes running with water. The poet would thus be saying here that his own eyes have affected him more than all professional wailing could have done. I consider it is better to take מן as comparative here.

Forgotten and Forsaken by God (Lam 5:19-20)

צ 3:52 They hunted me like a bird, my enemies, for no cause.[155]

3:53 In a pit they put an end to my life; they threw a stone over me.[156]

3:54 Waters flowed over my head; I thought, "I am cut off."

ק 3:55[157] I called on your name, O Yhwh, from the depths of the pit.

3:56 You heard my voice, "Do not hide your ear from my cry for help!"[158]

155. The word חנם can be taken in two ways: (1) "my enemies without cause"; see NRSV, NAB, NAS, Hillers, *Lamentations*, 112; Westermann, *Lamentations*, 163; or (2) the actions of the enemies are unprovoked; see Berlin, *Lamentations*, 80; O'Connor, *Lamentations and the Tears of the World*, 54; Salters, *Lamentations*, 190 and 263. Both interpretations are possible; I opt to follow the second one.

156. Some scholars prefer to read the singular אבן as collective and interpret the phrase as "they threw stones at me"; see Gordis, *Song of Songs and Lamentations*, 144; Westermann, *Lamentations*, 164; Hillers, *Lamentations*, 112; Salters, *Lamentations*, 265. I prefer to interpret the singular according to the image of a covering stone on top of a cistern, thus my rendering "they threw a stone over me"; see also Berlin, *Lamentations*, 81; O'Connor, *Lamentations and the Tears of the World*, 54.

157. Scholars are divided on the import of the tenses in vv. 55–62. The traditional view is to read the perfects as simple past tenses, as do the majority of scholars. An alternative view renders them as precatives, expressing a desire or request; see Gordis, *Song of Songs and Lamentations*, 186; Hillers, *Lamentations*, 118; Berlin, *Lamentations*, 83; Dobbs-Allsopp, *Lamentations*, 126–27. Provan ("Past, Present and Future in Lamentations III," 164–75) presents the strongest arguments for reading these perfects as precatives. Provan argues that Lam 3:52–66 refers to a single situation of distress, the one currently being endured, rather than two situations, one past, the other present. He claims that to read the perfects as precatives results in an entirely coherent reading of 3:52–66 and of the chapter as a whole. I agree that Provan's approach does result in a more coherent reading of the passage and the chapter; however, some problems remain. Parry (*Lamentations*, 123–24) critiques Provan's position and raises these weak points: (1) precatives are very rare in MT such that "no perfect should be taken to be a precative unless there is a strong reason to do so"; (2) given the dire situation of the poet, it would be better for him to use rhetorically more effective imperatives rather than weaker precatives to avoid misunderstanding; and (3) Provan and others who prefer the precative reading translate the perfects, imperatives, and imperfects in 3:52–66 in exactly the same way, i.e. all as imperatives; but then one wonders why the poet would have shifted among three different forms if there is no difference among them. Thus, I follow majority of scholars and read the perfects as simple past tenses.

158. The MT phrase לרוחתי לשועתי is difficult to interpret. LXX has εἰς τὴν δέησίν μου, "to my prayer" in v. 56, and εἰς τὴν βοήθειάν μου, "to my help" at the beginning of v. 57. Salters (*Lamentations*, 267) holds that the phrases' displacement in LXX is probably not original but due to faulty transmission. *BHS* suggests deleting one phrase. The word רוחה occurs elsewhere in the Hebrew Bible only at Exod 8:11 where it clearly means "respite, relief"; Provan (*Lamentations*, 107) takes the root as רוח "to breathe" and renders the word as "gasping." The word לשועתי is from the root שוע, "cry for help." A number of scholars understand the two words as forming a hendiadys, meaning "to

Exegesis of Lamentations

3:57 You came near on the day I called you; you said, "Do not fear!"

ר 3:58 You have championed my cause,[159] O Adonai, you have redeemed my life.

3:59 You have seen the wrong done to me, O Yhwh; judge my cause.[160]

3:60 You have seen all their vengeance, all their plots against me.

ש 3:61 You have heard their insults, O Yhwh, all their plots against me.

3:62 The lips of those rising[161] and their murmurs are against me all day long.

3:63 Whether they sit or rise[162]—look, I am the object of their taunt-songs.

ת 3:64 Pay them back for their deeds,[163] O Yhwh, according to the work of their hands!

3:65 Give them anguish of heart;[164] your curse be on them!

---

my cry for help"; see NRSV, Gottwald, *Studies*, 14; Renkema, *Lamentations*, 453; Berlin, *Lamentations*, 83. Salters (*Lamentations*, 268), however, points out that a hendiadys is defined as two nouns joined by *and* to form one concept, which is not what we have here. However, Salters's understanding of hendiadys seems too narrow; a hendiadys is usually formed by two nouns, but is not limited to noun combinations; Watson (*Classical Hebrew Poetry*, 328) lists Lam 3:56 as an example of hendiadys used to generate rhyme. Accordingly, I understand the two words as a hendiadys, "to my cry for help."

159. Salters (*Lamentations*, 270) points out that the word רבת, from the root ריב "to plead someone's legal cause," is the only occurrence of the verb in Lamentations, where it is construed with the cognate plural noun ריבי here in 3:58.

160. LXX has ἔκρινας τὴν κρίσιν μου, "you judged my cause" for MT's imperative שפטה משפטי, "judge my cause." Schäfer (*BHQ*, 130*) considers MT's שפטה (masculine singular imperative + paragogic ה) as the *lectio difficilior*. Salters (*Lamentations*, 272–73) holds that even though the MT imperative is difficult in a context of perfect verbs, the speaker may be recounting past experience of Yhwh's positive interventions as a base for his plea for present deliverance. I retain the MT vocalization.

161. MT קמי is a masculine plural participle from קום, which literally means "those who rise against me." NRSV and NAS read "my assailants," while NAB has "my foes." I render the form literally here.

162. The MT phrase שבתם וקימתם, "their sitting down and rising up" is probably a meristic idiom encompassing all daily activities. Hillers (*Lamentations*, 119) renders "in everything they do."

163. Since the letter ת is required by the acrostic here, the poet chose to begin these three lines with second-person imperfects commencing with letter ת but having the force of imperatives.

164. The meaning of the MT phrase מגנת־לב is uncertain. LXX has ὑπερασπισμὸν καρδίας, "a shielding of the heart," probably deriving the root from גנן, "to cover, defend,"

89

Forgotten and Forsaken by God (Lam 5:19-20)

3:66 Pursue them in anger and destroy them from under Yhwh's heavens.

Comments

Lamentations 3 does not open with a dirge-like exclamation איכה as do chapters 1, 2 and 4, but rather with the statement אני הגבר ראה עני, "I am the man who has seen affliction" (3:1).[165] This man's voice dominates the entire chapter, with the word גבר being reiterated in vv. 27, 35, and 39. He gives the reader a different perspective from the female voice of Zion as he tries to confront the reality of suffering and come to terms with it. Dobbs-Allsopp puts it well: "this distinctly male voice complements and contrasts with Zion's equally distinct female voice, providing the sequence with a feeling of gender balance—the suffering and misery engulfed men as well as women."[166]

Lamentations 3 is not as clearly structured as the previous two chapters; scholars vary in their divisions of the chapter. I divide the chapter into four parts. In the first part (vv. 1-18), the man describes the affliction he experienced at the hands of a "him," an unidentified figure throughout vv. 1-16, only specified as Yhwh at the very end of the section in v. 18; the language here resembles that of a personal lament. In the second part (vv. 19-39), the man employs conventional wisdom language and expresses hope in Yhwh, but this hope is not sustained, even in this section. In the third part (vv. 40-47), we hear the man exhorting the community to return

---

a meaning reflected in translations such as "hardness of heart" (Provan, *Lamentations*, 109) and "obstinacy of heart" (O'Connor, *Lamentations and the Tears of the World*, 56). But these translations seem weak in the context; I follow Hillers (*Lamentations*, 119) and Berlin (*Lamentations*, 83), who render it as "anguish of heart."

165. A lot of ink has been spilled over the identity of the man. Even though it has been a scholarly consensus that the man in Lamentations 3 is not Jeremiah, Hannes Bezzel ("'Man of Constant Sorrow', 254-65) holds that identifying the man as Jeremiah helps us understand Lamentations 3 better. Saebø ("Who is 'the Man' in Lamentations?," 302) identifies the man as Zedekiah. Albrektson (*Studies in the Text and Theology of Lamentations*, 126-28) and Gordis (*Song of Songs and Lamentations*, 170-71) hold that the man represents a collective voice of the people. Berges (*Klagelieder* 183-85) suggests that the man represents personified Lady Zion. Renkema (*Lamentations*, 350) considers him a prominent resident in Jerusalem. Lanahan ("Speaking Voice in the Book of Lamentations," 45) suggests that the man is a frustrated veteran, while O'Connor (*Lamentations and the Tears of the World*, 47) holds that he is a defeated "strong man." Hillers (*Lamentations*, 122) argues that he is an "Everyman," a figure who represents any man who feels that God is against him, as does Dobbs-Allsopp (*Lamentations*, 106-9). I simply translate הגבר here as "the man," i.e. a typical male voice that is different from Zion's.

166. Dobbs-Allsopp, *Lamentations*, 105.

to Yhwh; the first person common plural "we" is employed, and the genre is that of a communal lament. In the chapter's final part (vv. 48-66), the man recalls Yhwh's previous act of deliverance and pleads with Yhwh to act; the chapter ends with a prayer for vengeance in vv. 64-66.[167]

Lam 3:1-18: Afflictions the Man Experienced

Lam 3:1-18 is the man's description of Yhwh's personal attacks on him. Dobbs-Allsopp notes that this section "constitutes Lamentations' third and final depiction of God as adversary."[168] The man's lament in 3:1-18 forms a fitting counterpart to Zion's testimony concerning Yhwh's violent acts against her in 1:13-15. Lam 3:1-18, together with 1:13-15, constitutes an envelope structure, with the series of God's destructive actions done out of anger in 2:1-9 standing at the center.[169] The man describes himself as the one "who has seen affliction" (3:1). The word ראה, "to see," recurs throughout the book, functioning as a *Leitwort*. It reminds us of Zion's repeated call on Yhwh (1:9c, 11c, 2:20a) and the passersby (1:12a) to look at and see her pain; it also points to the community's final plea to Yhwh to see (5:1). The man here "sees affliction"; as such, he may serve as a witness for Zion and her complaint. The phrase בשבט עברתו, "under the rod of his wrath" reminds the reader of the wrath of God so emphatically described in 2:1-9; the same word עברה "wrath" is used in 2:2 as well.

The man's voice is "as intimate, personal and anguished" as that of Daughter Zion.[170] A series of strong verbs and images are employed in Lam 3:1-18. "He," the (initially) unidentified attacker, acted like a bad shepherd; he drove the man and led him into darkness (3:2);[171] he turned his hand against

---

167. It is worth noting that ideas in Lamentations 3 are usually "conjoined across the stanzas" as delimited by the intensified triple acrostic; e.g., v. 3 goes with v. 4, 6 with 7, 12 with 13, 18 with 19-20, 21 with 22ff., 42 with 43, 48 with 49-51, and 60 with 61-63; see Hillers, *Lamentations*, 120; Dobbs-Allsopp, *Lamentations*, 106.

168. Dobbs-Allsopp, *Lamentations*, 109.

169. Ibid., 109-10.

170. O'Connor, "Book of Lamentations," 1046.

171. Van Hecke ("Lamentations 3,1-6," 264-81) argues that Lam 3:1-6 was conceived as a reversal of Psalm 23. God in Psalm 23 is a good shepherd and the psalmist takes comfort from God's rod while walking "through a valley of deepest darkness" (Ps 23:4); God in Lam 3:1-6 is a very bad shepherd who not only leads the man into darkness, but also tears away his skin and flesh, and makes him sit in darkness like the dead of long ago.

Forgotten and Forsaken by God (Lam 5:19–20)

the man (3:3),[172] wore away his skin and flesh, and broke his bones (3:4).[173] The imagery turns then to imprisonment: the attacker besieged the man, encircled him with bitterness, and made him sit in darkness like the dead of long ago (3:5–6);[174] he put heavy chains on him and blocked him up with no way of escape (3:7–9). The persecutor next acted like various wild animals, a bear in wait, a lion in hiding, tearing the man to pieces (3:10–11),[175] then like an archer who shot into the man's innards (3:12–13). His persecutor filled the man with bitterness and made his teeth grind on gravel (3:15–16). The man becomes a laughingstock to his own people,[176] he is bereft of peace and happiness (3:14, 17). He has no future, no hope from Yhwh (3:18).

Lam 3:19–39: Hope Expressed But Not Sustained

The man is totally crushed and feels extremely bitter (3:19–20). However, at the lowest point in his life, in the midst of hopelessness, the man startles readers by claiming that he has hope (3:21); he then recalls the positive attributes of God in vv. 22–25 and 31–33. This passage contains the only explicit message of hope in the book. Words derived from יחל "to wait, hope for" and קוה "to wait" are repeated six times in 3:18–29. The first such usage has a negative sense: "*vanished* are my future and my hope from Yhwh" (3:18), while the final one ends on a very uncertain note: "*perhaps* there is hope" (3:29).

> 3:18 And I said "vanished are my future and my hope (ותוחלתי) from Yhwh." יחל
> 3:21 This I call to mind; therefore, I have hope (אוחיל) יחל
> 3:24 therefore I will hope in him (אוחיל) יחל
> 3:25 Yhwh is good to those who wait for (לקוו) him קוה
> 3:26 Good it is to wait (ויחיל) quietly for the salvation of Yhwh יחל
> 3:29 perhaps there is hope (קוה לקוו)

---

172. The hand of God is mentioned elsewhere in Lamentations: God's hand tied Zion's transgressions into a yoke in Lam 1:14; God withheld his right hand before the enemy in 2:3, but did not withhold his hand from destroying the walls and strongholds of Judah in 2:8.

173. The man's broken bones recall Zion's burning bones in 1:13 and point ahead to the dry bones of Jerusalem's nobles in 4:8.

174. The same phrase "like the dead of long ago" of Lam 3:6 is used in Ps 143:3; the sufferer is described as those among the dead in Pss 31:12; 88:6; Isa 59:10 as well.

175. God is depicted as a bear and a lion in Hos 13:8, and compared with a lion in Amos 3:8.

176. Such "laughingstock" imagery is often used in laments, see, e.g., Job 12:4; Jer 20:7.

In the midst of affliction, bitterness and despair (3:19–20), the man hopes and waits; he is waiting for God to do something about his desperate situation. Bergant holds that the primary focus here is on the man's waiting.[177] The man appeals to a covenantal God in 3:22–24. The man's hope is clearly rooted in God's character: steadfast love and mercy that are new every morning (3:22–23a), and it is here that the man addresses God for the first time: "Great is *your* faithfulness" (3:23b). The man then affirms: "Yhwh is my portion, therefore I will hope in him" (3:24). Prompted by suffering and rooted in God, the man's hope is "neither innocent nor lacking in its own claims on God."[178] The man lays claim on God who promised David to maintain his line "forever" (2 Sam 7:15; Ps 89:28–37). Dobbs-Allsopp holds that "such hope both indicts God for the current miseries that imply God has in fact 'renounced his covenant' (Ps. 89:40) and calls God back to covenant faithfulness."[179]

The man's sudden change of mood from despair to hope is due to his change of mind: "This I call to mind; therefore I have hope" (3:21). His circumstances have not changed since he will return again to his misery in 3:48–54 and again call upon God to see the suffering of his people and his own in 3:50 and 63; rather, the change occurs within him, in his renewed hope in the covenantal God he knew.[180]

The man then evidences his proper response to suffering by utilizing traditional wisdom language (3:25–30):[181] it is good that one wait quietly, bear his yoke from youth, sit alone in silence, put one's mouth in the dust, give one's cheek to the smiter, and be filled with insult. Yhwh will not reject forever, nor would he afflict willingly (3:31–33); it is the Most High who ordains both good and bad; one should not complain about the punish-

---

177. Bergant, *Lamentations*, 90.

178. Dobbs-Allsopp, *Lamentations*, 118.

179. Ibid., 119; Dobbs-Allsopp also states that the references to God's "steadfast love," "mercy," and "faithfulness" allude to God's covenantal loyalty as promised in the Davidic covenant (e.g., 2 Sam 7:15; 1 Kgs 8:23; Pss 89:2, 14, 24–37; Isa 55:3).

180. The positive characteristics of Yhwh that the man recalls are those featured in Yhwh's self-description at Sinai in Exod 34:6–7: "The Lord, the Lord, a God merciful and gracious, slow to anger, and abounding in steadfast love and faithfulness, keeping steadfast love for thousandth generation, forgiving iniquity and sin, yet by no means clearing the guilty, but visiting the iniquity of the parents upon the children and the children's children to the third and the fourth generation."

181. There are a number of parallel Old Testament passages: "Yhwh's goodness" in Ps 119:68; Hos 3:5; Neh 9:25; etc.; the idea of "waiting for God" in Pss 25:3, 5, 21; 27:14; 37:9, 34; 40:2; etc.; "wait in silence for the salvation of Yhwh" in Pss 37:7; 39:3, 8; 62:2, 6; Isa 30:15, etc.; "put one's mouth in the dust" as a gesture of humility in Ps 72:9; Mic 7:17; etc.; "Adonai does not reject forever" in Ps 103:8–9; and God the Most High who establishes justice in the world in Ps 82:1–8.

ment for one's sins (3:37–39). The protesting man, who sounded very much like Job in 3:1–20, now assumes the role of Job's friends;[182] the emphatic first- person subject *I* recedes into the background and didactic third person statements come to the fore. Yet, within this very section, the man also states that Adonai does not see the injustice of the world (3:34–36). Dobbs-Allsopp holds that the view of suffering and God articulated in chapter 3 as a whole proves to be broader, more complicated than that reflected in vv. 21–33. He further states that there are challenges to this section's ideology throughout the book, e.g., its image of the passive sufferer stands in stark contrast to the active lamenters and protesters in chapters 1 and 2, as well as to the man's own assertions in 3:1–20 and those of the community in chapter 5; moreover, the phrase "to sit alone in silence" (3:28) recalls Zion's sitting alone, and she is anything but silent! Furthermore, while the man denies that Adonai will reject forever in 3:31, this is called into question in 2:7a (Yhwh rejected his altar), and more generally in 5:20–22. In addition, the man's claim "although he causes grief, he will have compassion" (3:32) stands in tension with the claims that Yhwh killed לא חמל, *without mercy* (3:43), destroyed לא חמל, *without mercy* (2:2a), demolished לא חמל, *without mercy* (2:17b), slaughtered לא חמל, *without mercy* (2:21c).[183]

For the suffering man, there is no one to go to but Yhwh, the covenantal God; there is nothing else he can do except hope. His hope is real, but it has to be measured against the larger reality of suffering. His positive claims about God have to be balanced by the book's counterclaims. The poem itself does not resolve the contradictions; neither need we.

Lam 3:40–47: Call to Communal Confession and Divine Responsibility

The man now speaks as part of the community, using the first person plural voice "we." This part manifests traits of a communal lament: accusation against God, complaint about the enemies, and explicit lament.[184] The man first exhorts the community to examine its ways and return to Yhwh. The word שוב is used here to indicate a complete and sincere, external and internal transformation (3:40). There follows a call to pray with lifted hands as well as hearts. Then we hear a confession of sin: "we have transgressed and rebelled" (3:42a), after which we expect to hear a specification of the community's misdeeds or a prayer asking for forgiveness, but instead we

---

182. See Dobbs-Allsopp, *Lamentations*, 120.
183. Ibid., 120–22.
184. Bergant, *Lamentations*, 98.

Exegesis of Lamentations

meet the statement, "You have not forgiven." The people's sin is alluded to only in general, abstract and conventional terms.[185] Moreover, a contrast is set up by utilizing the antithetical personal pronouns: "we" and "you," i.e. between the positive confession by the "we" and the negative assertion about the "you"—God's actions.[186] The poet is accusing God of not fulfilling his covenantal duties: we have done our part, but you have not done yours.

A series of accusations against God follow in 3:43-45. Dobbs-Allsopp points out that the language here echoes that found in both 3:1-18 and 2:1-9: divine anger (2:1ac, 2b, 3a, 6c; 3:1, 43); "pursued us" (1:3c; 3:43); "killing without mercy" (2:2a, 17b, 21c); the cloud imagery (2:1; 3:44); and "filth and rubbish among the peoples" (3:14, 45).[187] This section ends with a description of the total collapse of the social, political and emotional order in v. 47 via its utilization of two pairs of words: פחד ופחת, "panic and pitfall," and השאת והשבר, "devastation and destruction." The repetition of both consonantal and vowel sounds and the assonance here reinforce what is being expressed and amplify the suffering spoken of.[188] The situation is hopeless indeed.

Lam 3:48–66: Description of Personal Misery

The individual voice *I* reemerges for the remainder of the chapter. The image of eyes flowing with unceasing tears dominates 3:48-51. The man, like the narrator in chapter 2, is deeply moved by the destruction of Jerusalem, identified as "daughter of my people" in v. 48 and the suffering of the people. The man, like Zion before him, pleads with Yhwh "to see" (v. 50). As Dobbs-Allsopp puts it, "the poem's flood of words match the man's flood of tears in an effort to goad, flatter, shame, or otherwise compel God into acting in deliverance."[189] The following three verses (vv. 52-54) recount the man's personal suffering, now not at Yhwh's hands, but at those of human enemies. The man who previously associated suffering with punishment for sin now describes the enemies' acting against him "without cause" (v. 52). The man is down in a pit, defenseless, helpless, cut off, and totally lost (v. 54).

From the depth of the pit, we hear again words of confidence and petition: "I called on your name, O Yhwh" (3:55). In the following 3:56-61, we encounter a series of perfect verbs, which some scholars understand as

---

185. O'Connor, *Lamentations and the Tears of the World*, 53.

186. Dobbs-Allsopp, *Lamentations*, 123; he also points out that personal pronouns are used only here in chapter 3, except for the "I" in vv. 1 and 63.

187. Ibid., 123-24.

188. Bergant, *Lamentations*, 100.

189. Dobbs-Allsopp, *Lamentations*, 125.

Forgotten and Forsaken by God (Lam 5:19–20)

precatives; I understand them as simple perfects referring to past actions (see n. 156). The man is recalling past divine favor in order to nourish hope that God will act again to alter his present plight. God is described as having "heard" (vv. 56, 61), "come near" (v. 57), "having taken up," "redeemed" (v. 58), and "having seen" (v. 60). The man then asks God to "look" (הביטה in v. 63; see also 1:11; 2:20). The chapter ends with a prayer for vengeance in vv. 64–66: the man asks God to "repay them according to their deeds," "give them anguish of heart," "curse them," "pursue them in anger" and "destroy them." The man has experienced God's outburst of fury, he wants the same to befall his enemies, to balance the scales, to restore justice.

To sum up, the suffering "the man" of chapter 3 experiences is no less acute than that of Zion as articulated in chapters 1–2, and his voice no less passionate. In his attempt to navigate such suffering, he tries to find hope in the midst of hopelessness for himself and for his community. He utilizes conventional wisdom language and recalls God's beneficent actions in the past, and appeals to the covenantal God he knew before. From despair, his hope arises, more though from a change of mind than from any improvement in his circumstances. Then, his hope fades, the devastation all around him is too overwhelming; subsequently, his confidence returns a bit, only to fade again. As happened with the narrator and Zion before him, the suffering of the people makes the man's tears flow; like them, he repeatedly calls upon God to look and see, to act on their behalf.

Exegesis of Lamentations

Lamentations 4: Unlimited Suffering

Translation of MT With Textual Critical and Translational Notes

א 4:1 How the gold has grown dim, how the pure gold is changed!¹⁹⁰
    The sacred stones lie scattered at every street corner.¹⁹¹

ב 4:2 The precious children of Zion, worth their weight in fine gold;¹⁹²
    how they are reckoned as earthen pots, the work of a potter's hands!

ג 4:3 Even jackals¹⁹³ offer their teat, suckle their young,
    but my people has become cruel, like ostriches¹⁹⁴ in the wilderness.

ד 4:4 The tongue of the baby stuck to the palate from thirst.
    Little children begged for food, no one gave them a crumb.

190. LXX has πῶς ἀμαυρωθήσεται χρυσίον ἀλλοιωθήσεται τὸ ἀργύριον τὸ ἀγαθόν, "how gold will grow dim; the good silver will be altered!" LXX sticks closely to the Hebrew here and translates MT's imperfects as future tenses. Salters (*Lamentations*, 285) points out that MT's imperfects in the verse describe an existing state of affairs; thus, they are not futures and are better rendered as presents. Hillers (*Lamentations*, 137–38) holds that while MT as it stands is linguistically possible, it does not yield a satisfactory sense since: (1) gold stays bright and does not grow dark in any conspicuous way; (2) nowhere else does the Old Testament speak of the color of gold, only of its value; (3) the image of gold recurs in v. 2, where it serves as a comparison with the precious children of Zion, who, once worth their weight in fine gold, are regarded as cheap pottery; the image of gold here refers to value, not color. Based on these reasons, Hillers emends יועם, "to grow dim" to יועב, "to be despised," and ישנא, "to change" to ישנא, "to be hated." Stokes ("I, Yhwh, Have Not Changed?" 271) follows him. I prefer to read the MT since the poet here combines "gold" with the "impossible" quality of "growing dim" for shock effect; moreover, the image of "gold growing dim" in 4:1 parallels the mention of "night" in 1:2, the image of cloud in 2:1, and the man being led into darkness in 3:2. Each chapter of Lamentations 1–4 thus begins with an image of darkness.

191. MT בראש כל־חוצות literally means "at the head of every street."

192. MT המסלאים is a *hapax legomenon*, a Pual participle from the root סלא, a variant of סלה, "to weigh." Berlin (*Lamentations*, 98) regards the ב here as comparative, and renders the whole as "worth more than fine gold." I follow the majority of scholars, who adopt a literal understanding of the phrase: children are weighed in terms of fine gold, thus my rendering "worth their weight in fine gold." Cf. NRSV, NAS; Albrektson, *Lamentations*, 174; Hillers, *Lamentations*, 135; O'Connor, *Lamentations and the Tears of the World*, 59; Salters, *Lamentations*, 288–89.

193. MT Ketib תנין, Qere תנין. Schäfer (*BHQ*, 130–31*) points out that the Ketib is ambiguous: it can be taken either as the singular תנין, "sea monster," "snake" or as the plural of תן, "jackal," a variant of the usual form תנים. LXX's δράκοντες, "dragons" certainly points to a plural form in the Hebrew. Schäfer reasons that the ambiguous Ketib seems to be the *lectio difficilior*, while the Qere is an attempt to eliminate the ambiguity.

194. MT Ketib כי ענים makes no sense in the context, Qere כיענים is probably a variant form of the plural noun יען, "ostrich." Scholars generally take the Qere as the correct reading; see Schäfer, *BHQ*, 131*; Salters, *Lamentations*, 292.

Forgotten and Forsaken by God (Lam 5:19-20)

ה 4:5 Those who ate delicacies are desolate in the streets.
Those brought up in scarlet huddle against[195] dunghills.

ו 4:6 And greater is the chastisement of the daughter of my people than the punishment of Sodom,[196]
The overturning was in a moment, though no hands were raised against her.[197]

---

195. The word חבק literally means "embraced" (e.g., Gen 29:13; 33:4; 48:10; 2 Kgs 4:16). I follow Berlin (*Lamentations*, 101), who holds that here it has the sense of "huddle against" or "cling desperately to," as in Job 24:8 חבקו־צור, "huddled against a rock."

196. The Hebrew word עון normally means "iniquity," חטא "sin"; both terms can also be used to refer to punishment for sin (cf. Lam 3:39; 4:22; 5:7; elsewhere 1 Sam 28:10; Zech 14:19). Scholars choose to translate the two words in one way or the other, but always note that they call to mind both moral deficiency and its consequences; see, e.g., Hillers, *Lamentations*, 139. Parry (*Lamentations*, 128) tries to retain the two meanings in his translation and has "Indeed, greater was the transgression-punishment of the daughter of my people than the sin-punishment of Sodom"; he further notes that a focus on punishment seems likely in Lamentations 4 with its description of the dreadful situation in Jerusalem and the prolonged suffering there. Since the focus is more on punishment for sin than on iniquity committed, I opt for "chastisement" and "punishment," but the concept of Israel's sinfulness should be kept in mind as well.

197. The verb חלו is difficult and can be understood in three ways: (1) from the root חלה, "to become weak, sick" (so LXX and Syriac, which read "no hands become weak in her"); this reading in turn is rather ambiguous: it could refer either to others, who were not much affected by Sodom's downfall, or to Sodom's inhabitants, who did not have the time to grow weak since its destruction came so swiftly; (2) from the root חול "to dance, to twist," thus generating the sense that no hands were wrung over the fate of Sodom; (3) from the root חול, but with the meaning "to turn against" (e.g., 2 Sam 3:29; Jer 23:19; 30:23; Hos 11:6): Sodom was destroyed by God's punishment; no human hands were turned against it. I opt for this last interpretation since it sets up a sharp contrast between the fate of Sodom and the fate of Jerusalem, with its prolonged suffering and siege at the hands of foreign rulers. See the more detailed discussion in McDaniel, "Philological Studies in Lamentations I," 45-48; Parry, *Lamentations*, 128-29, 136; Salters, *Lamentations*, 297-99.

Exegesis of Lamentations

ז 4:7 Her noble ones[198] had been brighter than snow, whiter than milk;
their bodies[199] ruddier than coral, their hair like sapphire.[200]

ח 4:8 Now they look darker than soot,[201] not recognized in the streets.
Their skin shrivels on their bones, it has become as dry as wood.

ט 4:9 Better off were those pierced by the sword than those pierced by hunger,
whose life drains away, deprived of the produce of the field.[202]

    198. It is very unlikely that MT נזיריה refers to Nazirites here. Rather, the allusion is to persons of a high rank, as in Gen 49:26 and Deut 33:16; see Albrektson, *Lamentations*, 180; Schäfer, *BHQ*, 131*; Salters, *Lamentations*, 299.

    199. MT עצם literally means "their bones," which most scholars understand as a reference to "their bodies"; see Schäfer, *BHQ*, 131*; Berlin, *Lamentations*, 99; Salters, *Lamentations*, 301. LXX reads ἐπυρρώθησαν ὑπὲρ λίθους, "they became redder than stones," and leaves עצם untranslated. Kotzé ("LXX Lamentations 4:7 and 4:14," 256–58) compares the translation of עצם in various contexts of the LXX; he shows that the Greek translator intentionally left the word עצם in Lam 4:7 untranslated since it simply signifies "they themselves" in the eyes of the translator. I translate "their bodies," which tries to capture the sense of "they themselves."

    200. The meaning of the phrase גזרתם ספיר is difficult to determine, and translations vary. The word גזרתם literally means "their cutting," or "their separation" (BDB, 160), which some scholars understand as "their form" (RSV; Gottwald, *Studies in the Book of Lamentations*, 16; O'Connor, *Lamentations and the Tears of the World*, 60) or "their physique" (Berlin, *Lamentations*, 99; Wilkins, *Lamentations and the Social World*, 142). Hillers (*Lamentations*, 135) renders "their beards" and holds that "the word must refer to a part of the body that can be compared to a dark blue substance" since elsewhere ספיר refers to sapphire or lapis lazuli (see BDB, 705). I follow the NRSV, Salters (*Lamentations*, 302–3), and Parry (*Lamentations*, 129) who render גזרתם as "their hair"; thus, my translation "their hair like sapphire."

    201. The word שחור is a *hapax legomenon*, which most likely refers to "blackness." LXX has ὑπὲρ ἀσβόλην, "than soot," whence my rendering "darker than soot" here.

    202. This line is obscure in MT. Scholars try to make sense of it by emending the MT, their efforts yielding various translations. Hillers (*Lamentations*, 136), e.g., gives, "Those killed by the sword were more fortunate than those killed by famine, those who perished of wounds than those who lacked the fruits of the field"; Berlin (*Lamentations*, 99) proposes, "Better off were those slain by the sword than those slain by famine, who bleed slowly, stabbed by the lack of produce of the field"; O'Connor (*Lamentations and the Tears of the World*, 60) suggests, "Better off those pierced by the sword than those pierced by hunger, than those who waste away, pierced by (no) produce from the field." I, however, follow those scholars who retain the MT; Renkema (*Lamentations*, 517–18), e.g., argues that MT can stand as it is if we accept a figurative meaning for the verbs in the second line as well as in the first. The verb זוב basically means "to flow," thus, יזובו could refer to the life of starved people as "drained away"; the Pual participle מדקרים, which literally means "pierced" could be understood in a figurative sense like חלל in the first line, while מדקרים would correspond to the double חללי—those starved were "pierced" for lack of produce in the field, thus my translation: "whose life drains away, deprived of the produce of the field." See also Provan, *Lamentations*, 115–16; Salters,

Forgotten and Forsaken by God (Lam 5:19-20)

י 4:10 Hands of compassionate women have boiled their own children;
they became their food[203] when my people was ruined.

כ 4:11 Yhwh gave full vent to his wrath; he poured out his hot anger,
he kindled a fire in Zion, and it consumed her foundations.

ל 4:12 Neither the kings of the earth nor any of the inhabitants of the world believed,
that foe or enemy could ever enter the gates of Jerusalem.

מ 4:13 It was for the sins of her prophets and the iniquities of her priests,
who shed the blood of the righteous[204] in the midst of her.

נ 4:14[205] They wandered blindly through the streets, defiled with blood,
so that no one could touch their garments.[206]

Lamentations, 306–8.

203. MT's לִבְרוֹת is construed with ל + בָּרוֹת. Schäfer (*BHQ*, 132*) points out that בָּרוֹת can be regarded as a conflate form of the infinitive construct בְּרוֹת and the noun בָּרוּת, both derived from the root ברה "to eat." All ancient versions take בָּרוֹת as a noun: LXX, Syriac and Targum render "for food," while Vg reads "food."

204. The Old Greek has αἷμα δίκαιον, "righteous blood" for MT's דַם צַדִּקִים, "blood of the righteous." Albrektson (*Studies*, 186) holds that the Greek wording reflects "an inner-Greek corruption," as does Schäfer (*BHQ*, 132*). Ziegler restores a Greek equivalent to the MT in his reading αἷμα δικαίων, "blood of the righteous." There is no question that the MT represents the original reading.

205. Hillers (*Lamentations*, 142) considers vv. 14–15 the most difficult verses of the book; various proposals regarding these two verses have been made, but none is completely satisfactory. Salters (*Lamentations*, 315) points out that vv. 14–16 are fraught with problems, not only because the subject of the verbs is not clear, but also because the content of the verses is complicated. Hillers (*Lamentations*, 149–50) and Provan (*Lamentations*, 117–20) consider the "they" in vv. 14–15 to refer to the people as a whole; Westermann (*Lamentations*, 202) takes vv. 14–16 as a unit and identifies the "they" as "priests and elders." I follow the majority of scholars, who suggest that the pronoun "they" refers to "prophets and priests"; so, e.g., Renkema, *Lamentations*, 530–37; House, *Song of Songs; Lamentations*, 444–45; Berlin, *Lamentations*, 109; O'Connor, *Lamentations and the Tears of the World*, 65; Salters, *Lamentations*, 315–16. I opt for this interpretation because various groups of people have been mentioned in previous verses in the chapter as experiencing tragic reversals: the children, nobles, mothers; hence, it is likely that prophets and priests are described here in vv. 14–15, as are the priests and elders in v. 16.

206. Albrektson (*Studies*, 187) regards the phrase בלא יוכלו as a relative clause governed by יגעו, which is normally construed with ב, and renders "what they are not allowed, they touched with their cloths"; he takes the subject as the priests, "who had been anxious to keep all the cultic rules of purity [and] cannot avoid contact with unclean things," i.e. they touched the unclean things with their (cultic) cloths. But I prefer to take the subject of v. 14b as the common people, who cannot touch the blood-contaminated garments of priests and prophets; see also Berlin, *Lamentations*, 101–2; O'Connor, *Lamentations and the Tears of the World*, 64.

ס 4:15 "Away! Unclean!"²⁰⁷ they call to them; "Away! Away!²⁰⁸ Do not touch!"
So they fled²⁰⁹ and wandered; they said "Among the nations, they may no longer reside."

ע 4:16²¹⁰ The face of Yhwh²¹¹ scattered them, he regards them no longer; The faces of the priests were not lifted up, the elders were not honored.

פ 4:17 Our eyes ever wasted away, looking in vain for help; from our watchtower we watched²¹² for a nation that could not save.

צ 4:18 They hunted²¹³ our steps so we could not walk in our streets; our end drew near; our days were numbered; for our end came.

207. MT סורו טמא, LXX ἀπόστητε ἀκαθάρτων, "Away from the unclean ones!" LXX keeps the imperative of the first word סורו, but changes MT's singular טמא to a plural form. Vg reads *recedite polluti*, "Away, unclean ones!" Schäfer (*BHQ*, 133*) points out that the picture remains unclear because the versions present different syntactical interpretations of the Hebrew; he further states that MT seems to be preferable in any case because the plural in the versions can be regarded as a stylistic facilitation. See also Salters, *Lamentations*, 319–20. I retain the MT and regard the call here as addressed to the priests and prophets of 4:13 with their blood-stained garments.

208. MT has סורו סורו, BHS suggests deleting the second term as a dittography; but Schäfer (*BHQ*, 133*) points out that 5QLama and the versions unanimously confirm the repetition, so I retain the MT.

209. MT's נצו is a *hapax legomenon*. BDB (663) suggests that the stem is from נצה "to fly," while HALOT (682) lists it under נוץ, "to flee." I take the meaning as "to flee" in light of the following נעו, "they wandered."

210. The פ verse precedes the ע verse in Lamentations 4 as it does in chapters 2 and 3. Schäfer (*BHQ*, 133*) points out that although 5QLama is fragmentary, it clearly follows the MT order.

211. A number of scholars rightly point out that MT פני יהוה, "the face of Yhwh" is equivalent to Yhwh himself, MT's paraphrastic wording being required by the acrostic; see Westermann, *Lamentations*, 197; Berlin, *Lamentations*, 100; Salters, *Lamentations*, 322. I prefer to render in accordance with the phrase's literal meaning because "the face of Yhwh" is usually used in a positive sense (see, e.g., Exod 33:14; Num 6:24–26), but here, in pointed contrast, refers to Yhwh's anger.

212. In MT's phrase בצפיתנו צפינו, צפיה is a *hapax legomenon*, a feminine noun from צפה "to watch"; BDB (859) gives the meaning as "lookout post," HALOT (1048) as "observation point," thus my rendering "from our watchtower we watched." Berlin (*Lamentations*, 100 and 102) understands the phrase as "from our watching we watched" and translates "as we watched and watched."

213. Albrektson (*Studies*, 192) points out that the Hebrew verb צדו is derived sometimes from צוד "hunt," sometimes from צדה "lie in wait for, after"; he holds that "it is doubtful whether it is really possible to distinguish clearly between the two roots." LXX has ἐθηρεύσαμεν μικροὺς ἡμῶν τοῦ μὴ πορεύεσθαι ἐν ταῖς πλατείαις ἡμῶν, "we

Forgotten and Forsaken by God (Lam 5:19-20)

ק 4:19 Swifter were our pursuers than eagles in the heavens;
on the mountains they chased[214] us, in the wilderness they ambushed us.

ר 4:20 The breath of our nostrils, Yhwh's anointed, was caught in their traps,[215]
of whom we have thought, "In his shadow we shall live among the nations."

שׂ 4:21 Rejoice and be glad, Daughter Edom, you who dwell[216] in the land of Uz;
To you also, the cup shall pass; you shall become drunk and strip yourself bare.

ת 4:22 Your punishment is completed, Daughter Zion, he will keep you in exile no longer;
but your iniquity, O Daughter Edom, he will punish, he will uncover[217] your sins.

Comments

We encounter a certain diminishment in Lamentations 4 in both form and content. The three lines of the alphabetic acrostic found in the proceeding

---

hunted our little ones, so that they may not walk in our streets." Albrektson thinks that the first-person plural in LXX may be influenced by the form ἀπεσκοπεύσαμεν, "we kept watching" in the preceding line. Salters (*Lamentations*, 327–28) reads the verb as צָרוּ rather than צָדוּ, a reading attested in one Hebrew manuscript, according to the BHS note; he renders "our movement is restricted so that we cannot walk in public." I prefer to follow the MT and render "they hunted our steps."

214. The Hebrew verb דלק has two meanings: "to burn, set on fire" (e.g., Ps 7:14; Isa 5:11; Obad 1:18), and "to hotly pursue" (Gen 31:36; 1 Sam 17:53; Ps 10:2). The latter is clearly the meaning meant here in Lam 4:19b.

215. LXX has ἐν ταῖς διαφθοραῖς αὐτῶν, "in their destructions" for MT's בִּשְׁחִיתוֹתָם, "in their traps." Albrektson (*Studies*, 193–93) contends that the Greek translator thought the root to be שׁחת "spoil, destroy," here. LXX probably does not presuppose a different *Vorlage* from MT; see Schäfer, *BHQ*, 134*; Salters, *Lamentations*, 332–33. The word שַׁחַת may refer to a "pit" or "trap."

216. Ketib יוֹשַׁבְתִּי, Qere יוֹשֶׁבֶת. The Ketib is an archaic form with a parogogic *yod*, while the Qere represents the normal form. Schäfer (*BHQ*, 134*) regards the Ketib form as "justified and representing the *lectio difficilior*," and thus the original reading. See also Joüon, *A Grammar of Biblical Hebrew*, 260.

217. The two verbs, פָּקַד and גִּלָּה, are prophetic perfects, thus entailing that the poet functions here like a prophet who views these actions as already completed; see Berlin, *Lamentations*, 102; Salters, *Lamentations*, 338.

chapters are shortened to two. The pouring out of emotions and passion that dominate Lamentations 1–3 are replaced with the tired voice of the narrator in 4:1–16, who matter-of-factly reports the horrifying scenes of post-war Jerusalem. Moreover, there is no explicit appeal to God—the divine name Yhwh is mentioned in v. 11 and 16, but God is not addressed anywhere in the chapter. At the same time, we also note a broadening effect in Lamentations 4. Dobbs-Allsopp holds that chapter 4 plays a pivotal role in the book structurally by expanding the primarily individual and personal voices of Lamentations 1–3. Chapter 4 focuses on various groups of the population and finally breaks into the communal "we" in 4:17–20, which will be the primary speaker throughout chapter 5.[218]

The phrase "in the streets" recurs throughout Lamentations 4 (חוצות in v. 1; בחוצות in vv. 5, 8, 14; קצינו in v. 18 [*bis*]), which serves as a *Leitwort* for the chapter. The situation is more gruesome than in previous chapters, yet the description is more restrained. Prolonged suffering and its deepened lingering effects have worn out the people's spirits as well as their bodies.

I divide the chapter into four parts: everything grows dim in vv. 1–10; reasons for Yhwh's actions are cited in vv. 11–16; dashed hopes of the community are voiced in vv. 17–20; and a wish for revenge on Edom and a hope for Zion's exile to end expressed in vv. 21–22. The speaker in the first two parts is most probably the same narrator as in chapters 1–2.[219]

Lam 4:1–10: Everything Grows Dim

Lamentations 4 starts with a familiar, dirge-like exclamation איכה that appears twice in vv. 1–2. Lam 4:1–2 functions as a general introduction to the chapter, setting up its theme of reversal with a series of images: gold has grown dim, pure gold is changed; holy stones are scattered at every street corner; the precious people of Zion, worth as much as gold, are considered worthless pottery, easily broken and discarded. The inconceivable has happened. The image of gold turning dim captures the dimming effect of famine endured by all groups among the people. The following vv. 3–8 are very fragmentary, held together only by the acrostic. The reversal here is focused now on the starving children (4:4, 10), the most vulnerable in a famine. Children, people's hope for the future, are perishing because of thirst and hunger. The people, worse than jackals and as cruel as ostriches in the desert, are not providing for them, or, more likely, have nothing with which to provide for them. Starvation degrades humanity and affects everyone. The

---

218. Dobbs-Allsopp, *Lamentations*, 129–30.
219. Bergant, *Lamentations*, 109.

privileged fare no better (4:5): those who ate delicacies pant on the streets and those who were brought up in scarlet cling to ash heaps.

The punishment of Zion is even greater than that of Sodom (4:6), according to the narrator.[220] Sodom was destroyed by God in an instant, Jerusalem was seized by the enemy, her suffering was prolonged, and its effect lingers. The nobles who were whiter than snow before, now are blacker than soot; those who earlier were endowed with physical beauty and strength, are now as dry as wood; they have changed so much that they cannot even be recognized in the streets (4:7-8). Indeed, it would have been better to be pierced by sword, than to suffer famine; to die brutally but quickly is better than enduring the agony of hunger. Even worse: hands of compassionate (רחמניות, from רחם "womb love") women have boiled their own children for food (4:10; cf. 2:20b)! This is the most horrible reversal of all, a reversal of human nature and a destruction of domestic order. As in Lam 2:20b, maternal cannibalism here might be a literal or a symbolic fulfillment of the curse in Deut 28:53-57 which describes what will happen if Israel breaks its covenant with God. However, the horror of the situation and its terrible effect on little children certainly call into serious question whether Israel's sin deserves this kind of punishment, or whether there is any correlation between sin and suffering.

Lam 4:11-16: Reasons Provided for Yhwh's Actions

In the middle of Lamentations 4, the narrator attempts to provide a theological explanation for Zion's calamities: Yhwh gave full vent to his wrath and poured out his hot anger (4:1a; cf. 1:12; 2:1 [bis], 2, 3, 6, 21, 22; 3:1, 43). Yhwh kindled a fire in Zion that devoured her foundations. Destroyed are not just Zion's Temple, city, buildings and gates, but her social, political, religious and domestic order. The narrator then gives a reason for Yhwh's anger: the prophets and priests have committed sin by shedding innocent blood in Zion (4:13). O'Connor regards the term "righteous blood" here as both literal and metaphoric. Aside from sin committed against the innocent, the phrase may also refer to the city's economic welfare, destroyed by the disregard for justice, i.e. putting trust in the deceptive words "this is the temple of the Lord," while oppressing the alien, the orphan, and the widow, or shedding innocent blood as described in Jeremiah's temple sermon (Jer 7:1—8:3).[221] Those who are supposed to see visions are blind, wandering in

---

220. Renkema (*Lamentations*, 485) regards Lam 4:6 as the "thematic center" of the chapter.

221. O'Connor, *Lamentations and the Tears of the World*, 67.

the streets (4:14), while those who are called to guarantee purity are defiled with blood, shunned by others (4:15). They wander about like lepers, with no place in the city, no place among the nations. Yhwh himself scattered them and looks at them no more (4:16); Zion's plea to Yhwh to "look" (1:12; 2:20) has met a negative response. Yhwh's face turned against them, and so the faces of the priests are not lifted up, and those of the elders not honored (4:16). Society has collapsed, the leaders are gone; what is left is a consuming fire beneath Zion's foundation, a raging famine that devours all. To survive is to endure the unendurable; it is better to be dead.

Lam 4:17–20: Dashed Hopes of the Community

Lam 4:17–20 is the community's first direct retelling of the invasion. They recall their futile hope before the invasion (4:17), the pursuit of the enemy during the invasion (4:18–19) and dashed hopes after the invasion (4:20). These succinct words are a matter-of-fact report, similar to the narrator's in their emotional restraint.[222]

With the abrupt shift to the communal "we" in 4:17, "our eyes" searching for help come into focus. The word "eyes" here reminds the reader of the eyes of Zion, the narrator and the man flowing with tears as cited previously in 1:16 (bis); 2:11, 18; 3:48, 49, 51. Eyes worn out with tears hurt; eyes looking for help in vain hurt no less (4:17). "A nation that could not save" in 4:17b is not specified; it might refer to Egypt or Edom (cf. 4:21, 22b). In any case, the expected help did not come. Images of entrapment follow in 4:18–19 (cf. 1:3, 6; 3:52–54): the enemies hunted their victims in their streets; there is nowhere to escape, whether to the mountains or to the wilderness, since the pursuers are swifter than eagles in their pursuit. It really feels as though their end has come. Two epithets, "the breath of our life," and "the anointed of Yhwh," both refer to the king (4:20), under whose shadow the people are to live among the nations (2 Samuel 7); yet, the king has been captured. With the king's capture, the people's confidence and hope that God would protect them was lost as well.

Lam 4:21–22: Revenge and Hope

The poet's vengeful and sarcastic words against Edom here are uttered in a context of prophetic curses and blessings; they are more like a wish. There is also a glimpse of hope that Zion's iniquity might be pardoned and her exile

---

222. Ibid., 66–67.

Forgotten and Forsaken by God (Lam 5:19-20)

ended (4:22a). For Hillers, this segment "comes closer to being an expression of hope than almost anything else in the book."²²³ The community's raw rage at suffering's deep hurt may release emotion and foster the people's desperate need to cling to life; yet, Dobbs-Allsopp rightly notes that the faint hope voiced here is short-lived—as the following communal lament in chapter 5 will make clear.²²⁴

To sum up, the narrator tours the ruined city of Jerusalem in Lamentations 4 and reports the desperate situation of different groups in the streets. All are deeply shattered by prolonged starvation, and society has totally collapsed. A further reason is given for Yhwh's wrath: the prophets and priests shed innocent blood in the midst of Zion (4:13; cf. 2:14). The communal voice then breaks in and, for the first time, recounts the people's experience of the invasion (4:17-20), with their dashed hopes of external aid and crushed confidence in God's protection. The curse on Edom and hope for an end to exile (4:21-22) introduces some emotion at the end of a dry report elsewhere in the chapter. Yet, this momentary glimmer of hope itself fades into the following communal lament in Lamentations 5.

Lamentations 5: Communal Lament Prayer

Translation of MT With Textual Critical and Translational Notes

> 5:1²²⁵ Remember, O Yhwh, what has happened to us; look,²²⁶ and see our disgrace!
>
> 5:2 Our inheritance is turned over to strangers, our houses to aliens.²²⁷
>
> 5:3 We have become orphans, fatherless;²²⁸ our mothers are like widows.

223. Hillers, *Lamentations*, 153.

224. Dobbs-Allsopp, *Lamentations*, 137-39.

225. A number of Greek manuscripts title Lamentations 5 προσευχή, "a prayer," others προσευχὴ Ιερεμίου, "a prayer of Jeremiah." I retain the MT, which does not have such a title.

226. Ketib הביש, Qere הביטה. The Ketib is an irregular form of the masculine singular Hiphil imperative of נבט; the Qere is the regular form with a paragogic ה. Schäfer (*BHQ*, 134*) suggests that the Ketib is preferable as the *lectio difficilior*, although there is no difference in meaning.

227. MT has לנכרים, while 5QLama has a longer form, i.e. לנוכריאם. Schäfer (*BHQ*, 135*) notes that the editor of the fragment 5QLama, J. T. Milik, regards the longer form as metrically more satisfying than MT (Baillet et al., *Les "petites grottes" de Qumran* 1:175). I, however, retain the MT here.

228. Ketib אין, Qere ואין. The Qere most probably represents a stylistic facilitation. I prefer the Ketib which is followed by LXX, Vg, Syriac and the Targum.

Exegesis of Lamentations

5:4 We must pay for the water we drink; our firewood comes at a price.

5:5 Upon our necks we are pursued;[229] we are worn out, we are allowed no rest.

5:6 We extended a hand to Egypt and Assyria to get enough bread.[230]

5:7 Our ancestors sinned, they are no more; we bear their punishment.[231]

5:8 Slaves rule over us; there is no one to deliver us from their hand.

5:9 We get our bread at the risk of our lives because of the sword in the wilderness.

5:10 Our skin is black[232] as an oven from the scorching heat of famine.

229. LXX has ἐπὶ τὸν τράχηλον ἡμῶν ἐδιώχθημεν, "upon our necks we are pursued," which corresponds to MT's על צוארנו נרדפנו, also followed by Syriac and the Targum. Symmachus adds ζυγός (= על), "yoke." A number of interpreters follow Symmachus and translate the phrase as "A yoke is upon our necks, we are pursued"; see RSV, NRSV, NAB, Hillers, *Lamentations*, 153; Salters, *Lamentations*, 347–48. Albrektson (*Studies*, 197), however, finds that the MT makes good enough sense as it stands: "it is a way of expressing the imminence of the danger and the persistency of the persecutors." Other scholars who retain the MT are: Provan, *Lamentations*, 126–27; Gordis, *Song of Songs and Lamentations*, 195; Renkema, *Lamentations*, 600–601; Berlin, *Lamentations*, 119; O'Connor, *Lamentations and the Tears of the World*, 72. I, too, prefer the MT.

230. The Hebrew phrase יד נתנו can be understood in different ways: (1) It can refer to a past alliance Israel made with Egypt and Assyria, which is condemned as showing disloyalty to Yhwh (cf. Hos 5:13; 7:11); on this understanding, Lam 5:6 is read together with v. 7 to refer to past wrongdoings; and the phrase יד נתנו means "to signal a pact." (2) It can refer to the present situation wherein Israel asks for help from neighboring countries to relieve its need for food. "Assyria" can be understood symbolically as a generic reference to Mesopotamia; see Berlin, *Lamentations*, 119. In my view, it is more probable that the phrase refers to the present desperate situation of trying to find food in all possible ways. Salters (*Lamentations*, 349) points out that Judah was now a province of Babylon and so not in a position to make contact with other states; Wilkins (*Lamentations and the Social World*, 197), however, notes that Judah's survivors did benefit from some trade activity with neighboring peoples. Thus, I am inclined to adopt the second of the above alternatives.

231. The Hebrew word עון can mean both iniquity and punishment; the emphasis here is on "punishment" as in Lam 4:6 (see n. 195 above).

232. MT's עורנו כתנור נכמרו is problematic. First, its subject עורנו is singular while the verb נכמרו is plural; perhaps, the plural suffix of the subject influenced the verb. Schäfer (*BHQ*, 136*) points out that the versions change either the subject into the plural or the verb into the singular; these changes, however, are translational adjustments that may not presuppose a different Hebrew *Vorlage*. MT is confirmed by 5QLama and the Targum. I take the verb as expressing a singular sense here. Second, the meaning of the verb is itself uncertain. It can mean: (1) "to grow warm, hot"; see BDB, 485; Berlin, *Lamentations*, 115; O'Connor, *Lamentations and the Tears of the World*, 72; (2) "shriveled up, wrinkled"; LXX adopts this meaning and reads τὸ δέρμα ἡμῶν ὡς κλίβανος

Forgotten and Forsaken by God (Lam 5:19-20)

5:11 Women in Zion are raped, virgins in the cities of Judah.

5:12 Princes are hung up by their hands;[233] no respect is shown to the elders.

5:13 Young men pulled the millstone,[234] and boys stagger under loads of wood.

5:14 The elders have gone from the city gate, the young men from their music.

5:15 Gone is the joy of our hearts; our dancing has turned into mourning.

5:16 The crown has fallen from our head; woe to us, for we have sinned!

5:17 Because of this our hearts are faint; because of these things our eyes are dim.[235]

5:18 Because of Mount Zion which lies desolate; jackals[236] prowl over it.

5:19 But you, O Yhwh, sit forever; your throne is from generation to generation.

ἐπελειώθη, "our skin is shriveled up like an oven"; see also NAB, Salters, *Lamentations*, 354–55; (3) "to be black"; see Lam 4:8 and Job 30:30, which refer to "blackening" of skin due to famine. I opt for the third meaning here; see also Hillers, *Lamentations*, 158.

233. The meaning of בידם is unclear. It could refer to the hands of the princes that were hung up as a punitive treatment, or to the hands of slave-rulers [(5:8), who slaughtered the princes by hanging them. I am inclined to think that the phrase is suggestive of ignominy rather than execution; the princes were hung up, a cruel and humiliating treatment. See the more detailed explanation in Salters, *Lamentations*, 357–58.

234. The word טחון is a *hapax legomenon*. I follow the majority of scholars, who understand it as "millstone" in the context of grinding; see Berlin, *Lamentations*, 115; O'Connor, *Lamentations and the Tears of the World*, 73; Salters *Lamentations*, 359–60.

235. The problem with this verse concerns whether זה and אלה refer backward to vv. 2–16 or forward to v. 18. RSV, NRSV, NIV, Renkema (*Lamentations*, 619), and Berlin (*Lamentations*, 124) regard the two words as pointing forward to v. 18. Hillers (*Lamentations*, 159), however, rightly points out that על plus the demonstrative pronoun זה at the beginning of a sentence usually refers to what proceeds rather than to what follows (see, e.g., Ps 32:6; Isa 57:6; 64:11; Jer 31:26; Amos 8:8); he further states that it is not likely that the plural אלה refers to the single situation described in v. 18. I follow this view and take זה as referring to "sin" in v. 16 and אלה to the situations described in vv. 2–16, so Westermann, *Lamentations*, 215; Provan, *Lamentations*, 132; House, *Lamentations*, 467; Dobbs-Allsopp, *Lamentations*, 147; O'Connor, *Lamentations and the Tears of the World*, 73.

236. The Hebrew word שועלים could mean either "fox" (BDB, 1043) or "jackal" (HALOT, 1445). I follow Salters (*Lamentations*, 368), who points out that foxes are solitary creatures whereas jackals roam in groups, the animal behavior that seems to be envisioned here.

Exegesis of Lamentations

5:20 Why have you forgotten us for so long, forsaken us these many days?

5:21 Return us to yourself, O Yhwh, that we may return; renew our days as of old

5:22 unless you have utterly rejected us, and are angry with us beyond measure—

Comments

Lamentations 5 prepares the reader for closure by changing the book's governing patterns of repetition, i.e. the alphabetic acrostic and the *qinâ* meter.[237] This chapter is not written in an acrostic, though it is alphabetic in that it consists of twenty-two lines; neither does it follow the "limping" *qinâ* meter, exhibiting more balanced lines. Its genre is that of a communal lament: it starts with an address to God in v. 1, proceeds to describe the miserable condition of the community in vv. 2–18, and ends with a petition for help in vv. 19–22. It is noteworthy that the description of misery is very long, while the petition is rather short.

O'Connor points out that the lack of alphabetic acrostic in Lamentations 5 signifies "an abandonment of efforts to contain suffering within a recognizable alphabetic order" and implies "accelerating hopelessness."[238] The first-person common plural suffix נו occurs thirty-four times in this short chapter. It holds together the distinct lines which are not unified by the use of an acrostic as are the previous chapters.[239]

LAM 5:1–18: COMPLAINT OF A COMMUNITY

Lamentations 5 opens with three imperatives that recall previous petitions made by Zion, the narrator and the man: remember (3:19), look and see (1:9c, 11c, 20a; 2:20a; 3:59–61). Dobbs-Allsopp holds that this conscious lexical echoing of previous chapters counterbalances chapter 5's effort to otherwise differentiate itself from previous chapters; as a result, closure is

---

237. Smith (*Poetic Closure*, 34) states that closure allows the reader to be satisfied with the absence continuation to a text. Dobbs-Allsopp (*Lamentations*, 140) notes that one of the most common and effective ways to conclude a sequence of poems is simply to modify the patterns of repetition that dominate the main body of the text.

238. O'Connor, *Lamentations and the Tears of the World*, 71.

239. Grossberg, *Centripetal and Centrifugal Structures*, 93–94; Dobbs-Allsopp, *Lamentations*, 142.

Forgotten and Forsaken by God (Lam 5:19-20)

achieved smoothly and in a fitting and appropriate way in chapter 5.[240] The community asks Yhwh to "remember" what had happened to them, i.e. all the misery described in the previous chapters: the word *remember* carries a very rich meaning; Bergant points out that "to ask God to remember in a distressful situation is to ask God to remedy it."[241] The word "disgrace," for its part, highlights the image of suffering and underlines all the miseries described in vv. 2–18.

Lam 5:2–18 describes the present struggle to survive in the land, a daily endeavor in a devastated world. This section contains a laundry list of miseries endured by all groups of people, comparable to Zion's lament in 1:12–22 and the man's in 3:1–20. It piles complaint upon complaint, pleading with God to "pay attention" and to "see" all these. This section starts with the phrase "our inheritance has been turned over to strangers," which refers to the vulnerable situation of the covenant people even within their own country.[242] The word *inheritance* has in view not only the land, but also the covenantal relationship between God and the chosen people; the first person plural suffix "our" is noteworthy here, i.e. the reference is to "our" instead of "your" inheritance as in Ps 79:1, thus highlighting the people's relationship to the land, and consequently to God as well.[243] The people's inherited land has been turned over to strangers, and they live like strangers in their own land with their houses occupied by aliens (5:2). It is very hard for the people to survive, and meeting their daily needs has become a constant challenge. They have to pay for water and wood in their own land (5:4), a "disgrace" (5:1) indeed! They are being hunted all the time, driven hard and have no rest in the land where God had promised to give them rest (5:5; cf. Deut 25:19). In order to survive, they have to forge agreements with their enemies to get enough bread (5:6), yet, their bread is far from enough. The community laments that they bear the punishment of their ancestors' sins (5:7). Their doing so does not imply that they themselves are innocent, for they admit their own guilt as well (5:16); however, they do not dwell on that guilt; rather, their focus is constantly turned to the current situation.

The people are ruled by slaves, probably minor officials from Babylon who are in charge of occupied Judah. These slaves rule with severity, and there is no deliverance for the people (5:8). To make things worse, they must risk their lives to obtain bread; food remains scarce and they are exhausted

240. Dobbs-Allsopp, *Lamentations*, 142–43.

241. Bergant, *Lamentations*, 126.

242. See Helberg, "Land in the Book of Lamentations," 373.

243. Cf. Ps 79:1 "O God, the nations have come into *your* inheritance; they have defiled *your* holy temple; they have laid Jerusalem in ruins." See also Salters, *Lamentations*, 343–44.

by famine (5:10). Their women and maidens are not protected in their own land, but are being raped throughout Judah (5:11); the princes are captured and tortured; the faces of the elders are not honored (5:12), just as those of the priests are not favored (cf. 4:16). Their young men are compelled to do the works of a slave and their boys are exploited for hard labor (5:13). The social order had collapsed; there are no more gatherings at the city gate, nor celebrations and music-making (5:14). Their community life has ceased, and so too has the joy of their hearts (5:15). They are left to struggle, to mourn, to take the blame for their own sin, to feel their shame, to taste bitterness, and to waste away in famine. Their hearts are sick and their eyes grow dim (5:17) from shame, guilt and weariness. Worst of all, Zion lies desolate (5:18). Zion was desolate at the beginning of the book (1:4) and now she is still desolate and jackals prowl over her. Zion, the seat of Yhwh (2:1), the perfection of beauty and joy of all the earth (2:15), remains desolate throughout the book of Lamentations.

Lam 5:19–22: Refusal of a Conclusion

Right after the preceding heart-wrenching depiction of desolate Zion, we hear an affirmation of Yhwh's reign: "You, O Yhwh, sit forever, your throne endures from generation to generation" (5:19). Where though would Yhwh "sit" while Zion remains desolate? Where would Yhwh's throne be, now that Jerusalem is destroyed? Now comes the thundering "why" question: why have you forgotten us for so long, forsaken us these many days (5:20)? The "why" that has been suppressed thus far is now finally uttered, to the "You," the only one who can make a difference, to the only "you" who is so addressed in the book of Lamentations (1:21; 3:42; 5:19). This "why" echoes all the complaints made by Zion, the narrator, the man, and the community in the book; its sound lingers while suffering drags on.

The community pleads with God again: "Return us to yourself, O Yhwh, so that we may return; renew our days as of old" (Lam 5:21). The community asks for a mutual return: God to them, and they to God. They know very well that it is only when God returns to them that they will be able to return to God. The initiative has to come from God. The community asks for a renewed relationship, in which they will know God intimately, in which God will be close to them. God will be enthroned among them, in their hearts, wherever they are. Yet, the community is far from certain whether this is possible: unless you have uttered rejected us, angry with us beyond measure—

Forgotten and Forsaken by God (Lam 5:19–20)

In a way, the closure of Lamentations 5 is achieved smoothly through its balancing of changing patterns of repetitions and echoing of previous chapters' words and images. However, the book's conclusion is not a real closure. It is a half sentence, that awaits God's completing it. The book ends without an end, a failure of closure. As F. Landy puts it, Lamentations' success depends on its failure; its discourse which attempts to explain, illustrate and mitigate catastrophe communicates its own inadequacy, while the final silence exhausts its cries and questions.[244]

To sum up, Lamentations 5 reiterates the suffering in the land endured by all groups of people. The book's final chapter is as desperate as the previous ones; any momentary glimpse of hope fades. God remains silent, even as any future for the people depends on a response from God. Lam 5:19–20 affirms that God's reign is for generations, but also utters a "why" question concerning all the sufferings endured by the community. The book ends without an end. All that can be said has been said, the community is exhausted, but its cry for God to remember, to see, to pay attention, and to return echoes, lingering on in time and in space, until a reaction by God occurs.

---

244. Landy, "Lamentations," 329.

4

Mood Change in Lamentations and Related Old Testament Laments

INTRODUCTION

IN THE PREVIOUS CHAPTER, we have seen that different voices in Lamentations form an ongoing dialogue. Given the final absence of God's voice, the book ends without an ending, even as its ongoing dialogue goes even beyond the boundary of Lamentations, both within and without biblical literature. Thus, Deutero-Isaiah (Isaiah 40–55) clearly echoes Lamentations and tries to provide the positive response from God which is lacking in Lamentations.[1] Later, in the Lamentations Targum, God's voice is heard in three places (1:1; 2:20; 4:13); the Targum thereby demonstrates God's continued engagement with the people in exile.[2] Scholarly attention has been given to the dialogic interaction between Lamentations and the prophetic books, especially Deutero-Isaiah, that does provide a response from God—whether one considers this response adequate or not.[3] However, the book of Lamentations remains a tragedy, where the voice of God is missing even at the very end. Lamentations thus is part of a small group of biblical laments that do not end in praise, but in lament, in contrast, e.g., to the overall movement of the book of Psalms.

A certain mood change can, however, be perceived in the book of Lamentations. It contains three passages of hope and praise (3:21–33; 4:22;

---

1. Tull, *Remember the Former Things*, 48–50; O'Connor, "Speak Tenderly to Jerusalem," 290–91; Mandolfo, *Daughter Zion Talks Back*, 104.

2. Alexander, *Targum of Lamentations*, 29–31.

3. See detailed discussion in Mandolfo, *Daughter Zion Talks Back*, 103–19.

Forgotten and Forsaken by God (Lam 5:19-20)

5:19); the book moves from lament to hope in Lam 3:21-33, then falls back into lament, reaffirms hope and praise momentarily in 4:22 and 5:19, but then reverts to lament and remains in lament at the end. The book's momentary glimpses of hope and praise are thus not sustained; Lamentations does not move from lament to final praise. Accordingly, the widely held scholarly view that biblical laments regularly lead to praise needs to be revisited.

This chapter will focus on the mood change in biblical laments both outside and inside Lamentations, and the question of whether such mood change is invariably from lament to praise or rather also from praise to lament. This chapter will first give an overview of the scholarly discussion on mood change in biblical laments; it will then study mood change in several selected lament psalms (i.e. Psalms 12, 44, and 88; see below); and finally address the question of how Lamentations as a communal lament that ends in lament might enrich scholarly understanding regarding mood change in biblical laments. Thus I will suggest, the dialogic interaction between Lamentations and the Book of Psalms might help us appreciate biblical laments more holistically.

SCHOLARLY DISCUSSION OF MOOD CHANGE IN BIBLICAL LAMENTS

Scholars have long noticed a sudden change of mood in biblical laments and the emphasis has been on the positive dimension of such changes: without obvious reason, the psalmist changes from lament to praise or thanksgiving (e.g., Psalms 3, 6, 13, 35, and 59).

Emphasis on the Certainty of a Hearing

Various reasons have been proposed for this sudden change of mood, the best known of which adduces a cultic explanation of the phenomenon: J. Begrich argued that the sudden change of mood was prompted by a salvation oracle from Yhwh addressed to the worshiper who had just uttered a lament;[4] Other explanations have been proposed as well, e.g., A. Weiser suggests that a covenant renewal ceremony highlighting God's kingship brought about the change of mood;[5] J. W. Wevers holds that the psalmist gains confidence by invoking the divine name יהוה,[6] while E. K. Kim avers

---

4. Begrich, "Das Priesterliche Heilsorakel," 81-92.
5. Weiser, *Psalms*, 80.
6. Wevers, "A Study in the Form Criticism of Individual Complaint Psalms," 80-96.

that the abrupt change of mood is grounded in holy war ideology and faith in Yhwh, the warrior God who will surely defeat the enemy.[7] S. B. Frost explains mood change through "asseveration by thanksgiving,"[8] while Sung-Hun Lee believes that the cause of the move from lament to praise is God's חסד.[9] H. G. M. Williamson argues that lament psalms that contain the element of mood change arise out of situations where the psalmist has already received an answer from God; these psalms are thus actually thanksgiving psalms.[10] These studies focus on one direction of the mood change, i.e. from lament to praise, this feature also being called "certainty of a hearing,"[11] or "assurance of being heard."[12]

Lament Has No Meaning in and of Itself

Lament is devaluated when an exclusive emphasis is placed on a one-directional mood change from lament to praise and the focus is on certainty and resolution; this tendency occurs even among scholars who advocate the importance of lament in biblical tradition. Claus Westermann is one such scholar who brings to the fore the importance of lament. He divides the psalms into two major categories: lament/petition and praise, which he considers as the two literary forms that characterize the Psalter as a whole and are related as "polar opposites."[13] Westermann tries to keep the dialectic tension of praise and lament by affirming that "praise can retain its authenticity and naturalness only in polarity with lamentation."[14] Nevertheless, Westermann views lament only in relation to praise. He states "there is no, or almost no, such thing as 'mere' lament and petition . . . by nature it cannot be *mere* petition or lament, but is always underway from supplication to praise."[15] Westermann even claims that "there is not a single Psalm of lament that stops with lamentation. Lamentation has no meaning in and of itself."[16] Such a claim is certainly inaccurate; Psalm 88 is a pure lament without any expression of hope or praise (see below). For Westermann, praise is the goal

---

7. Kim, *Rapid Change of Mood in the Lament Psalms*, 224–26.
8. Frost, "Asseveration by Thanksgiving," 380–90.
9. Lee, "Lament and the Joy of Salvation," i224–47.
10. Williamson, "Reading Lament Psalms Backwards," 3–15.
11. Bellinger, *Psalmody and Prophecy*, 78–82; Day, *Psalms*, 30.
12. Baumgartner, *Jeremiah's Poems of Lament*, 35.
13. Westermann, *Praise and Lament*, 11.
14. Ibid., 267; see also, Westermann, "Role of Lament," 27.
15. Westermann, *Praise and Lament*, 75 (italics original).
16. Ibid., 266.

and no matter how important lament is, it always moves toward praise, such that praise has the final word.

Brueggemann follows Westermann and delves into the importance of lament in relation to doxology and praise.[17] Brueggemann studies the literary shape of the Psalter and holds that the theological thrust of the book of Psalms is from obedience to praise.[18] Psalm 1 situates the Psalter within the context of torah obedience, while Psalm 150 is the book's culmination in praise. Brueggemann holds that the move from glad duty to utter delight is made possible through "candor about suffering and gratitude about hope."[19] He sketches the psalmic spiritual journey as moving from orientation, to disorientation, and then to new orientation.[20] Brueggemann highlights the importance of lament and considers it indispensible for authentic faith and genuine dialogue with God, the loss of which results in "psychological inauthenticity and social immobility."[21] He rightly points out that "much Christian piety and spirituality is romantic and unreal in its positiveness ... we have censored and selected around the voice of darkness and disorientation, from victory to victory."[22] Brueggemann has done much work to direct scholars' attention to the neglected lament tradition. However, his presentation gives one the impression that lament is a situation to be overcome, a necessary phase in life to be eventually transcended. He asserts that lament surely moves toward praise, yet, the other possible movement (i.e. from praise to lament) that is present in biblical laments is not mentioned in his studies.

A Lacuna in Scholarship: Mood Change from Praise to Lament

The scholarly focus on the movement from lament to praise in mood change actually accounts for only a part of the individual lament psalms. There are other individual lament psalms that move from praise to lament (e.g., Psalms 9/10, 27, 40) or alternate between the two (e.g., Psalms 28, 31, 35). Most of the communal laments do not end with the expression of a certainty of hearing; some of them contain elements of hope that the community will survive to praise God (e.g., Pss 79:13; 80:18; 85:6), but these are not the kind of confident statements with which some of the individual laments conclude.[23]

17. Brueggemann, "Costly Loss of Lament," 57–71.
18. Brueggemann, "Bounded by Obedience and Praise," 63–92.
19. Ibid., 72.
20. Brueggemann, *Message of the Psalms*, 20.
21. Brueggemann, "Costly Loss of Lament," 67.
22. Brueggemann, *Message of the Psalms*, 11.
23. See Williamson, "Reading the Lament Psalms Backwards," 5–6.

Mood Change in Lamentations and Related Old Testament Laments

A number of scholars have, in fact, observed that the mood change in biblical laments is not one-directional; it can move from praise to lament.[24] As Villanueva points out, it is unfortunate that the accent on mood change in biblical laments falls on "the element of certainty, on resolution and the overcoming of the situation of lament."[25] Just as in life, a person's mood may change from lament to praise or verse versa, so in the lament psalms, the movement runs both ways.

Villanueva focuses on the movement from praise to lament in the individual lament psalms in Book I of the Psalter. He names this movement "the uncertainty of a hearing," and tries to fill a gap in scholarship regarding the change of mood, given the prevailing assumption that the movement is from lament to praise even though the movement from praise to lament is also present in biblical texts.[26] Villanueva points out that scholars seek to "impose the one way linear movement lament-praise on every psalm where the two elements are present. Some even go to great length, including changing the text and the order of a psalm just to fit them into their framework."[27] Villanueva further notes that "the important shift from praise to lament in the communal psalms has not been given the attention it deserves."[28] The book of Lamentations may also serve as a notable example of communal lament that does not end in praise.

J. Goldingay responds to Brueggemann's article "Psalms and the Life of Faith," and points out that Brueggemann understates the presence of "a

---

24. Johnson ("Psalms," 169–70) notes that the so-called certainty of a hearing is by no means always present; and where it is present, there is occasionally a marked rise and fall in the psalmist's mood: he can sink back to renewed lamentation after expressions of assurance. Kim (*Rapid Change of Mood*, 123–25), in his analysis of Psalm 12, notes that a complaint (v. 9) occurs after a salvation oracle (v. 6) and expressions of confidence (vv. 7–8).

25. Villanueva, *The "Uncertainty of a Hearing,"* 1.

26. Ibid., 27–28.

27. Ibid., 28; Villanueva (ibid., 102–3) cites Psalms 9/10 as an example. Scholars generally agree that Psalms 9/10 form a unity given (1) the use of the acrostic that runs through the two segments, (2) the absence of a title for Psalm 10, (3) LXX's combining the two psalms into one. But since the two psalms move from thanksgiving to lament, some scholars have tried to rearrange the order of the two parts so that lament will be followed by thanksgiving. Dahood, *Psalms*, 1:54), e.g., holds that the movement from thanksgiving to lament raises "logical difficulties." John Strugnell and Hanan Eshel ("Psalms 9 and 10 and the Order of the Alphabet," 42) regard the two psalms as thematically reversed; Psalm 9 should follow Psalm 10 from the standpoint of literary flow and the Psalter's typical forms. But this position is problematic since the MT order in Psalms 9/10 is confirmed by LXX, and changing the order of the two psalms disrupts the acrostic that continues from Psalm 9 into Psalm 10.

28. Ibid., 257.

movement from praise to petition, or of an interweaving of praise and lament as the psalmist wrestled to be true both to his past experience and the convictions of his faith, and also to the reality of his present experience of affliction."[29] There are two movements present in the psalms: lament can lead to praise, but praise can also lead to lament (e.g., Psalms 22, 42, 43, 44, 74, 85, 89, and 106). Goldingay further states that the actual hermeneutical circle is really more of a spiral: "a question provokes an answer, but the answer provokes a different question, and thus another answer, and yet another question."[30] The journey of faith is more dynamic than a one-directional movement from lament to praise.

D. Erbele-Küster likewise emphasizes on the importance of uncertainty in the mood change in lament psalms.[31] She finds Begrich's salvation oracle theory unsatisfactory since actual examples of salvation oracle are virtually absent in the psalms (there is only one clear instance of such, i.e. Ps 12:6: "Because of the devastation of the afflicted, because of the groaning of the needy, now I will arise," says Yhwh, "I will grant safety to whoever longs for it"; see below). Erbele-Küster further argues that psychological explanations of the shift even out the tension between praise and lament, stating: "A psychological explanation is not appropriate, because this would make the despair much more understandable."[32] Erbele-Küster likewise affirms that even given the experience of "certainty of a hearing," the psalmist may still lament and the psalm end with a *Leerstelle* (i.e., a blank space). She cites Psalms 40 and 70 as examples of the phenomenon. There are other psalms where petition has the last word (e.g., Psalms 20, 25, 27, 28, 31, 38, 39) and those that end precisely with a *Leerstelle* (e.g., Psalms 12, 39, 88). Erbele-Küster asserts that the tension between lament and praise should not be resolved; it is unfortunate that scholars are uncomfortable with the uncertainties and ambiguities of mood change and so try to define its movement in a unidirectional way. She holds that the psalmic *Leerstellen* should not be filled and that the tension should not be explained away.[33]

---

29. Brueggemann, "Psalms and the Life of Faith," 3-32; Goldingay, "Dynamic Cycle," 86.

30. Goldingay, "Dynamic Cycle of Prayer and Priase in the Psalms," 88. Brueggemann ("Response," 141) notes that the word "spiral" that Goldingay finally adopts is more appropriate than the word "cycle," which he uses in the title of his article since there is no return to the previous orientation.

31. Dorothea Erbele-Küster, *Lesen als Akt des Betens*, 141-78.

32. The original German is, "Es geht nicht um eine psychologische Erklärung, denn diese würde die Verzweiflung viel eher verständlich machen"; see Erbele-Küster, *Lesen als Akt des Betens*, 161-62.

33. Ibid., 153-54.

Mood Change in Lamentations and Related Old Testament Laments

To sum up, even though scholars recognize that mood change in biblical laments is dynamic, studies of the phenomenon have often focused on the uni-linear movement from lament to praise; emphasis has been on "certainty of a hearing." The opposite movement from praise to lament has not been given the attention it deserves; as a consequence, lament is mostly understood simply as a prelude to praise.

MOOD CHANGE IN SELECTED LAMENT PSALMS AND THE SCHOLARLY DISCUSSIONS OF THESE

I will now study mood change in three selected lament psalms. Since much scholarly work has been done on the movement from lament to praise, my focus is on the opposite movement from praise to lament. The following psalms have been selected for this purpose given their respective distinctive character. Psalms 12 contains the only clear example of a "salvation oracle" in the Psalter,[34] but the psalm ends in lament. Psalm 44 is the Psalter's initial communal lament;[35] it starts with affirmation and ends in uncertainty and lament; a number of other communal lament psalms will also be discussed in connection with it. Finally, Psalm 88 is an individual lament psalm, the bleakest psalm in the Psalter, devoid of words of hope or thanksgiving.

Psalm 12: Return to Lament after a Salvation Oracle

Psalm 12 presents several noteworthy features: first, as noted above, it contains the only clear example of a salvation oracle (12:6) in the Psalter; second, it starts with petition (vv. 2–3), then after revelation and affirmation from the side of Yhwh (vv. 6–8), returns to lament (v. 9). Thus contrary to Begrich's claim that the mood change from lament to praise is evoked by a salvation oracle, lament occurs again following reception of a salvation oracle in this psalm.

Psalm 12 displays a chiastic structure:[36]

---

34. Williamson, "Reading Lament Psalms Backwards," 6.
35. Mays, *Psalms*, 170; DeClaissé-Walford, "Psalm 44," 745.
36. See Terrien, *The Psalms*, 152–53; Villanueva (*The "Uncertainty of a Hearing,"* 134) proposes a slightly different chiastic structure for Psalm 12:
A *Absence* of the upright/faithful (v. 2),
  B Words of the wicked—vain (v. 3),
    C Petition/wish: that the wicked be cut off (v. 4),
      D Speech of the wicked (v. 5),
      D' Speech of Yhwh (v. 6),

Forgotten and Forsaken by God (Lam 5:19–20)

  A Lament over absence of faithful ones from humankind (vv. 2–3)

    B Vain words of the wicked (vv. 4–5)

      C The Divine Promise (v. 6)

    B' Pure words of Yhwh (vv. 7–8)

  A' Return to Lament over Presence of the Wicked All Around (v. 9)[37]

The beginning and ending of Psalm 12 form an *inclusio* involving the words בני אדם, "children of humankind" (vv. 1 and 9). The speech of the wicked in v. 3 is described as שוא, "vanity/emptiness," in contrast to the pure words of Yhwh (v. 7). Assurance from Yhwh in v. 8 corresponds to petition made in v. 4. The chiastic structure of the psalm goes together with shifts in the personal pronouns applied to Yhwh: vv. 2–3 is addressed to Yhwh in the second-person "you"; vv. 4–5 are a wish/petition to Yhwh in the third person; v. 6 occupies the center of the psalm and contains statements by Yhwh in the first person; v. 7 refers to Yhwh in the third person; v. 8 is addressed to Yhwh again in the second person; the psalm's final verse corresponds to the first with an emphasis on the pervasiveness of wickedness.[38] The salvation oracle in v. 6 is the center of one of five occurrences of divine name יהוה in the psalm (vv. 2, 4, 6, 7, 8). The absence of the godly and faithful and the presence of the wicked all around are reinforced by the *inclusio* formed by vv. 1 and 9. The psalm begins and ends as a lament over the destruction of social order due to vain words and smooth tongues.

Part A: Lament over Absence of Faithful Ones among Humankind (vv. 2–3)[39]

> 2 Rescue, O Yhwh, for the loyal is gone,
> for vanished are the faithful ones[40] from humankind.

    B' Words of Yhwh—pure (v. 7),
    C' Assurance: Yhwh will protect us (v.8),
A' *Presence* of the wicked (v. 9).

Erich Zenger (*A God of Vengeance?*, 27) also detects a concentric structure in Psalm 12, which is similar to the one I outlined above, the only difference being that Zenger reads vv. 8–9 as a unit; cf. McCann, *Psalms*, 724.

37. The verse numbers of the psalms as cited in this volume follow those of the MT.

38. Cf. Zenger, *A God of Vengeance?*, 27.

39. Translations of the Psalms in this chapter are my own.

40. I follow the majority of scholars, who translate אמונים as "faithful people," which sets up a better parallel with חסיד "faithful or loyal one" in the first colon (e.g., NAB, NAS, NRSV; Villanueva, *The "Uncertainty of a Hearing*," 136). Alter (*The Book of Psalms*, 35), however, holds that the noun אמונים refers to the quality of faithfulness, not to the people; Terrien (*The Psalms*, 152) takes the same position.

3 Falsehood every man speaks to his fellow,
   smooth talk, with two hearts they speak.

Psalm 12 opens with an imperative: הוֹשִׁיעָה, "Rescue," "Save," or "Help"; Ps 69:2 is the only parallel to such an opening. J. Goldingay points out that it might seem impolite to begin a prayer with the bold imperative, "rescue";[41] nonetheless, this is certainly acceptable to, even welcomed by Yhwh, since the psalmist prays with such heartfelt urgency. The imperative הוֹשִׁיעָה lacks an object here, but the gravity of the situation is immediately clear: the loyal and faithful ones have disappeared from society due to the vain words and smooth talk of the wicked (12:3). Villanueva discerns a broadening of scope from the singular חָסִיד to the plural אֱמוּנִים; this generalizing movement is underscored by the use of the phrase בְּנֵי אָדָם, which refers to the whole human race. The complaint of the psalmist is mainly focused on the speech of the wicked. The image is vivid: they speak vanity, with smooth lips and a double heart, they say one thing but think otherwise, their actions and intentions are incoherent, their mind and life not integrated. Their words thus become effective weapons—they boast, leaving the righteous unable to express their faith and loyalty. The situation is described well in Proverbs: "When the wicked rise, people hide themselves; but when they perish, the righteous increase" (Prov 28:28; cf. 28:12).

Part B: Vain Words of the Wicked (vv. 4–5)

4 May Yhwh cut off all smooth-talking lips,
   the tongue that speaks of big things.

5 Those who said, "With our tongue we will prevail,
   Our lips are our own, who is master over us?"

Villanueva points out that vv. 4 and 5 form a minichiastic structure based on their uses of שָׂפָה and לָשׁוֹן:[42]

שָׂפָה

לָשׁוֹן

לָשׁוֹן

שָׂפָה

The psalmist asks Yhwh to destroy the lips and tongues of the wicked, weapons that enable them to prevail over the righteous and cause society to become dysfunctional. The wicked not only boast, "speak of big things"

---

41. Goldingay, *Psalms* 1:197.
42. Villanueva, *The "Uncertainty of a Hearing,"* 138.

Forgotten and Forsaken by God (Lam 5:19–20)

(v. 4), they actually challenge the very existence of God. They trust more in their power to boast and bluff with their lips and tongues; they question "who is master over us?" (v. 5)

Part C: The Divine Promise (v. 6)

> 6 "Because of the devastation of the afflicted, because of the groaning of the needy, now I will arise," says Yhwh, "I will grant safety to whoever longs for it."[43]

A number of scholars find indications of a salvation oracle in this verse because of the presence of the decisive עתה, "now" and the verb קום, "arise."[44] What is significant here is that it is Yhwh who responds to the petition and affirms that "I will arise"; further, Yhwh's speech stands in clear contrast to the words of the wicked: the wicked boast of their own power, while Yhwh's words are orientated toward others, toward the afflicted and needy.

The phrase אשית בישע literally means "I will set in salvation/deliverance," and corresponds to the imperative הושיעה in v. 1; the two words בישע and הושיעה derive from the same root, ישע. Yhwh has now answered the prayer of the psalmist.

Part B': Pure Words of Yhwh (vv. 7–8)

> 7 The words of Yhwh are pure words;
> as silver refined in a furnace on the earth, purified seven times.
>
> 8 You, O Yhwh, will keep them,
> You will guard them from this generation forever.

A further contrast is now formulated between Yhwh's words and those of the wicked. Yhwh's words are like silver of uttermost purity, tested in fire and reliable, the opposite of the vain and boasting words of the wicked uttered with smooth tongue and a divided heart. R. J. Clifford points out that after the double occurrences of אמרות, "words" in v. 7a, there is no further

---

43. The two words יפיח לו of MT in v. 6 are problematic. The root פוח can mean "to breathe, to blow" or "to pant for, to long for." The phrase then can be understood in two ways: (1) with the verb פוח in the sense of "to long for" and לו as the object of such longing, thus "I will grant him security to whoever longs for it" (NAS, NAB, RSV); (2) with the verb פוח in the sense of "to blow" and the phrase יפיח לו as the object of אשית, thus "I will set him in security against whom one blows"; Zenger (*A God of Vengeance?*, 26), e.g., renders "I will bring rescue to the one against whom they are snorting." I adopt the first rendering, which I consider to fit the context better.

44. Villanueva, *"Uncertainty of a Hearing,"* 139; Westermann, *Praise and Lament*, 72–73.

reference to speech in the poem. God's words in vv. 6–7 silence all those of the wicked.[45]

Part A': Return to Lament over Presence of the Wicked all around (v. 9)

> 9 On every side, the wicked walk about,
> as the worthless are exalted among humankind.

After the salvation oracle and the assurance of Yhwh's deliverance in v. 6, and the affirmation of the reliable words of Yhwh in v. 7, the psalmist returns to lament with a description of the wicked people all around, who walk about arrogantly. Moral disorder remains a social reality with the worthless being exalted.

Quite a number of interpreters find this last line problematic. C. Broyles calls it "a disappointing anticlimax."[46] Some prefer to read v. 9 as a continuation of v. 8's affirmation of trust in Yhwh by adding a particle "even though" at the beginning of v. 9.[47] However, as Kim notes, there is no grammatical or textual reason to insert a conjunction in v. 9; Psalm 12 shows that a lament can (re-)occur even after a salvation oracle.[48] Clifford holds that Psalm 12 thus "ends with a realistic appreciation of a broken world."[49] To sum up, Psalm 12 starts with a petition to Yhwh over the vain speech of the wicked (vv. 2–5), then cites a salvation oracle from Yhwh (v. 6), affirms that Yhwh's words are pure and reliable (v. 7) and expresses trust in Yhwh (v. 8). Finally, the psalmist returns to lament again (v. 9). The mood of the psalm moves from lament to trust, then back to lament again. The psalmist remains aware of the grim reality—even after receiving a divine oracle.

Psalm 44: A Communal Lament from Trust to Lament

Mood change in communal laments is not as abrupt as that in the individual laments. Even though Williamson observes that communal laments never finish with an expression of a certainty of hearing,[50] we do perceive a certain mood change in the communal lament psalms; some move from lament to trust and confidence (e.g., Psalms 14; 58; 60); some move in the opposite

---

45. Clifford, *Psalms 1–72*, 83.

46. Broyles, *Psalms*, 84.

47. See, e.g., Weiser, *Psalms*, 158; Dahood, *Psalms* 1:72–75; Craigie, *Psalms 1–50*, 139; Zenger, *A God of Vengeance?*, 26.

48. Kim, *Rapid Change of Mood*, 124–25.

49. Clifford, *Psalms 1–72*, 84.

50. Williamson, "Reading the Lament Psalms Backwards," 5.

Forgotten and Forsaken by God (Lam 5:19-20)

direction from confidence to lament (e.g., Psalm 44); still others alternate between confidence and lament (e.g., Psalms 74; 89). R. J. Clifford makes two observations about the communal lament psalms: first, the psalmist chooses to recall a particular significant event in the past that corresponds to the present crisis; second, the specific language of lament and the recall of the primal past event can occur in a different order in the various psalms: lament may occur before or after the recalling of the key event.[51] Psalm 44, e.g., laments over a military defeat and recalls the divine planting of the people in the land; here, the recalling comes first and is followed by the lament; the reverse is the case in Psalm 77, while in Psalms 74, 80, and 83, lament forms a frame with the saving event cited in the middle.[52]

Psalm 44 is a typical communal lament which, at the same time, also exhibits a remarkable feature: it firmly professes the people's innocence in the covenant relationship (vv. 18-23).[53] Psalm 44 lays the responsibility for destruction on God, while the human enemy recedes into the background (cf. Lamentations 2; Psalms 80; 89). It thus accuses God of becoming the enemy of his own people and reflects the "unorthodox" views that it is God who has violated the terms of the covenant.[54]

L. Crow observes a loose chiastic structure in Psalm 44 (my terminology below differs from Crow's):[55]

A God's saving act in the past (vv. 2-4)
  B Communal expression of trust in God in the present (vv. 5-9)
    C Lament over God's rejection and present community's shame (v. 10-17)
  B' Community's fidelity to God in crisis (vv. 18-23)
A' Urgent petition to God to act (vv. 24-27)

Part A: God's Saving Act in the Past (vv. 2-4)

> 2 O God, we have heard with our ears, our ancestors have told us,
> a deed[56] that you did in their days, in the days of old:

---

51. Clifford, "Psalm 89," 40.

52. Ibid.

53. Mays, *Psalms*, 176.

54. Dalit Rom-Shiloni ("Psalm 44," 683-84) notes that the mainstream "orthodox" way of thinking justifies God at all costs and thus blames the people for their horrible circumstances; this is the approach of "prophetic, priestly, and historiographic circles," in contrast to the "unorthodox" view as expressed in the book of Lamentations, communal laments, and various "quotations" of the audience found in Jeremiah and Ezekiel (e.g., Jer 6:24-25; 8:19-20; 14:19-22; 22:10; Ezek 18:2).

55. Crow, "Rhetoric of Psalm 44," 394; see also Clifford, *Psalms 1-72*, 219.

56. MT פֹּעַל, "deed" is singular. The psalmist recalls one significant deed, namely, the giving of the land of Canaan to the people; it is not a question of plural "deeds," as

Mood Change in Lamentations and Related Old Testament Laments

3 You, your hand drove out the nations, but them you planted;
you afflicted the peoples and sent them away.

4 For not by their own sword did they take hold of the land,
nor did their own arm give them victory;
but your right hand and your arm,
and the light of your face, for you favored them.

The psalmist recounts the giving of the Promised Land by God as the positive counterpart to the present crisis of loss of the land and exile. The ancestors have followed the command of Deut 6:20–25 by narrating the story of exodus from Egypt generation after generation. It is "you"—God who brought the people to the land, with your right hand and your arm, since you favored them (vv. 3–4). The second person pronoun and suffix in reference to Yhwh occur twelve times in these two verses; as Alter puts it, "the fluidity of biblical Hebrew in pronominal reference is especially evident here."[57] The psalmist moves from what "we" (the present generation) have heard to what "you" (God) did to "them" (our ancestors): their coming into the land was "your" (God's) work, not their own doing.

Part B: Communal Expression of Trust in God (vv. 5–9)

5 You are my King, O God;
ordain the victories of Jacob.

6 Through you we push down our foes;
through your name we trample those against us.

7 For not in my bow do I trust,
nor can my sword save me.

8 For you have saved us from our foes,
and those who hate us you put to shame.

9 God we praise all day long,
and your name we acclaim for all time. Selah

The psalmist embraces the sovereign God who acted on behalf of the forefathers and declares that God is his own king (Ps 44:5). He then utilizes first-person plural to express the present generation's trust in God to bring salvation to them again (Ps 44:6–8). The psalmist avers that he does not trust his own bow and sword (Ps 44:7), since it is not the people's own power that

---

RSV and NRSV have it.
  57. Alter, *The Book of Psalms*, 154.

Forgotten and Forsaken by God (Lam 5:19–20)

gives them victory (Ps 44:4). The saving act has rather to come from God (Ps 44:8). The psalmist declares his praise for God at all times (Ps 44:9); Goldingay notes that the terms "all day long" and "for all time" suggest the "regularity and consistency of this confessional praise and its permanent nature."[58]

Part C: Lament over God's Rejection and Present Community's Shame (vv. 10–17)

> 10 Yet you rejected and ashamed us,
> and you did not go out with our armies.
>
> 11 You made us turn back from the foe,
> and our enemies took their plunder.
>
> 12 You made us like sheep to be eaten,
> and scattered us among the nations.
>
> 13 You sold your people for no wealth,
> and set no high price upon them.
>
> 14 You made us a shame to our neighbors,
> derision and mockery to those around us.
>
> 15 You made us a byword among the nations,
> a laughingstock among the peoples.
>
> 16 All day long my disgrace is before me,
> and shame has covered my face,
>
> 17 from the sound of revilers and cursers,
> from the sight of the enemy and the avenger.

The tone changes abruptly via the particle אף, "yet" in v. 10; the mood shifts from confidence and trust (vv. 4–9) to lament (vv. 10–17). It is noteworthy that each verse in vv. 10–15 starts with a second person pronoun ת, "you": *you* made us turn back from the enemy; *you* made us like sheep to be eaten; *you* sold your people for a very low price; *you* made us a shame, derision and mockery; *you* made us a byword and object of scorn. Clifford describes the above sequence as creating "a staccato effect."[59] God is no longer driving back the enemy; rather, he made his people turn back; God made them ashamed and a mockery among the nations, in contrast to his previous favor. The same God who ransomed them from the land of Egypt

---

58. Goldingay, *Psalms* 2:41.
59. Clifford, *Psalms 1–72*, 220–21.

has now sold them, at a very low price. It is all the doing of God—"you"; the people are utterly ashamed in the face of others' mocking (vv. 16–17).

Rom-Shiloni observes that "the triangular relationship of God-people-enemy has drastically shifted" between vv. 2–9 and 10–17; the two parts form a chiastic structure, even as they display themes of reversal:[60]

3 אתה ידך גוים הורשת ותטעם תרע לאמים ותשלחם You, your hand drove out the nations, but them you planted; you afflicted the peoples and sent them away. גוים לאמים	11 תשיבנו אחור מני־צר ומשנאינו שסו למו You made us turn back from the foe, and our enemies took their plunder. צר משנאינו
5 אתה־הוא מלכי אלהים צוה ישועות יעקב You are my King, O God; ordain the victories of Jacob. יעקב	12 תתננו כצאן מאכל ובגוים זריתנו You made us like sheep to be eaten, and scattered us among the nations. גוים
6 בך צרינו ננגח בשמך נבוס קמינו Through you we push down our foes; through your name we trample those against us. צרינו קמינו	13 תמכר־עמך בלא־הון ולא־רבית במחיריהם You sold your people for no wealth, and set no high price upon them. עמך
8 כי הושעתנו מצרינו ומשנאינו הבישות For you have saved us from our foes, and those who hate us you put to shame. צרינו משנאינו	15 תשימנו משל בגוים מנוד־ראש בל־אמים You made us a byword among the nations, a laughingstock among the peoples. גוים אמים

The voice of constant praise, "God we praise all day long" (v. 9), is now replaced by what Rom-Shiloni calls "permanent self-contempt": "All day long my disgrace is before me, and shame has covered my face" before the enemy (vv. 16–17).[61]

Part B': Community's Fidelity in God in Crisis (vv. 18–23)

Crow argues that this section features "the same thing argued twice," with two parallel segments in vv. 18–20 and vv. 21–23. In each part, the first two verses insist on the people's fidelity, while the last verse (vv. 20 and 23) accuses God of betrayal with an asseverative כי (a strong "yet") at the beginning.[62]

60. Rom-Shiloni, "Psalm 44," 687.
61. Ibid.
62. Crow, "Rhetoric of Psalm 44," 397–98.

Forgotten and Forsaken by God (Lam 5:19-20)

A 18 All this has come upon us, yet we have not forgotten you,
or been false to your covenant.

A 19 Our heart has not turned back,
nor have our steps departed from your way,

B 20 yet you thrust us down to the sea monster's place,
and covered us with deep darkness.

A 21 If we had forgotten the name of our God,
or spread out our hands to a strange god,

A 22 Would not God discover this?
For he knows the secrets of the heart.

B 23 Yet because of you we are being killed all day long,
and accounted as sheep for the slaughter.

The community claims that they have not been false to their covenant with God—even in secret. The present disaster is not caused by the community's wrongdoing and the psalmist rejects the simple cause and effect theology laid out, e.g., in Deut 28:15-68. The community is suffering because of God, "because of you we are being killed all day long" (v. 23a). The phrase כל היום, "all day long," or "constantly" appears for the third time here after its prior uses in vv. 9 and 16. Rom-Shiloni points out that "the repetition of the phrase marks the general movement through the psalm as it expresses the decline in the people's condition"; the psalmist starts with praise and thanksgiving in v. 9, changes to an emphasis on disgrace and shame in v. 16, and finally to defeat and death in v. 23.[63]

Part A': Urgent Petition to God to Act (vv. 24-27)

24 Rouse yourself! Why do you sleep, O Adonai?[64]
Awake, do not cast us off forever!

25 Why do you hide your face?
Why do you forget our affliction and oppression?

26 For we sink down to the dust;
our bodies cling to the ground.

27 Rise up, come to our help.
Redeem us for the sake of your steadfast love.

---

63. Rom-Shiloni, "Psalm 44," 689.

64. For an analysis of the sleeping deity motif, see Batto, "Sleeping God"; Mrozek and Votto, "Motif of the Sleeping Divinity."

This final petition ties the whole psalm together. The psalmist is urging God to wake up from sleep; God's neglect of the people has gone on too long (v. 24). God is present, but has been hiding his face (v. 25a). It is not the people who forgot God, as often affirmed in Deuteronomistic and prophetic literature (e.g., Hos 2:15; 4:6; Jer 2:32b; 13:25; 18:15a; 20:11; Isa 65:11, etc.); rather, Psalm 44 laments the community's being forgotten by God, in this aligning itself with a small number of biblical passages that accuse God of forgetting his people (Lam 5:20; Pss 74:19; 77:10; Isa 49:14).[65] The psalmist ends his petition with a further plea for help in v. 26: "we sink down to dust; our bodies cling to the ground," with a double sense: we were brought very low and we humble ourselves before you.[66]

To sum up, Psalm 44 does not end in praise. It does not follow the structure of the communal lament genre outlined by Westermann, from lament to petition to praise.[67] Praise simply serves as an introduction in Psalm 44, which ends in petition. Neither does the psalm attain to a new orientation as Brueggemann's scheme would suggest—it remains an unanswered lament.

Psalm 88: A Psalm of Pure Lament

Psalm 88 is a unique psalm; it is a pure complaint. C. Mandolfo describes Psalm 88 as "the only psalm in the Psalter that exhibits no shift to thanksgiving, no vow of praise, and no third person didactic voice."[68] It does not even appeal explicitly for help.[69] Lament and protest permeate Psalm 88; petition appears at the beginning, in the middle and toward the end (vv. 2, 10b, 14). Irene Nowell holds that Psalm 88 possesses "a compelling simplicity";[70] the sole focus of the psalmist is Yhwh who has been afflicting him. The psalmist does not claim innocence or appeal for forgiveness; he has only one appeal to make, that Yhwh "listen" (Ps 88:2). However, Yhwh remains silent and no light penetrates the dark world of the psalmist, whose last word is מחשך, "darkness" (v. 19).

I follow the majority of scholars who divide Psalm 88 into three parts: vv. 2–10a, 10b–13, 14–19.[71] Each part starts with persistent cries of lament

---

65. See the analysis in Preuss, "שכח," 674–77; and Broyles, *Conflict of Faith and Experience*, 70–73.
66. Clifford, *Psalms 1–72*, 221.
67. Westermann, "Role of Lament," 26–27.
68. Mandolfo, "Psalm 88," 155.
69. Culley, "Psalm 88," 293.
70. Nowell, "Psalm 88," 105.
71. Nowell, "Psalm 88," 114–15; Clifford, *Psalms 73–150*, 87; Hossfeld and Zenger,

Forgotten and Forsaken by God (Lam 5:19–20)

to Yhwh—"you": "day and night," (vv. 2–3); "everyday" (v. 10bc); and "in the morning" (v. 14). The first and third parts are followed by the description of a crisis (vv. 4–10a; 15–19), while the second part leads into an appeal consisting of six urgent questions (vv. 11–13).[72] Clifford notes that the first and third parts are parallel in theme (personal suffering) and syntactic structure.[73] He further states that the argument is developed progressively over the course of the psalm: part 1 asks only that the lament of a dying wretch be heard; part 2 provides a motive for God to act (i.e., that once dead, the psalmist can no longer praise God); part 3 restates part one with an intensified accusatory tone.[74]

Part 1: First Petition "My Life Draws Near to Sheol" (vv. 2–10a)

2 O Yhwh, God of my salvation,
  I cry out by day, and at night, in your presence,

3 let my prayer come before you;
  incline your ear to my cry.

4 For I am sated with troubles,
  and my life draws near to Sheol.

5 I am counted among those who go down to the Pit;
  I became like a man without strength,

6 among the dead cast away, like the slain, those who lie in the grave,
  whom you remember no more, and they are cut off by your hand.

7 You put me in the depths of the Pit,
  in darkness, in the depths.

8 Your wrath lay heavy upon me,
  and you afflict me with all your waves. Selah

9 You distanced my friends from me,
  you made me disgusting to them.
  Imprisoned, I cannot get out.

10a My eye grows dim from affliction.

Psalms 2, 391–92; Goldingay, *Psalms* 2:644.
72. Hossfeld and Zenger, *Psalms 2*, 392.
73. Clifford, *Psalms 73–150*, 87.
74. Ibid.

Mood Change in Lamentations and Related Old Testament Laments

The psalmist addresses Yhwh by name and title: "God of my salvation" (v. 2). The psalmist prays with "urgency and persistence" and pleads with Yhwh to hear his cry which is uttered day and night (v. 3).[75] The following three verses, vv. 4–6, focus on the miserable condition of the psalmist, with repeated use of "I" and "my." Nowell points out that vv. 4–6a are the only verses in the psalm in which there are no second person suffixes or verbs.[76] The images the psalmist evokes are of those of death and darkness which have almost engulfed him.[77] He is sated with troubles and his life draws near to Sheol (v. 4); he is counted among those going down to the Pit (v. 5); worse, he is among the dead cast away, like those killed in battle, lying in a grave (v. 6a). The Hebrew word חפשי usually refers to people "freed" from slavery (e.g., Exod 21:2, 5, 26–27; Deut 15:12–13, 18), but here the reference is to an outcast, who is excluded from the human community.[78] Verse 6b serves as a transition, with Yhwh being identified as the one who caused the near death and isolation of the psalmist. Yhwh is the subject of all verbs in vv. 7–9a: rather than simply being forgotten by Yhwh, the psalmist is convinced that it is Yhwh who personally thrust him into sheer darkness in the depth of the Pit (v. 7); Yhwh's wrath overwhelms the psalmist (v. 8); Yhwh not only isolates the psalmist, but makes him an abhorrence to his friends (v. 9a). The psalmist is imprisoned and cannot get out (v. 9b); his eye grows dim from affliction (v. 10a); the two words עיני, "my eye," and עני, "affliction" engender a pun: that the psalmist's eye grows dim from affliction is "particularly significant in a psalm in which darkness is the symbol for affliction."[79]

Part II: Second Petition "Is Your Steadfast Love Declared in the Grave?" (vv. 10bc–13)

> 10bc Every day I call on you, O Yhwh;
> I spread out my hands to you.
>
> 11 Will you work wonders for the dead?
> Will the departed spirits rise up to praise you? Selah
>
> 12 Is your steadfast love declared in the grave,
> your faithfulness in perdition?

---

75. Nowell, "Psalm 88," 116.
76. Ibid., 112.
77. Alter (*The Book of Psalms*, 308) notes that Psalm 88 distinguishes itself from other psalms due to its concentration on the terrifying darkness of the realm of death.
78. See the more detailed discussion in Clifford, *Psalms 73–150*, 88.
79. Nowell, "Psalm 88," 113.

Forgotten and Forsaken by God (Lam 5:19–20)

> 13 Will your wonders be known in the darkness,
> your righteous deed in the land of forgetfulness?

The psalmist has been calling upon Yhwh day in and day out in a gesture of helplessness and desperation (10b–c). The six rhetorical questions in vv. 11–13 serve to create a sense of heightened urgency. These questions come at a point in the lament where we might expect a confession of guilt or a protestation of innocence, but instead, as Nowell notes, the psalmist focuses entirely on Yhwh.[80] The psalmist provides motivations for Yhwh to act right now: otherwise, he will soon disappear among the dead, into the darkness, with the result that the steadfast love, faithfulness, wonders and righteous deeds of Yhwh will be forgotten (vv. 12–13). The psalmist recalls Yhwh's "steadfast love and faithfulness" (חסד and אמונה), Yhwh's covenantal character; as well as his righteous and wondrous deeds (צדקה and פלא); צדקה can only be understood in the context of a relationship while פלא refers to Yhwh's saving act in bringing the people out of Egypt (Exod 3:20; 15:11).[81] It is in Yhwh's own interest to act, to revive the psalmist, so that all Yhwh's faithful traits will be displayed in the life of the saved psalmist.

Part III: Third Petition (vv. 14–19)

> 14 But I—to you, O Yhwh, I cried out;
> in the morning my prayer comes before you.
>
> 15 Why, O Yhwh, do you reject me?
> Why do you hide your face from me?
>
> 16 I was afflicted and about to die from my youth on,
> I have borne your terrors; I am desperate.
>
> 17 Over me your wrath has passed;
> your horrors destroy me.
>
> 18 They surround me like water all day long;
> they encircle me completely.
>
> 19 You distanced lover and friend from me;
> my acquaintance is darkness.[82]

---

80. Ibid., 117.
81. See Achtemeier, "Righteousness in the Old Testament," *IDB* 4:80.
82. The words מידעי מחשך in MT v. 19 can be understood in two ways: (1) the psalmist's friends are nothing but darkness to him since they rejected him and distanced themselves from him, thus "my companions are in darkness" (e.g., RSV; NRSV; NAS); (2) the only friend or acquaintance left to the psalmist is darkness (e.g., NAB; Alter, *The Book of Psalms*, 310). I adopt the second interpretation.

Mood Change in Lamentations and Related Old Testament Laments

The final section of the psalm focuses on its two main characters: the psalmist and Yhwh, or rather, on the psalmist's holding on against all odds to Yhwh who has been the source of his affliction. Having received no answer from Yhwh to his questions, the psalmist nonetheless continues his crying out to Yhwh; every day and every morning, the psalmist cries out to the "you" to whom he clings (v. 14). The psalmist feels rejected; he still cannot see the face of Yhwh after a long search (v. 15). His affliction, desperation, and the terrors he has been enduring continue; he has been like the dead since his youth (v. 16). Yhwh's wrath passed over him, its effects and terror still surround him, permeating him totally like water (vv. 17-18). The psalmist is avoided by lovers and friends; he is left in total darkness, his only companion. The psalmist suffered, lamented, pleaded like Job; but still God's voice is not heard—there is no vindication, no restoration, unlike what happens in the Book of Job (cf. Job 42:7-7-17). The psalmist remains an outsider to the community, an outsider from the realm of Yhwh; his physical suffering continues; his spiritual turmoil remains unabated; his only companion is total darkness.

To sum up, no mood change occurs in Psalm 88; despair and darkness pervade the entire psalm. A few scholars see a glimpse of hope in the title "God of my salvation" in v. 1; if, however, there is some sort of hope at the beginning, this recedes ever more into darkness. The psalmist does not ask God to relieve his pain; he asks only that God hear his cry and show his face; however, his wish is not granted, darkness prevails. In total darkness, the psalmist continuously cries out, to Yhwh—"you" (v. 14); his cry persists, leaving its mark on the darkness.

We have seen that while in Psalms 12 and 44, the mood can shift from confidence to lament; any movement toward praise is absent in the lament-oriented Psalm 88. Nevertheless, these psalms are positioned in a Psalter that moves toward final praise (Psalms 146-50). The book of Lamentations, on the contrary, starts and ends with lament. Accordingly, I now turn to the topic of mood change in Lamentations.

MOOD CHANGE IN THE BOOK OF LAMENTATIONS

Mood change occurs in the Book of Lamentations, and the book ends in lament as do Psalms 12, 44, and 88 analyzed above. As noted previously, Lamentations contains three passages of hope or praise. The longest one is 3:21-33, positioned in a chapter where the suffering man alternates between despair and hope. The two much shorter ones are 4:22 and 5:19; 4:22 affirms that God will no longer keep Zion in exile and will punish Edom's sins, but this line is followed by chapter 5, a communal lament; 5:19 declares that God's reign endures from generation to generation, but is followed by two "why" questions in v. 20, and a final assertion of Yhwh's rejection and anger in v. 22.

Mood Change in Lamentations 3

Lamentations 3 is fraught with tensions. This chapter differs from the other chapters in the Book of Lamentations in its combining "descriptions of suffering with theological inquiry into that suffering."[83] At the same time, Lamentations 3 is like the other chapters in its refusing to solve the issues it presents to the reader. Lamentations 3 addresses the quest for meaning and outlines the proper attitude in suffering, but does not come to a resolution. It "alternate[s] between despair and hope, as if the speaker wants to convey his changing feelings as he ponders the events and their implications."[84]

The opening of Lamentations 3 is unique: "I am the man who has seen affliction" (Lam 3:1); the name of God is not invoked until v. 18.[85] Dobbs-Allsopp points out that, by contrast, even the "dark" Psalm 22 opens by addressing God: "My God, My God, why have you forsaken me?" According to him, it was customary and even obligatory to "name God in some fashion in the opening line or couplet of a psalm."[86] Yet, God is not directly mentioned at the start of Lamentations 3, which thereby "betrays an attempt to highlight the absence of God, or more specifically God's failure to 'see' the suffering of the people."[87]

The chapter's first change of mood occurs in vv. 21-24, where it moves from despair to hope, after a long description of the man's suffering under "him" (vv. 1-18), at a juncture where the man is at the lowest point in his life (vv. 19-20), feeling extremely bitter and very low. It is at this lowest point that the man affirms that he has hope. C. Westermann holds that the sequence of themes in vv. 1-25 corresponds to "the normal pattern for the genre of the personal lament," moving from accusation against God in vv. 1-19 to praise in vv. 20-25.[88] However, Lamentations 3 does not end on this hopeful passage; it moves on. Westermann views vv. 26-41 as an ex-

---

83. Berlin, *Lamentations*, 86.

84. Ibid.

85. It is clear that the phrase "the rod of his wrath" in Lam 3:1 refers to God, and NRSV introduces a mention of God here: "under the rod of *God's* wrath." However, it is better to keep the third-person pronoun "his" unspecified as it is in MT.

86. Dobbs-Allsopp, *Lamentations*, 110.

87. Villanueva, *The "Uncertainty of a Hearing,"* 223.

88. Westermann, *Lamentations*, 169-70.

pansion of the personal lament in vv. 1–25, while vv. 42–51 would be a communal lament taken out of its original context since the explicit vow of praise is lacking in this part; finally, he regards vv. 52–58 and vv. 59–66 as two fragments appended to Lamentations 3.[89] Westermann's approach is constrained by his prior form-critical view that lament has to move to praise; as a result, he considers the materials after the praise in Lam 3:21–25 as fragments that were added later.

The words of hope in Lam 3:21–24 are followed by a wisdom-like section in vv. 25–39 that cites proper behaviors for a suffering person (vv. 25–30). Yet, even within this "wisdom" interlude, one can sense the tension between hope and despair. As Villanueva puts it, "there is a strong attempt to 'defend' God (31–33) and an equally strong opposition to doubt the assertions being made (34–36)."[90] It is within this section that we find the line "Yhwh does not see" (Lam 3:36) which constitutes a negative answer regarding the book's preceding calls for Yhwh to "see" (Lam 1:9, 11, 20; 2:20); Villanueva notes that this is the first and only time in the book that we find a direct accusation of God for his failure to "see."[91]

The poet then exhorts the community to return to Yhwh by examining their ways (Lam 3:40–42). The poet admits that "we have transgressed and rebelled," but there follows a strong accusation against God, "you have not forgiven" (3:42). Villanueva points out that the words of Lam 3:42a reflect the spirit of the prayers of confession found in Ezra 9; Nehemiah 9; and Daniel 9; of these texts, Daniel 9 is particularly relevant since it contains the word סלח, "forgive" (vv. 9, 19), used also in Lam 3:42b.[92] In the prayers in Ezra 9; Nehemiah 9; and Daniel 9, confession moves to a petition for forgiveness; the immediate turn from confession to accusation of Yhwh within a single verse in Lam 3:42 is thus unusual. Lam 3:42 sets up a stark contrast between the positive confession of the "we" and the negative, unforgiving "you." A number of scholars try to "soften" the accusatory tone here, e.g., W. Rudolph follows Luther in rendering Lam 3:42b as "Darum hast du *billig* nicht verschonet," i.e. "therefore you have not forgiven *lightly*."[93] House suggests "indeed you have not forgiven" since "the sheer mention of repentance by even a true penitent may not necessarily signal actual repentance of the whole group," and the people remain rebellious.[94] This line of interpretation does not, however, fully

---

89. Ibid., 189–91.
90. Villanueva, *The "Uncertainty of a Hearing,"* 219.
91. Ibid., 232.
92. Ibid., 233.
93. Rudolph, *Das Buch Ruth; Das Hohe Lied; Die Klagelieder*, 242.
94. House, *Song of Songs; Lamentations*, 422.

take into account Lam 3:42's juxtaposed cola without a linking *waw*: "*billig*" or "indeed" are translational insertions. Furthermore, Lam 3:42 introduces another shift of mood within the chapter, not from lament to hope this time, but from hope to lament in vv. 43–47, now with added intensity as well.[95]

The suffering man returns to personal lament in vv. 48–66. He recalls God's past saving acts and pleads for deliverance from present misery in vv. 55–60. Begrich takes Lam 3:57 ("Do not fear") as reflecting an essential moment in the lament process when the salvation oracle is given.[96] However, Begrich takes the verse out of its context, according to which the poet is referring to a past experience of Yhwh. Villanueva shows that Lam 3:55–60 intertwines past experience of deliverance and present need for divine action.[97] Thereafter, the man again asks Yhwh to "see" his misery in v. 63 and to punish those persecuting him according to their malice (vv. 64–66).

Lamentation 3 alternates between hope and despair, assurance of Yhwh's goodness and uncertainty as to whether Yhwh will deliver the suffering man. It ends with a petition for Yhwh to see and to act.

Remaining in Lament in Lamentations

Lamentations as a communal lament remains in lament; it does not move on praise to God. It ends on uncertainty and despair: "unless you have utterly rejected us and are angry with us beyond measure –" (Lam 5:22). The book ends, but the grieving process of the community is not yet over. L. Allen holds that the traditional synagogal practice of repeating 5:21 after v. 22 in order to leave the community with a positive note "misses the point."[98] The extreme conclusion in Lam 5:22 functions as "a sting in the tail," designed to force God to face up his covenant obligations.[99]

I think that the time for grieving, no matter how long this may take, has to be respected. The grieving community in Lamentations remains true to its authentic feelings, which is the only way to remain faithful in one's relationship with God. There are momentary glimpses of hope in the book,

---

95. See my interpretation of Lam 3:40–47 in Chapter 3, 121–22.

96. Begrich, "Das Priesterliche Heilsorakel," 83.

97. Villanueva (*The "Uncertainty of a Hearing,"* 240–41) lays out the structure of Lam 3:55–60 as follows: what Yhwh has done in the past (55–56a), prayer that Yhwh act in the present: "Do not cover your ears . . ." (56b), what Yhwh has done in the past (57–59a), prayer that Yhwh act in the present: "Judge my cause" (59b), What Yhwh has done in the past (60).

98. Allen, *A Liturgy of Grief,* 164.

99. Ibid.

but they are not sustained. The mood changes a bit from lament to hope, but then falls back into lament and remains in lament.

However, Lamentations is not a book of despair; its hope does not lie in its hopeful messages, conveyed in words. Its hope runs deeper than a mood change could capture, more profound than what words can express. The hope in Lamentations lies in its insistence on keeping God as a dialogic partner, the "You" who can make a difference. God is the only "you" in Lamentations, where the second person pronoun אתה occurs three times (1:21; 3:42; 5:19), all in reference to Yhwh.

Unlike the community in Psalm 44, the community in Lamentations does not claim innocence; they admit that they have sinned and rebelled, but they have also confessed and expect, more than anything else, a reply from God. God is silent and seems absent; it is the community that tries to keep the relationship and dialogue with God going.

CONCLUSION

Mood change in biblical laments is far more complex than a uni-directional movement from lament to praise. The change is not only from lament to praise, but also from praise to lament or to alternate between the two. Communal laments usually do not end with certainty of a hearing; likewise, a number of communal lament psalms and the book of Lamentations do not end in praise; lament and petition remain to the end in these communal laments. At the same time, these laments insist that God continues to be their dialogue partner, and the community holds God accountable for the present miserable situation, regardless of whether the community is innocent (Psalm 44) or sinful (Lamentations).

Still, admission of sin and guilt is present in the book of Lamentations and how this is to be understood influences one's understanding of the overall message of the book. Admission of guilt is also present in some other Old Testament laments; accordingly, I will focus on the function of admission of guilt in Lamentations and related Old Testament texts in the next chapter.

5

Admission of Guilt in Lamentations and Related Old Testament Laments

INTRODUCTION

I have shown in chapter 1 that scholars who consider the message of hope in Lam 3:22–33 as the "core" of the book of Lamentations tend to emphasize the meaning of suffering in Lamentations; an alternative view has been advanced by other scholars who pay more attention to the expression of pain articulated by various voices throughout the book. A major difference between the two approaches lies in the question of how the admissions of sin and guilt should be interpreted in Lamentations. In this connection, it is important to note that the book of Lamentations is part of a transition in the exilic/postexilic literature, with its shift of emphasis from lament to penitential prayers, found especially in Ezra 9; Nehemiah 9; and Daniel 9.

In chapters 2 to 4 of the book, we have seen that Lamentations is a perfect unity of literary form and content (chapter 2) in which various voices form an on-going dialogue, a dialogue without an end; a final word or a reply from God remains to be uttered (chapter 3). Moreover, no obvious mood change from lament to praise occurs in Lamentations; Lamentations remains tragic, starting with the loneliness of Zion and ending with the question of why God has forgotten and forsaken the people for so long; the book concludes with a half sentence, the other half of which can only be supplied with a reply from God (chapter 4).

Overall, Lamentations remains a lament and protest against God, who has punished disproportionately, beyond measure. It is thus a valid assertion

Admission of Guilt in Lamentations and Related Old Testament Laments

that Lamentations is more an expression of pain through its different voices than a search for meanings behind the pain. However, admission of guilt remains as a valid interpretative response to the fall of Jerusalem among others that focus on disaster and pain; its significance and function in the book deserve attention. Lamentations thus belongs to a group of biblical texts that hold lament and confession in tension (e.g., Isa 63:7—64:12; Jer 14:1—15:9; and Psalm 79).[1]

This chapter will look into the dialogic interaction between Lamentations and the above-mentioned three texts regarding admission of guilt. I will study first scholarly discussions of the historical development of biblical laments and penitential prayers and the relationship between these two forms of prayer, then the function of admission of guilt in the three passages, and finally the function of admission of guilt in the book of Lamentations.

RELATIONSHIP BETWEEN BIBLICAL LAMENTS AND PENITENTIAL PRAYERS

In the historical development of biblical laments, admission of guilt is a late feature; its occurrence and heightened importance in penitential prayers are related to the fall of Jerusalem, the destruction of the temple, and consequently the disappearance of cultic liturgy.

Historical Development of Biblical Laments

Claus Westermann is the most influential scholar to have tracked the historical developments of laments. He considers two types of biblical prayer to be of primary importance (i.e. praise and lament) and lays out the characteristic structure of both forms. Westermann further identifies three stages in the historical development of lament.[2] The primary stage consists of laments of the individual found in early narrative texts (Gen 25:22; 27:46; Jer 20:18). The lament and complaint in these laments are directed to God and concern the meaning of existence; they do not require a cultic setting or mediator. These early laments are "a self-contained call to God" (Josh 7:7-9; Judg 15:18;

---

1. Werline (*Penitential Prayer in Second Temple Judaism*, 42–43) points out that the coupling of lament with confession of sin in the Old Testament occurs in Psalm 79; Isa 63:7—64:12; Jeremiah 14; and Lamentations.

2. Westermann, *Praise and Lament*, 165–213. Balentine (" 'I Was Ready to Be Sought,' " in *Seeking the Favor of God, 1: The Origins of Penitential Prayer in Second Temple Judaism*, 4–5) provides a summary of Westermann's analysis of the three stages of laments.

21:3);[3] there is "no actual complaint about the enemy."[4] The laments in this earliest stage in their simplest form consist only of the "why" question (Exod 5:22–23; 17:3; Num 11:11; Judg 6:13, 22; 21:3). Westermann emphasizes that the lament of the early period is "essentially a complaint against God" and that these prose laments always relate to a particular given situation.[5]

In the second stage, the once simple, one-sentence, prose laments are "fused into poetic/psalmic laments."[6] Lament, complaint against God and petition are held in balance in these later laments.[7] These laments comprise both laments of the community and of the individual. Laments directed to God are predominant in the communal laments, often introduced with the question, why?, less frequently with, how long?[8] The "why" questions ask why God has rejected (Ps 74:1; Jer 14:19), abandoned (Lam 5:20), or forgotten (Ps 44:24; Lam 5:20) his people. Westermann holds that these why questions assume that "what has been suffered has its origin in God's alienation."[9] The question of "how long" focuses on the duration of the speaker's distress (e.g., Pss 79:5; 80:4; 85:5; 89:46; Jer 3:5; Hab 1:2). In these "why" and "how long" questions, words of anger predominate. These questions often appear in the laments of the individual as well, and with "startling bitterness."[10] Westermann points out that the individual laments tread a thin line between reproach and judgment, but never condemn God since their statements remain personal, never objective.[11] Confession of sins seldom occurs in the laments of the second stage, which often combine complaint against God with protestations of innocence.[12]

In the third and final stage in the historical development of biblical laments, the focus is on the destruction of Jerusalem, beginning with Lamentations and continuing through to 4 Ezra.[13] A major shift occurs at this stage: penitential prayers without a lament or with mere traces of lament become

3. Westermann, *Praise and Lament in the Pslams*, 197.
4. Ibid., 201.
5. Ibid., 198–99.
6. Balentine, " 'I was Ready to Be Sought Out,'" 4.
7. Westermann, *Praise and Lament*, 171.
8. Ibid., 176.
9. Ibid., 177.
10. Ibid.
11. Ibid.
12. Westermann (*Praise and Lament in the Pslams*, 206) points out that the prayer of repentance in its fully developed form is not to be found in the Psalter; only in a few psalms (e.g., Psalm 51) does the motif of the confession of sins begin to shape the whole psalm.
13. Ibid., 172.

the most prevalent type of prayer.[14] No firm line of development can be drawn from lament to penitential prayer and there are many transitional forms.[15] During this stage, the complaint against God is silenced by repeated claims that everything that happened is justified, with the accompanying praise of the righteous God. Here, the poetic form of lament that dominated the second stage is replaced by the prose penitential prayers that first appear biblically in Nehemiah 9; Ezra 9; and Daniel 9.[16] The confession of sins becomes a powerful and ever more pervasive motif. The lament was "gradually pushed more and more into the background" and finally excluded altogether from the prayer of repentance.[17] However, lament could not be suppressed, and so it broke forth anew, now separated from penitential prayers (e.g., Baruch 4–5; 1 Macc 2:6, 8–13; 3:50–54). Westermann considers the "free-standing" lament alongside penitential prayers in this late period as the "most surprising phenomenon" in the history of the lament.[18]

Balentine regards Westermann's survey of the historical development of lament as very important since Westermann provided "the base line for the assessment of penitential prayers" for the following fifty years.[19] Westermann attributes the silencing of lament and the emphasis on admission of guilt to the trauma of exile: the experience was so devastating that the exilic community had no alternative but to take its cue from the Deuteronomistic theologians. As a result, the earlier polarity between praise and lament disappeared. Westermann's proposal that penitential prayers originated from laments is supported by the majority of scholars.[20] However, the relationship between communal lament and penitential prayers seems more complex, since, as Westermann himself points out, lament was never totally suppressed but survived alongside penitential prayers in the postexilic era. To their relationship we turn next.

---

14. Ibid., 201.

15. Ibid.

16. Westermann (ibid., 206) points out that the penitential prayers occur among extracanonical prayers as well, e.g., 1 Esdras (3 Ezra) 8:73–90, the Prayer of Manasseh, *Psalms of Solomon* 9, and Bar 1:15—13:8.

17. Ibid., 206–7.

18. Ibid.

19. Balentine, "'I was Ready to Be Sought Out,'" 4.

20. Balentine, *Prayer in the Hebrew Bible*, 117.

Forgotten and Forsaken by God (Lam 5:19-20)

Relationship between Communal Laments and Penitential Prayers

M. J. Boda builds on Westermann's research and traces the shift from lament to penitential prayer.[21] Admission of the sins of the community, both past and present (as found in Ezra 9:6-7, 10, 13-15; Neh 1:6-8; 9:33-35, 37; Dan 9:5-11, 13-16, 18), is essential to penitential prayers. Boda argues that penitential prayers emerged as a liturgical convention in the Jewish community in the Persian period, in the wake of the Deuteronomistic and Priestly traditions. Boda further notes that admission of guilt occurs in a certain number of communal laments, e.g., the book of Lamentations and Jer 14:1—15:9, which can be viewed as proto-penitential prayers. Boda, like Westermann, sees penitential prayer as originating from the lament.

Dalit Rom-Shiloni accepts Boda's definition of penitential prayer as "a type of prayer which reveals close affinities with Priestly-Ezekielian emphases drawing on a base of Dtr orthodoxy."[22] However, she disagrees with Westermann, Balentine, Boda and other scholars who argue that penitential prayers originated from communal laments. She proposes, instead, that "penitential prayers do not simply continue communal laments diachronically, with certain generic-formal transformations. Rather, during the sixth century BCE penitential prayers polemicize *against* communal laments, suggesting 'orthodox' alternatives to them."[23] According to Rom-Shiloni, laments and penitential prayers do share some common elements: complaint, petition and confession of sins; however, the transformative tactic of silencing the lament and accentuating confession of sin and guilt is not simply a shift of emphasis, but rather an "intentional theological innovation in the penitential prayers" designed to affirm the orthodoxical prophetic/historiographic/priestly perspectives by differentiating itself from the non-orthodoxical views of the laments.[24]

Rom-Shiloni restricted her study to the recurrent issue of the God-people relationship in both penitential prayers and communal laments.[25] In the communal laments, the emphasis is on God's obligation to provide military aid and salvation from enemies; the people often loudly declare their innocence (Pss 44:18-23; 80:19); their destruction is perceived as initiated by human enemies or as a direct act of God; the people urge God to return

---

21. Boda, *Praying the Tradition*, 43-73; Boda, "Priceless Gain of Penitence," 51-75.

22. Boda, *Praying the Tradition*, 197; Rom-Shiloni, "Socio-Ideological Setting or Settings for Penitential Prayers?," 51.

23. Rom-Shiloni, "Socio-Ideological Setting, or Settings for Penitential Prayers?" 52-53 (italics original).

24. Ibid., 55.

25. For a more detailed discussion, see ibid., 57-64.

and bring the people back; and God is the one who rejects, forgets, and abandons. In contrast, in the penitential prayers, God establishes the covenant, and the people are obligated by its demands; the sinful people is set in contrast to the faithful and mighty God; it is always the people who violate the covenant with disastrous results; God is often described as mighty and righteous and as justified in his judgments; God's continued commitment to the covenant is affirmed such that there is no expectation of divine renewal of the covenant; and God is motivated to act for God's own sake.[26]

The relationship between communal laments and penitential prayers is complex. Rom-Shiloni affirms that penitential prayers cannot be taken simply as "a linear evolution of communal laments"; they are, rather, a "contemporaneous polemical response to communal laments."[27] She describes the relationship of the two genres as one of explicit and implicit rejection on the one hand and implicit acceptance on the other. Penitential prayers explicitly reject the claim that God abandoned God's people as often stated in communal laments; they reject implicitly the concept of God who is sometimes perceived as an enemy in communal laments. Penitential prayers distance themselves from communal laments and intentionally set out to justify God and accept his judgment, even as they subtly distinguish the present generation from the sinfulness of the past (see e.g., Nehemiah 9), thus implicitly affirming communal laments.[28]

I am inclined to agree with Rom-Shiloni that penitential prayers are not simply linear developments of communal laments with heightened emphasis on admission of sin and guilt. Penitential prayers represent an intentional distancing from communal laments in an effort to affirm orthodox Deuteronomistic concepts of God and the people. This supposition explains the fact that even as penitential prayers flourished in the post-exilic period, communal laments receded into the background, but never totally disappeared. Communal laments remained a persistent marginal voice alongside penitential prayers.[29]

---

26. Balentine, *Prayer in the Hebrew Bible*, 108.

27. Rom-Shiloni, "Socio-Ideological Setting or Settings for Penitential Prayers?" 64.

28. In Nehemiah 9, there are explicit confessions of sin on behalf of previous generations—"they" in vv. 16–18, 26, 28–31; the first-person plural "we" appears only in vv. 33–34 and in the closing description of distress in vv. 36–37. See more detailed discussion in Rom-Shiloni, "Socio-Ideological Setting or Settings for Penitential Prayers?," 66.

29. Walter Brueggemann ("A Shape for Old Testament Theology, I," 28–46; and Brueggemann, "A Shape for Old Testament Theology, II," 395–415) argues that although the mainstream of Old Testament theology functions to legitimate structure, the embrace of pain remains a crucial minority voice.

Forgotten and Forsaken by God (Lam 5:19-20)

In the course of the transition from communal laments to penitential prayers, a number of prayers maintain the tension between laments and confession. We will examine three of these prayers in the following part.

FUNCTION OF ADMISSION OF GUILT IN SELECTED OT LAMENTS

Generally speaking, there is a characteristic "vagueness" to the admission of sin in the Hebrew communal lament genre;[30] the nature of the sin usually is not specified. S. Mowinckel affirms that the psalmists usually speak in general terms of sin in order that their psalms might be applied on various occasions.[31] K. L. T. Nguyen holds that confession of sin usually occurs after the destruction of Jerusalem in the Deuteronomistic tradition, but its importance is still a matter of dispute.[32]

I will now focus on the three passages (Isa 63:7—64:11; Jer 14:1—15:9; and Psalm 79) within communal laments where there is a clear element of admission of guilt and which hold in tension lament and confession of sin, as happens in the book of Lamentations.

Isa 63:7—64:11: The Anger and Absence of Yhwh and the Straying of Israel

It is a scholarly consensus that the passage Isa 63:7—64:11 forms a literary unit.[33] J. Blenkinsopp further points out that the sequence of Isa 63:7—64:11 reads smoothly, it is thus unnecessary and undesirable to read the passage as a compilation of different strata, originating with Isa 63:7-16 and subsequently expanded to the final form we now have.[34]

30. Nguyen, "Lady Zion and the Man," 96-97.
31. Mowinckel, *The Psalms in Israel's Worship*, 2, 14.
32. Nguyen ("Lady Zion and the Man," 94-107) studies confession of sin in the Psalter; in her analysis, sin occurs in three "we" communal laments (Pss 79:8-9; 85:3; 90:8). If one looks closely, however, confession of sin actually occurs only in Ps 79:9, "Deliver us, and forgive our sins, for your name's sake"; in the other two psalms, sin is simply mentioned: Ps 85:3 reads "You forgive the iniquity of your people and covered all their sins"; Ps 90:8 has "you have set our iniquities before you, our secret sins in the light of your countenance."
33. Clifford, "Narrative and Lament," in *To Touch the Text: Biblical and Related Studies in Honor of Joseph A. Fitzmyer*, 93.
34. Joseph Blenkinsopp, *Isaiah 56-66*, 257. Compare Pauritsch (*Die neue Gemeind*, 144-71), who distinguishes four literary strata in Isa 63:7—64:11, i.e. (1) 63:11b-14a, 15-19a; (2) 64:4b-8; (3) 63:19b-64:4a, 9-11; and (4) 63:7-11a, 14b.

Scholars are also "virtually unanimous" in linking Isa 63:7—64:11 to the communal lament psalms (e.g., Psalms 44, 60, 74, 79, 80, 83, 85, 89, 90, 94).[35] Isa 63:7—64:11 indeed demonstrates a number of similarities with communal lament psalms: it contains a historical recital (Isa 63:7-14), a lament followed by an appeal (63:15—64:4a), a final appeal (64:4b-6) and a second lament (64:9-10).[36] Blenkinsopp also notes, however, several significant differences between Isa 63:7—64:11 and psalmic communal laments: first, it combines the historical recital of Yhwh's great deals with mention of Israel's rebellion; second, the deplorable situation in which the community finds itself is acknowledged as the result of its infidelity, but a tension is maintained in this regard since the community "goes some way toward attributing its sinful condition to the anger and indifference of the deity";[37] third, Isa 63:7—64:11 shares with the book of Lamentations a most significant peculiarity, i.e. the absence of a statement of confidence of being heard with which some of the communal lament psalms conclude (e.g., Pss 69:30-36; 79:13). No answer or response from God occurs in Isa 63:7—64:11, which thus—like Lamentations—does not end with the certainty of a hearing.[38]

The date of Isa 63:7—64:11 is difficult to determine. It most probably refers to the Babylonian invasion in 589-86 B.C.E. since there are references to foreign occupation, the destruction of Jerusalem, other Judean cities and the temple. The question remains, however, as to whether it stems from the early post-destruction period (between 586 and 539 B.C.E.) or much later.[39] Most scholars opt for the early post-destruction period and this is the stance I adopt as well.[40]

Structure of Isa 63:7—64:11

Isa 63:7—64:11 can be divided into four parts: (1) a historical recital (63:7-14); (2) lament and petition coupled with admission of guilt (63:15-19a);

---

35. Bautch, *Developments in Genre*, 35. Elizabeth Achtemeier (*The Community and Message of Isaiah 56-66*, 132) compares Isa 63:7—64:11 with Psalms 44, 74 and 79; Irmtraud Fischer (*Wo ist Yahwe?*, 32-72; 205-26) divides Isa 63:7—64:11 into six parts, i.e. 63:7-10; 63:11-14; 63:15-19a; 63:19b—64:4a; 64:4b-8; and 64:9-11; she then compares Isa 63:7—64:11 with Psalms 77; 78; 74; 79; and 106.

36. Bautch, *Developments in Genre*, 35-37.

37. Ibid., 258.

38. See the study of mood change in biblical laments in chapter 4, above.

39. Williamson ("Isaiah 63:7—64:11," 48-58) dates Isa 63:7—64:11 to the late postexilic period based on its similarities with Psalm 106 and Nehemiah 9.

40. Hanson (*The Dawn of Apocalyptic*, 87) dates Isa 63:7—64:11 to the middle of the sixth century B.C.E.

Forgotten and Forsaken by God (Lam 5:19-20)

(3) second petition also coupled with admission of guilt (63:19b-64:6); and (4) final plea and question (64:7-11).⁴¹

Isa 63:7-14 is a historical recital of Yhwh's gracious deeds and praiseworthy acts in the past. A historical recital is a regular feature of communal laments (e.g., Pss 44:2-9; 74:12-17; 77:12-21; 80:9-12; 83:10-13; 89:2-38). Clifford points out that the lamenter often carefully tailors the historical recital to fit the aim of the lament, with the same founding event of Israel's election as Yhwh's people being narrated in slightly different ways in line with the peculiarities of the current crisis.⁴² Isa 63:7-14 narrates its own version of the election of Israel as Yhwh's people and Yhwh's guidance of them out of the land of Egypt. Clifford further states that Isa 63:7-14 differs from most communal laments due to its including a narration of the people's apostasy, Moses' intercession, and the return of Yhwh's presence in the form of the spirit (Isa 63:14) in its historical recital.⁴³

Isa 63:7-14 starts with "I will recount" (אזכיר); the root "to remember" (זכר) appears four times in Isa 63:7—64:11 (63:7, 11; 64:4, 8), the first three times in reference to the people's remembering, while the last usage implores Yhwh "not to remember iniquity forever." The vocabulary employed in this passage highlights the covenant relationship between Yhwh and the people: it is Yhwh's covenantal characteristics—רחם and חסד—that are recalled (Isa 63:7); Yhwh's affirmation "surely they are my people" (Isa 63:8) is recalled as well; Yhwh is called the people's "savior" (מושיע) and "redeemer" (גאל). The emphasis on Yhwh's unique personal relationship with the people is unmistakable here: it was not a messenger or angel, but Yhwh's own presence (פניו) that saved them; their deliverance was not based on any merit on the people's part, rather, it was Yhwh's "love and compassion" (אהבה and חמלה) that rescued them (Isa 63:9). However, the people's rebellion is already alluded to in the historical recital ("they rebelled," והמה מרו) with the result that Yhwh himself became their enemy and fought against them (Isa 63:10).

The second part of the historical recital (Isa 63:11-14) commences with the declaration "his people *remembered* the days of old" (Isa 63:11a) followed by a narration of the exodus from Egypt. Blenkinsopp notes that the first step in restoring the broken relationship between Yhwh and the people

---

41. For different divisions of Isa 63:7—64:11, see Blenkinsopp, *Isaiah 56–66*, 251-54; Fischer, *Wo ist Jahwe?*, 32-72.

42. Clifford, "Narrative and Lament," 94-95.

43. Ibid., 95. Blenkinsopp (*Isaiah 56–66*, 261) notes that the expression "his holy spirit" (רוח קדשי) appears only here in Isa 63:10-11 and in Ps 51:11 ("Do not cast me off from your presence, do not take away from me your holy spirit [רוח קדשך])" in the Old Testament. The association of the spirit with the presence of God indicates that the spirit has become the object of theological reflection.

Admission of Guilt in Lamentations and Related Old Testament Laments

is to "remember" the traditions of the Exodus and wilderness journey—"the most prominent motifs in Deuteronomy" when Yhwh was actively engaged in Israel's history.⁴⁴ The emphasis here is on Moses and his leadership role: Moses was himself saved from the Nile, endowed with the spirit of Yhwh and saved the Israelite people from the sea by the power of Yhwh (Isa 63:11–14a). At the end of the historical recital, the previous reference to Yhwh in the third person gives way to a second person address in Isa 63:14b: "thus *you* led *your* people, to make for *yourself* a glorious name"; Yhwh will now be addressed in the second person throughout the rest of the passage.

Isa 63:15 begins the lament proper; it starts with a petition for Yhwh to "look" and "see" (ראה and הבט), two key words in the book of Lamentations (Lam 1:11, 12; 2:20; 5:1) as well. The community appeals to Yhwh's zeal, might, yearning of heart and compassion.⁴⁵ Isa 63:16 is noteworthy in its designation of Yhwh as the people's "father" (*bis*; also Isa 64:7) even as they are said to be disowned by Abraham and Israel.⁴⁶ The people lack any human support; their only resort is to appeal to Yhwh their father, the protector and defender of the powerless (cf. Ps 68:6).⁴⁷ The metaphor of "father" refers to Yhwh as Israel's defender and creator; Niskanen points out that these two meanings are evoked particularly via the pairing of "father" with the metaphors of "redeemer" in Isa 63:16 and "potter" in 64:7.⁴⁸ The following "why" question suggests that the people's "straying" from the right path is somehow Yhwh's own doing: "Why, O Yhwh, do you make us stray from your ways and harden our hearts, so that we do not fear you?" (Isa 63:17a). The people are

---

44. Blenkinsopp, *Isaiah 56–66*, 261.

45. Kitamori (*Theology of the Pain of God*, 151–67) notes that the same Hebrew words המון מעיך "yearning of your heart" (literally "the troubling of your internal organs") of Isa 63:15 are used in Jer 31:20 "Is Ephraim my dear son? Is he the child I delight in? As often as I speak against him, I still remember him. Therefore I am deeply moved for him (המו מעי, literally 'my bowels are troubled'); I will surely have mercy on him" (NRSV). Kitamori holds that the Hebrew word המה—the verb form of the noun המון—refers to Yhwh's pain and love simultaneously.

46. Niskanen ("Yhwh as Father," 398) notes that Old Testament passages explicitly identifying Yhwh as "father" (Deut 32:6; Ps 68:5; Jer 3:4, 19; 31:9; Mal 1:6 and 2:10) are often expressed hypothetically or in the form of a question; e.g., "Is he not your father, who created you?" (Deut 32:6); "And I thought you would call me, My Father, and would not turn from me" (Jer 3:19b); "If then I am a father, where is then the honor due me?" (Mal 1:6). Isa 63:16 "for you are our father" (כי אתה אבינו), "you, O Yhwh, are our father" (אתה יהוה אבינו), and 64:7 "Now, O Yhwh, you are our father" (ועתה יהוה אבינו אתה) stand out by contrast for their clear and direct invocation of Yhwh as "father."

47. Whybray (*Isaiah 40–66*, 260) holds that the address to God as father is closely connected to the emotional appeals in the previous verse, Isa 63:15; see also Niskanen, "Yhwh as Father," 399.

48. Nisakanen, "Yhwh as Father" 400.

impotent to change their current desperate situation; it is only through Yhwh's returning to them that they can return to Yhwh.[49]

In the poem's third part, Isa 63:19b-64:6, the people ask Yhwh to "come down" as he came down on Mount Sinai, with fire, power and might. The appeal here goes a step further than Isa 63:15 where Yhwh is only asked to "look down and see." The people desperately longs for Yhwh's revelation of his incomparable power and strength (Isa 64:3). At the same time, the community once again intimates that their sinning and transgression are partly Yhwh's doing: "But you were angry, and we sinned; because you hid yourself we transgressed" (Isa 64:4b-7). The people have become worthless, unclean, and filthy; they fade like a leaf (Isa 64:5). Yhwh has hidden his face and the people are unable to call on Yhwh's name, so they are helplessly carried away by their iniquities (Isa 64:6-7).

In the poem's final part (Isa 64:7-11), Yhwh is addressed not only as "father," but as "potter" as well. The community appeals to Yhwh to abate his anger and to look upon (הבט; cf. Isa 63:15) his people (Isa 64:8), now that their holy cities are in ruins and have become a wilderness; Jerusalem remains desolate and the temple has been burned by fire so that there is no place to praise Yhwh. The lament ends with a poignant question "After all this, will you restrain yourself, O Yhwh? Will you keep silent and punish us so severely?" (Isa 64:11). There can be no new beginning for the community if Yhwh does not return to them first.

Admission of Guilt in Isa 63:7—64:11

Yhwh's saving act and the people's rebellion are already juxtaposed in the historical recital of Isa 63:7-10. There are two passages in Isa 63:7—64:11 that hold in tension lament and admission of guilt: Isa 63:15a-17b and Isa 64:4b-6b. I will now look at the meaning of the admission of guilt in these two passages.

J. Gärtner shows that Isa 63:15a-17b forms a concentric pattern:[50]

> 15a Look down from heaven and see, from your holy and glorious habitation.
>
> 15b Where is your zeal, your might, the yearning of your heart and your compassion which have been withheld from me.

---

49. The tension between lament and admission of guilt here will be analyzed in more detail below.
50. Gärtner, "'...Why do You Let Us Stray from Your Paths,'" 147.

Admission of Guilt in Lamentations and Related Old Testament Laments

16aα For you are our father;

16aβ although Abraham does not know us and Israel does not acknowledge us;

16b You, O Yhwh, are our father; our Redeemer from of old is your name.

17a Why, O Yhwh, do you make us stray from your ways and harden our heart, so that we do not fear you?

17b Return for the sake of your servants, the tribes of your heritage.

The center of this structure is v. 16, which itself evidences a concentric pattern. Yhwh is twice addressed as "our father" with the second person "You" in the first and final parts of the verse, while the middle part of the verse expresses the people's feeling of alienation from their tradition, and from their founding fathers Abraham and Israel. The lamenting exilic community is experiencing an identity crisis, but still clings to Yhwh, "our father" and "our redeemer from of old." Gärtner points out that the כי at the beginning of v. 16 indicates that the people no longer recognize themselves as the heirs of the Abraham tradition, this suggesting their alienation in guilt from the very beginning.⁵¹ On the one hand, the noteworthy question "Why, O Yhwh, do you make us stray from your paths and harden our heart, so that we do not fear you?" (v. 7) shows the community's entanglement in guilt to be so deep that they cannot change unless Yhwh returns to them first (v. 17b); on the other hand, the guilt in question is not identified specifically, Gärtner further states that the above question is formulated, not to "claim innocence but with the knowledge that the possibility for conversion lies in Yhwh's hands alone."⁵² Lament, coupled with admission of guilt, functions persuasively in appealing Yhwh to return, to do something. The community, though guilty, is still Yhwh's servant and inheritance.

Gärtner structures the second passage, Isa 64:4b-6b, which holds lament and admission of guilt in tension as follows:⁵³

4b But when you grew angry, we sinned; when you hid yourself we transgressed.⁵⁴

---

51. Ibid., 148.
52. Ibid.
53. Ibid., 149. My translation of the verses above is slightly different from Gärtner's.
54. MT reads הן־אתה קצפת ונחטא בהם עולם ונושע; the meaning of the first part of the phrase is clear "but you were angry, and we sinned," although KJV and NAS interpret it as saying that Yhwh's anger is due to Israel's sin, "Behold, you were angry, for we sinned";

149

Forgotten and Forsaken by God (Lam 5:19-20)

> 5aα We have all become like one who is unclean,
>
> 5aβ and all our righteous deeds are like a filthy cloth.
>
> 5bα We all fade like a leaf,
>
> 5bβ and our iniquities, like the wind, take us away.
>
> 6aα There is no one who calls on your name,
>
> 6aβ or attempts to take hold of you;
>
> 6b for you have hidden your face from us, and have delivered us into the hand of our iniquity.

It is striking that Isa 64:4b-6 implies that divine anger preceded human sin. This passage further states that the community is entangled in iniquity and sin. The anger, alienation and absence of Yhwh only made the situation worse. The people are carried away in their iniquity, have trodden a downward path and cannot stop themselves. The longing for Yhwh to return is tangible in this lament.

J. Goldenstein regards Isa 63:7—64:11 as formulated as a literary unit which should be understood in the wider context of the book of Isaiah.[55] Gärtner reads the passage in the context of the entire book of Isaiah as well, especially in light of the motif of hardness of the heart found in Isaiah 6 and the figure of the servant of Yhwh in second Isaiah. The destruction prophesied in Isaiah 6 has been fulfilled, the lamenting community in Isa 63:7—64:11 refers to itself as "servants of Yhwh" (63:17b), and combines lament with petition because they know that only Yhwh can reverse his judging presence as announced in Isaiah 6.[56] Gärtner further notes that Isa 63:7—64:11 summarizes the book's main themes and, as such, most probably served as a conclusion to an earlier form of the book. The silence of Yhwh in Isa 63:7—64:11 prompted the appending of the following two chapters, Isaiah 65-66, where Yhwh does reply and the community is divided into the servants of Yhwh and those who persist in iniquity.

---

the Hebrew, however, implies the opposite since the verb order is perfect קצפת followed by imperfect ונחטא, thus "when you grew angry, we sinned"; see Gärtner,"'...Why Do You Let Us Stray from Your Paths," 149. The Hebrew of the second part of the colon is obscure, literally "in them a long time, and we will be saved." Most commentators agree that it is corrupt. It is possible that the phrase should read בהעלמך ונפשע, "because you hid yourself and we transgressed"; see NRSV; Blenkinsopp, *Isaiah 56-66*, 253.

55. Johannes Goldenstein, *Das Gebet der Gottesknechte: Jesaja 63,7-64,11 im Jesajabuch* (WMANT 92; Neukirchen-Vluyn: Neukirchner Verlag, 2001) 248-51.

56. Gärtner, "'...Why Do You Let Us Stray from Your Paths,'" 162.

To sum up, the lamenting community in Isa 63:7—64:11 admits their rebellion even in the historical recital. They combine lament with admission of guilt in order to appeal more persuasively to Yhwh, acknowledging that they themselves are incapable of change since they are entangled in guilt, unable to free themselves from its spell. It is only in virtue of Yhwh's prior return to them that they can return to Yhwh.

Jer 14:1—15:9: Appeal to Yhwh to Act "for Your Name's Sake"

While quite a number of scholars take Jer 14:1—15:9 as a literary unit,[57] others consider Jer 14:1—15:4 as the unit.[58] I follow the first option since Jer 15:5-9 is Yhwh's complex response to the punishment and devastation of Jerusalem spoken of in 14:1—15:4, and it thus an integral part of the sequence that begins in 14:1.

Jer 14:1—15:9 is another passage that holds in tension communal lament with admission of guilt. Boda holds that this passage reflects the transition from communal lament to penitential prayer.[59] The date of Jer 14:1—15:9 is open to discussion. Boda views it as pre-exilic, a liturgical prayer uttered in a time of draught, while Beuken and van Grol consider it post-exilic.[60] I consider Jer 14:17-21 as exilic or post-exilic since the passage most probably refers to the horrible situation of the land after the siege of Jerusalem by the Babylonians.

Structure of Jer 14:1—15:9

Poetry and prose intertwine in Jer 14:1—15:9. The passage can be divided into two major parts: the first part, 14:1-16, refers to the situation of drought, while the second one, 14:17—15:9, alludes to devastation in war; although war is already mentioned in 14:11-16. I follow Beuken and van Grol who provide the most extensive analysis of the structure of Jer 14:1—15:9, though with some modifications of their structural headings:[61]

---

57. Beuken and van Grol, "Jeremiah 14:1—15:9," 297-342; Clements, *Jeremiah*, 89.

58. Bright, *Jeremiah*, 97-104; Castellino, "Observations," 406-7; Mark J. Boda, "From Complaint to Contrition: Peering through the Liturgical Window of Jer 14:1—15:4," *ZAW* 113 (2001) 186-97.

59. See Boda, "From Complaint to Contrition," 197.

60. Ibid., 188-89; Beuken and van Grol, "Jeremiah 14:1—15:9," 297.

61. Beuken and van Grol, "Jeremiah 14:1—15:9," 308 and 326. Clements (*Jeremiah*, 89) divides Jer 14:1—15:9 as follows: 14:1-10, description of drought followed by a prayer of lamentation and oracular response; 14:11-16, dialogue between God and his

Forgotten and Forsaken by God (Lam 5:19–20)

14:2–6:   Report concerning the distressful situation of drought
14:7–9:   Lament of Judah bewailing the devastation
14:10–16:   Dialogue: distress interpreted as judgment
14:17–18:   Lament: Jeremiah's reaction to the judgment
14:19–22:   Lament of Judah: Why us, O Yhwh?
15:1–4:   Not even Moses and Samuel could change Yhwh's mind
15:5–9:   Lament: Yhwh's complex reaction to the judgment

Jer 14:2–6: Report Concerning the Distressful Situation of Drought

The beginning of the unit in 14:2–6 describes a distressful situation of drought. Beuken and van Grol point out that v. 2 places lamenting Judah at the center of attention (Judah mourns and her gates languish) with both a downward movement (they sink down gloomily on the ground) and an upward one (the cry of Jerusalem goes up).[62] The cistern is dry and the water jars empty (14:3). The ground is cracked since there has been no rain; the animals find no herbage, and so have to forsake their young (14:4–6). Everyone's survival is severely threatened. Beuken and van Grol further state that Jer 14:2–6 "evokes the lamentableness of the situation without being in itself a lament."[63]

Jer 14:7–9: Lament of Judah Bewailing the Devastation

A lament by the people follows in 14:7–9. The people admit their iniquities and apostasies; even if, however, they themselves do not deserve salvation, they still ask Yhwh to act "for your name's sake" (14:7).[64] Yhwh is called the "hope of Israel, its savior in time of trouble" (14:8). The root of the Hebrew word for "hope," מקוה, also refers to a gathering of waters (Gen 1:10; Exod 7:19; Isa 22:11; Lev 11:36). However, confession of sin quickly turns into bitter complaint in 14:8b–9. The people complain about Yhwh's inactivity and inattentiveness to their plight. At the same time, they express their unaltered trust in Yhwh and their bond with him: "we are called by your name" (14:9). Stulman holds that Jer 14:7–9 is an ideal prayer since "even its disputatious

---

prophet; 14:17–22, prophetic lament followed by a communal confession; 15:1–4, final oracular response; 15:5–9, final lamentation over the people's downfall. For other divisions of the passage, see Stulman, *Jeremiah*, 139–48.

62. Beuken and van Grol, "Jeremiah 14:1—15:9," 310.

63. Ibid., 313.

64. The meaning and function of the admission of guilt in Jer 14:1—15:9 will be explored in more detail below.

language reflects the most robust and compelling aspects of Israel's spirituality." Accordingly, one might expect a positive answer from Yhwh, of the sort Yhwh does give elsewhere (1 Sam 1:17; 2 Chr 20:1-12, 15, 17).⁶⁵

Jer 14:10-16: Dialogue: Distress Interpreted As Judgment

On the contrary, however, Yhwh's response as reported by the prophet is negative: "Yhwh does not accept them, now he will remember their iniquity and punish their sins" (14:10b). The anticipated positive answer is not given here; rather, it is affirmed that Yhwh's justice must be maintained. The section's following part, Jer 14:11-16, is a dialogue between Yhwh and the prophet; here we meet "a defiant prophet and a defiant God."⁶⁶ Yhwh commands the prophet "not to pray for the welfare of the people" (14:11; also 15:1); Yhwh is not going to accept the people's fasting, crying, burnt or grain offerings, and they are destined to be consumed by the sword, famine and pestilence (14:12). The prophet has to confront the people with a painful and hurtful "no" from Yhwh.

However, Jeremiah disregards Yhwh's command not to intercede on behalf of the people and "refused to acquiesce and relinquish his role as advocate for Israel."⁶⁷ In so doing, he shifts the blame onto the false prophets who have been deceiving the people (14:13). Stulman points out that Jeremiah is thereby indicating that "*God is ultimately responsible* for Israel's plight."⁶⁸

Yhwh's response is emphatic (14:14):

I *did not* send them (לא שלחתים)

I *did not* command them (לא צויתים)

I *did not* speak to them (לא דברתי אליהם)

The deceiving false prophets will encounter the very fate that they prophesied would not happen; they will be consumed by sword and famine (14:15), as will the people. The destruction will be total, with no one left to bury the dead (14:16).

---

65. Stulman, *Jeremiah*, 140.
66. Ibid., 141.
67. Ibid.
68. Stulman (*Jeremiah*, 142) calls this a bold and intriguing stance on Jeremiah's part since God is rarely blamed in Jeremiah.

Forgotten and Forsaken by God (Lam 5:19-20)

Jer 14:17–18: Lament: Jeremiah's Reaction to the Judgment

Jeremiah's lament reflects God's own mourning over the destruction and suffering of "the virgin daughter—my people" (14:17). The vocabulary and imagery used in Jer 14:17–18 resembles those in the book of Lamentations: tears running down, the people of God as virgin daughter; famine inside and sword outside; prophets and priests as irresponsible leaders.

T. Fretheim points out that "Jeremiah's mourning is an embodiment of the anguish of God, showing forth to the people the genuine pain God feels over the hurt that his people are experiencing."[69] God and Jeremiah both suffer for the people; their voices are intertwined, any sharp distinction between the two risks misrepresenting the text.[70]

Jer 14:19–22: Lament of Judah: Why Us, O Yhwh?

Jer 14:19–22 is a lament of the people. Once again, lament is coupled with admission of sin and guilt: "We acknowledge our wickedness, O Yhwh, the iniquity of our ancestors, for we have sinned against you" (14:20). The community confesses the sins of their ancestors and their own, and once again asks Yhwh not to spurn the people: "for your name's sake, do not dishonor your glorious throne, remember and do not break your covenant with us" (14:21). Jer 14:22 affirms that Yhwh is the ultimate cause of all that has happened, "it is you who do all this," and so "we set our hope on you." Clements holds that according to the text, God has indeed maintained a firm and loving relationship with Israel and that his inflicting grievous wounds upon the people is the result of God's righteous wrath against their sins.[71] This passage explores one of the most central themes of all theology: the relationship between divine justice and divine mercy; it testifies to the "ambiguities of the experience of human tragedy and suffering."[72]

Jer 15:1–4: Not Even Moses and Samuel Could Change Yhwh's Mind

Yhwh's response to the preceding lament prayer is a definitive "no"; the tone in 15:1 is even "more emphatic"[73] than in 14:11 since now it is declared that not even the greatest intercessors in Israel's history, Moses and Samuel—let

---

69. Fretheim, *The Suffering of God*, 161.
70. Stulman, *Jeremiah*, 144.
71. Clements, *Jeremiah*, 93.
72. Ibid.
73. Stulman, *Jeremiah*, 145.

Admission of Guilt in Lamentations and Related Old Testament Laments

alone the prayers of Jeremiah and the people—could alter the people's fate (14:7–9; 19–22). Stulman points out that the mention of Moses here has a double meaning.[74] The verb used in Jer 15:1, "sent them out" (שׁלח) is the same one Moses uses in summoning Pharaoh to "let my people go" in Exodus (e.g., 5:1; 7:16 [*bis*]; etc.). Moreover, the Hiphil verb of the root יצא "let them go" in Jer 15:1 is used in Exodus and Deuteronomy to describe Israel's going out of the land of Egypt to the promised land (e.g., Exod 6:13, 26–27; 7:4–5; Deut 4:20, 37; 5:6; 6:12). Here in Jer 15:1, these same verbs allude to the opposite movement from the Promised Land to the land of bondage and exile, to the four-fold destruction "pestilence, sword, famine, and captivity" (15:2) and to the four destroyers, "the sword to kill, the dogs to drag away, the birds of the air and the wild animals of the earth to devour and to destroy" (15:3). The Israelite people will be a "horror" to all countries and King Manasseh is mentioned as the one whose wickedness is responsible for these horrors (15:4).

Jer 15:5–9: Lament: Yhwh's Complex Reaction to the Judgment

The segment's ending in 15:5–9 shows Yhwh's complex reaction to Jerusalem's fate. Yhwh speaks to Jerusalem directly in vv. 5–6, then to a third person in vv.7–9. Stulman puts matters well: "Every word of Yahweh's speech enunciates disaster, although expressions of mourning are so intermingled with rage that it is difficult to tell the two apart."[75] Yhwh is grieving with the people and the prophet, and such grief, which "sometimes erupts as anger, sometimes as bewilderment, and at other times as uncontrolled sadness" is the first step toward healing.[76] Jerusalem is mourning alone, no one is concerned about her fate, no one cares for her (15:5); she is pitiful in her devastation, but she is not innocent; she rejected Yhwh and went backwards; Yhwh's relenting is no longer possible since Jerusalem has broken the covenant (15:6). A number of images are employed in 15:6–9 to describe the state of Jerusalem: winnowing as an act of Yhwh's judgment (v. 7); the fate of bereavement that befell most mothers whose number "became more numerous than the sand of the sea" (v. 8a), with terror and anguish at the death of their children striking them suddenly, at noonday (v. 8bc); the mother of seven—an image of fulfilled womanhood (Ruth 4:15; 1 Sam 2:5)—swoons at the news of her sons dying in battle and will never recover from the shock the rest of her days. These mothers are portrayed as "the ultimate victims of

---

74. Ibid., 145–46.
75. Ibid., 147.
76. Ibid.

war, caught up in the solidarity of national suffering."[77] They can no longer rely on their husbands and sons who have been killed in battle.

Jer 14:1—15:9 contains a lament over drought in 14:1–16 and a lament over military defeat in 14:17—15:9. Beuken and van Grol note that the segment's beginning in Jer 14:2–6 and its ending in 15:5–9 are thematically connected: drought and war may be different catastrophes, but their effects are the same—the destruction of all life.[78]

Function of the Admission of Guilt in Jer 14:1—15:9

The main message of Jer 14:1—15:9 is clear: even though the community admits its iniquity and sins (14:7, 20), its doing so is inadequate and comes too late to alter their fate. Yhwh will remember their iniquity and punish their sins (14:10). Even though the community appeals to Yhwh to act "for your name's sake" (14:7, 21), Yhwh will show justice instead of mercy. Yhwh rejects their prayers, just as he would those of powerful intercessors; no one now is able to change the course of events. War and famine will destroy them; the people are destined for captivity and ruin.

Boda, who considers Jer 14:1—15:9 as pre-exilic, argues that Jeremiah was "cognizant of a confession of sin that reflected the agenda set out in Lev 26."[79] In fact, our passage does employ a number of themes and vocabulary found in Leviticus 26, e.g., Yhwh's heart loathing Zion (Jer 14:19; Lev 26:11, 30, 44); the combination of מאס, "to reject" and געל, "to abhor" (Jer 14:19; Lev 26:15, 43, 44). Boda further argues that even though Yhwh rejects (Jer 15:1–4) the form of prayer found in 14:19–22, which combines lament with penitential confession, due to Yhwh's impending judgment, the passage Jer 14:1—15:4 reflects the transition from communal laments to penitential prayers, with the latter developing into a new form of prayer that involves a silencing of complaint.[80]

I agree with Boda that Jer 14:1—15:9 reflects a transitional type of prayer from communal lament to penitential prayer, but I also accept Rom-Shiloni's argument that penitential prayers developed alongside communal laments in order to offer a more "orthodox" view of suffering. The tension between lament and admission of guilt is clear in Jer 14:1—15:9: the lamenting community cannot claim innocence since God's message of upcoming punishment is strong and clear. The community accordingly confesses its

---

77. Allen, *Jeremiah*, 177.
78. Beuken and van Grol, "Jer 14:1—15:9," 323–25.
79. Boda, "From Complaint to Contrition," 196.
80. Ibid., 196–97.

Admission of Guilt in Lamentations and Related Old Testament Laments

sins, trying to persuade God to act not for the sake of the people, but for the sake of God's name. For the suffering community, the primary goal is to move God to act in their favor, rather than trying to find reasons for their suffering. The community holds onto God who is the initiator of all things; the God who punishes is also the God who is deeply affected by the people's suffering, a God who mourns with them (Jer 14:17–18; 15:5–9). The people take responsibility for causing their current plight, but their doing so does not leave God uninvolved in their suffering. If we take Jer 14:1—15:9 as an exilic or postexilic text, it envisages, now after the prophesied punishment has already occurred, a new future with renewed relationship with Yhwh.

Psalm 79 "Deliver Us and Forgive Our Sins for Your Name's Sake"

Psalm 79 is a communal lament that evidences a number of distinctive features: first, it is unusual that petition occupies the major part of such a psalm (vv. 5–12); not only that, as J. Goldingay points out, the petition in Ps 79:5–12 works out its agenda three times (vv. 5–7, 8–10a, 10b–12), with the petitioner each time asking God to punish the nations or deliver the people.[81] Second, the psalmist of Psalm 79 is someone "soaked in the psalms and/or the traditions that underlie psalmody" (e.g., Psalms 44; 74; 89; Jeremiah and Joel).[82] Third, Psalm 79 expresses particularly strong feelings of loss, anger, grief, shame, anguish and deeply felt yearning, with "guileless simplicity."[83] Finally, Psalm 79 features a sequence of laments that follow the "they, we, you" pattern, as J. L. Mays points out.[84] This pattern highlights the psalm's major actors—the nations, the people, God—and keeps the focus on the painful problem of their three-sided relationship.

Psalm 79, like the book of Lamentations, is not tied to a specific historical context. Hoppe points out that proposed dates for Psalm 79 range "from the preexilic to the Maccabean periods with no consensus developing around the question."[85] In any case, the situation presupposed by the psalm is the catastrophe of 587 BCE with invasion of the land, defilement of the temple and destruction of Jerusalem.[86] Psalm 79, like Lamentations

---

81. Goldingay, *Psalms* 2:518.

82. Ibid., 519; Hoppe ("Vengeance and Forgiveness," 2–7) lists a significant number of vocabulary items Psalm 79 shares with other parts of the Hebrew Bible.

83. Brueggemann, *Message of the Psalms*, 71.

84. Mays, *Psalms*, 260.

85. Hoppe, "Vengeance and Forgiveness," 8.

86. Tate (*Psalms 51–100*, 299) holds that the time after the fall of Jerusalem in 587 BCE is the most likely original setting for Psalm 79.

Forgotten and Forsaken by God (Lam 5:19-20)

and Isa 63:7—64:11, reflects the community's experiences of living out the consequences of destruction in the land. Goldingay notes that some Jewish communities recite Psalm 79 annually on the Ninth of Av, while others use Psalm 137 or the book of Lamentations on that occasion.[87]

Structure of Psalm 79

The structure of Psalm 79 is rather simple:

> vv. 1-4 Description of trouble
> vv. 5-12 Petitions
> > vv. 5-7 Petition I: How Long, O Yhwh?
> > vv. 8-10 Petition II: Help us for the sake of your name
> > vv. 11-12 Petition III: Rescue prisoners and punish scoffers of Yhwh
> v. 13 Conclusion

Ps 79:1-4 Description of Trouble

Psalm 79 starts with an invocation that is the shortest one possible: אלהים, "O God." E. Gerstenberger notes that this terseness of the invocation may signal a sense of urgency.[88] It is hard for the people to believe that the גוים, "nations," who should not be in the land, have come into Yhwh's inheritance, defiled his holy temple and laid the enduring city Jerusalem in ruins (cf. Ps 74:4; Isa 52:1; Lam 1:10b; Joel 3:17). Such anomalies are shocking. The nations have left behind a heart-wrenching scene in the land: the bodies of God's servants and faithful lie exposed in the open, without proper burial; there has been no "closure" achieved for the dead and for those who mourn them (79:2).[89] The psalm moves from "they" (vv. 1-2) to "we" (v. 3): the shame of God's people is beyond expression: they have become a taunt to their neighbors and are being mocked and derided by all around them. Such shame deepens their pain; they suffer even after the fighting is over.

---

87. Goldingay, *Psalms* 2: 520; see also Tate, *Psalms 51-100*, 299.
88. Gerstenberger, *Psalms Part 2 and Lamentations*, 100; see also Goldingay, *Psalms* 2:520.
89. See ibid., 521.

Admission of Guilt in Lamentations and Related Old Testament Laments

Ps 79:5–12 Petitions

The question of "how long?" in Ps 79:5 serves as a transition to petition. The anger and wrath of Yhwh are consuming Yhwh's people. The first petition of the people (vv. 6–7) is to ask Yhwh to pour out his anger on the nations who do not know Yhwh. Goldingay points out that the psalm's overall argument is not that the nations' punishment should fit their crime, but rather that these nations did not acknowledge or call on Yhwh when they had the opportunity to do so (cf. Isaiah 36–37).[90] They did not just mock Judah—they mocked Yhwh as well.

The second petition (vv. 8–10) again focuses on God's honor and the people's suffering, but now with an added element, i.e. confessing the iniquities of their ancestors and their own sins. In this connection, Mays notes that Psalm 79 is "the only corporate prayer for help that includes a confession of sin."[91] In v. 8, the community acknowledges the iniquities of previous generations (cf. Lam 5:7), the underlining message being that Yhwh's anger should not burn forever, there has been enough punishment and Yhwh should now show compassion. In v. 9 the community pleads with God to forgive their sins as a community, twice asking that this be done "for the sake of Yhwh's name." It is not only that the people's future is at stake, more importantly, God's reputation is threatened by the destruction of God's people, land and temple. Mays considers 79:10a "Why should the nations say, 'where is their God?'" as the climax of the psalm.[92] It is only via the assertion of Yhwh's power that the blood of Yhwh's servants will be avenged.

The final petition (vv. 11–12) focuses on "the groans of the prisoners" in v. 11. Although not exiles, but people living in Jerusalem, the speakers are captives in their own land under foreign rulers (cf. Lam 3:34).[93] They ask sevenfold revenge upon their neighbors in v. 12. This prayer reflects a twofold concern on the part of the people: forgiveness for themselves (v. 9) and a sevenfold revenge on their enemies (v. 12). Brueggemann points out that the speakers are honest and faithful enough to submit their yearning for revenge to Yhwh; meanwhile, they are inconsistent and divided since the center of their lives—the temple is gone; their desire is salvation for

---

90. Ibid., 524.
91. Mays, *Psalms*, 261; he points out (ibid., 25) that while clear examples of corporate prayers are few in number, e.g., Psalms 44, 74, 79, 80, 83, they hold immense theological importance. Among these psalms, the destruction of Jerusalem and its temple seems to be the occasion for Psalms 74 and 79.
92. Ibid.
93. For a more detailed explanation of this point, see Goldingay, *Psalms* 2:528.

Forgotten and Forsaken by God (Lam 5:19–20)

themselves and doom for their persecutors.[94] Goldingay affirms that "it is a remarkable act of restraint and trust in God" when victims of oppression by superpowers respond by urging God to do something rather than by acting in violence themselves.[95]

Ps 79:13 Conclusion

Psalm 79 concludes with anticipated thanksgiving for the moment when Yhwh hears the people's prayers. The community affirms to the very end that "we are your people, the flock of your pasture" (cf. Ps 100:3). Once restored by Yhwh, the community will give thanks and praise to Yhwh from generation to generation.

Function of Admission of Guilt in Psalm 79

The primary concern of Psalm 79 is the honor of Yhwh among the nations. The community recognizes the iniquities of their ancestors and urges God to end their suffering and show his compassion. The community also realizes that Yhwh is the one who forgives sins (כפר חטאתינו v. 9). The relationship between Yhwh and the people is not based on the people's faithfulness, prayers or offerings; rather, it is only through reliance on Yhwh that the people can move on. Mays holds that Psalm 79 does not stay with sin and punishment as the key to of Israel's current desolation; rather, it makes clear that the honor of God's name in the world is more important than even the sin and punishment of his people.[96]

The admission of guilt in Psalm 79 shows that the community recognizes that their suffering is God's righteous judgment on sin. However, the community also makes clear that their relationship with Yhwh is far more than a question of sin and punishment. The community is more concerned with Yhwh's name and honor and holds onto its status as Yhwh's chosen people, even when the going is rough and Yhwh seems absent.

The communities lamenting in Isa 63:7—64:11; Jer 14:1—15:9; and Psalm 79 admit their guilt for the purpose of persuading God to act on their behalf. They admit that they are entangled in guilt so a renewed relationship with Yhwh and a new future have to start with Yhwh. Since Lamentations was written in a similar context and reflects the tension between lament

---

94. Brueggemann, *Message of the Psalms*, 72–73.
95. Goldingay, *Psalms* 2:529–30.
96. Mays, *Psalms*, 261–62.

Admission of Guilt in Lamentations and Related Old Testament Laments

and admission of guilt as well, we now turn to the admission of guilt in Lamentations.

ADMISSION OF GUILT IN LAMENTATIONS

Occurrences of Admission of Guilt in Lamentations

Admission of guilt is one discernible feature in the book of Lamentations. E. Boase points out sixteen direct references to sin in Lamentations (1:5, 8, 9, 14, 18, 20, 22; 2:14; 3:39, 42, 64; 4:6, 13, 22; 5:7, 16); among these sixteen occurrences, three refer to the sins of the enemies of Jerusalem (1:22; 3:64; 4:22), while the rest allude to sins of Jerusalem.[97] We can make an immediate observation that admission of guilt figures most noticeably in Lamentations 1 since it occurs seven times in the chapter (1:5, 8, 9, 14, 18, and 20), and least in Lamentations 2 where it appears only once (2:14), as compared to three times in chapters 3 and 4 (3:39, 42; 64; 4:6, 13, 22) and twice in chapter 5 (5:7, 16). Boase further notes that on the whole the sin references in Lamentations lack specificity.[98]

The Hebrew words used to designate sin in Lamentations are: (1) פשע, "transgression" (1:5, 14, 22; 3:42); (2) חטא, "sin" (1:8 [*bis*]; 3:39 [*bis*]; 5:7, 16); (3) מרה, "rebellion" (1:18, 20 [*bis*]; 3:42); (4) עון, "iniquity" (2:14; 4:6, 13, 22; 5:7); and טמאה, "uncleanness" (1:9). I will analyze these occurrences chapter by chapter.

Lamentations 1 (vv. 5, 8, 9, 14, 18, 20, 22)

In Lamentations 1, both the narrator and personified Zion make references to sin and Zion's current miserable state. The narrator makes clear that Zion's suffering is God's just punishment for her sins in Lam 1:5: "Yhwh has made her suffer, upon the multitude of her transgressions (רב־פשעיה)." Here, a causal link is made between Zion's suffering and the multitude of her transgressions, but the nature of those transgressions is left unspecified. The narrator also links Jerusalem's sin with her uncleanness and shame: "Jerusalem sinned grievously (חטא חטאה), so she has become filthy. All who honored her despise her, for they saw her pudenda. Even she herself groans and turns away" (1:8); "Her *uncleanness* (טמאתה) was on her skirts, she gave no thought

---

97. See Boase, *The Fulfillment of Doom?*, 141.
98. Ibid., 173.

to her future" (1:9a). Again, although the "uncleanness" may refer to Zion's unfaithful conduct toward Yhwh, the nature of Zion's sins is not spelled out.

Zion herself admits that her transgressions weigh heavily on her: "Tied on is the yoke of my transgressions (עֹל פְּשָׁעַי), by his hand they are fastened together. They weigh on my neck, sapping my strength" (1:14). In Lam 1:18 and 20, Zion accepts the claim that Yhwh is in the right and she is in the wrong, but she is less concerned with any rationale for her fate, than with the suffering of her children: "Yhwh is in the right, for I have rebelled against his word (פִּיהוּ מָרִיתִי). Listen now, all peoples, and see my pain. My young women and men have gone into captivity" (1:18). In 1:20, Zion says: "See, O Yhwh, for I am in distress; my stomach churns. My heart is turned within me, for I have been very rebellious (מָרוֹ מָרִיתִי). Outdoors, the sword bereaves; indoors, death." The thought that Zion's own behavior has led to the suffering of her children only makes Zion's suffering worse. In Lamentations 1, Zion does not contest the connection between her sin and her suffering as God's punishment; however, her focus on the reality and extent of her suffering makes the reader ponder whether the suffering of Zion's little ones is indeed God's just punishment.

The final reference to sin in Lamentations 1 is in the context of the future fate of the enemy. God should deal with Zion's enemies according to the same principle that God has followed with Zion: "deal with them as you have dealt with me because of all my transgression" (1:22).

Lamentations 2 (v. 14)

References to sin are virtually absent in Lamentations 2, in contrast to chapter 1. In Lamentations 2, the narrator tries to find a reason for Zion's suffering. Here, the narrator is no longer blaming Zion for her misbehavior, but rather her false prophets who have been deceiving her: "Your prophets have seen for you false and deceptive visions. They did not reveal your iniquity (עֲוֹנֵךְ) so as to change your fortunes. They showed you false oracles and deceptions" (2:14). Boase points out two things regarding this statement: it is "non-confessional" and is concerned with false prophecy—a topic also highlighted in Jeremiah (Jer 2:8; 5:12–13, 30–31; 6:13–15; 8:10b–12; 14:13–16; 23:9–40; 28–29) and Ezekiel (13:1—14:11). Lam 2:14 thus voices one possible explanation for the fall of Jerusalem, i.e. the failure of its prophets to lead the people to repentance.[99]

---

99. Ibid., 182–83.

Admission of Guilt in Lamentations and Related Old Testament Laments

Lamentations 3 (vv. 39, 42, 64)

In Lamentations 3, the suffering man tries to apply traditional wisdom to ease the pain of the sufferer, urging her to find hope in a compassionate, loving and good God, and be patient and wait quietly (3:24–33). He asks in v. 39: "What living human will complain, a man of his sin/punishment?" The implication here is that Zion's punishment fits her crime. It is better for a sinful person to endure suffering as punishment and submit to the will of God in hope of a better future. However, in the context of Zion's vast suffering, this is easier said than done; the heart does not follow the will and refuses to be persuaded by a simple calculus of sin and punishment. "We have transgressed and rebelled, you have not forgiven" (Lam 3:42); the community declares. Even if there is a direct link between sin and suffering, we have done our part—we have suffered for our sins, but "you"—God, have not done yours. The emphasis here in on the inaccessibility of Yhwh, with Boase noting a link between Lam 3:42 and Jer 14:1—15:9. These passages express the post-exilic community's view that Yhwh's inaccessibility is increasing the community's suffering and negatively affecting their relationship with each other.[100]

Lamentations 4 (vv. 6, 13, 22)

In Lam 4:6, the reference to sin actually challenges the purported consequences of sin—judgment: "greater is the chastisement (עָוֹן) of the daughter of my people than the punishment (מחטאת) of Sodom; the overturning was in a moment, though no hands were raised against her." The narrator avers once again that the prophets and priests have not done what they were supposed to do, but rather sinned against the innocent and brought the nation to ruin: "it was for the sins (מחטאת) of her prophets and the iniquities (עונות) of her priests, who shed the blood of the righteous in the midst of her" (4:13; cf. 2:14).

Lamentations 5 (vv. 7, 16)

The two references to sin in Lamentations 5 stand in tension with each other. In v. 7, the community says of the sins of previous generations: "our ancestors sinned (חטאו), they are no more; we bear their punishment/guilt (עונתיהם)," while in v. 16, the sins of present generation are itself acknowledged: "The crown has fallen from our head; woe to us, for we have sinned!"

---

100. Ibid., 194.

Forgotten and Forsaken by God (Lam 5:19–20)

The issue of previous generations' guilt being passed on from one generation to the next also appears in exilic prophetic literature (Ezekiel 18; 33:10–20; Jer 31:27–30). Boase holds that it remained an issue for the post-exilic community as well.[101] Regarding the interpretation of Lam 5:7, two stances are taken by scholars: some understand its term עונתיהם more in the sense of "guilt" and read v. 7 in conjunction with v. 16: the community is thus confessing the sins of previous and current generations. Lam 5:7 and 16 hold onto traditional retribution theology according to this interpretation.[102] An alternative way of reading v. 7 is to understand עונתיהם more in the sense of "punishment," such that v. 7 would assert the innocence of the present generation that has been punished unjustly and excessively. Lam 5:7 would thus stand in dialogic tension with v. 16, a tension which Dobbs-Allsopp insists should not be resolved.[103]

Function of Admission of Guilt in Lamentations

The mention of guilt in Lamentations, especially in chapter 1, establishes a certain link between the community's suffering and their sinful behavior. The lamenting community in Lamentations does not totally reject the doctrine of retribution, but they do not accept it wholeheartedly either. The vast suffering they have been experiencing rules out any simple explanation for their condition, as well as any answer to the hard questions they have been posing to Yhwh.

A number of things can be said about the admission of guilt in Lamentations: First, the sin mentioned in Lamentations is never specified in the book. Comparing Lamentations with prophetic literature, Boase concludes that Lamentations shatters the correspondence between sin and punishment that is prevalent in the prophetic literature.[104]

Second, the relatively few, scattered, and nonspecific admissions of guilt in Lamentations stand in contrast to the expansive, detailed, and heart-wrenching descriptions of Zion's suffering. The purpose of the book is primarily to express pain through different voices and views, not to admit sin and guilt.

Third, admission of sin in Lamentations is one attempt to explain what had happened to Jerusalem and Judah. Such admission needs to be understood in relation to the much more expansive description of suffering and

---

101. Ibid., 196.
102. Westermann, *Lamentations*, 212.
103. Dobbs-Allsopp, *Lamentations*, 146.
104. Boase, *The Fulfillment of Doom?* 201.

depiction of Zion as a victim who gains the sympathy of the narrator and readers as well.

CONCLUSION

Admission of guilt appears at a late stage of communal laments. It attempts to give an explanation of the community's suffering; however, the expression of pain in these communal laments is often far more extended and stronger than any proposed rationale for its suffering.

The book of Lamentations, together with Isa 63:7—64:11, Jer 14:1—15:9, and Psalm 79 analyzed above, represents a transition from communal lament to penitential prayers. The writers of Lamentations must have been aware of the tendency to explain suffering as the punishment for sin, but their experience and understanding of suffering are far more complex. They surmise that there might be a connection between suffering and sin, and they admit their guilt; however, the reality of prolonged, unbearable suffering undermines simple answers and premature conclusions. Admission of guilt is one voice in Lamentations and it has to be understood in the context of the articulation of pain that dominates the book.

When penitential prayers finally gained the upper hand in the Persian period, communal laments became a minor voice, but this minor voice is never totally suppressed; it persists.

A suffering community, like the one in Lamentations, often laments, cries out, and asks questions of "why" the suffering has been so unbearably long and "how" the community is to move on to survive. Questions are uttered, usually with no adequate answers given. My next chapter will explore the significance of Lamentations, a polyphonic text, for suffering individuals and communities.

6

Significance of Lamentations for Suffering Individuals and Communities

INTRODUCTION

THE SUFFERING COMMUNITY IN Lamentations remains in lament throughout the book; the lament never turns into full-pledged praise and the community stays truthful to its life experiences. On the one hand, the community tackles pain in all its dimensions through different voices. Lamentations embraces a "tragic vision" within which its imagery and ideas are situated.[1] On the other hand, the community—the tragic hero in Lamentations according to F. W. Dobbs-Allsopp—refuses to accept the tragic event simply as is.[2] Even though Yhwh remains absent throughout the book and Zion is faced with divine abandonment from the beginning to the very end, the community tries all means imaginable to engage Yhwh, to bring Yhwh back into dialogue with the community. The focus of Lamentations is mainly on Yhwh.

1. Dobbs-Allsopp ("Tragedy, Tradition, and Theology," 30) points out that most recent discussions about tragedy in the Hebrew Bible fail to mention the book of Lamentations, mainly because it is poetry that lacks a typical tragic plot; however, Dobbs-Allsopp makes a compelling case that Lamentations shows the characteristics of a genuine tragic work. Exum (*Tragedy and Biblical Narrative,* 8) holds that "the Bible contains a profoundly tragic dimension, and we deny that dimension at the cost of our honesty about reality, and at the risk of losing a precious affirmation of the indomitable human spirit."

2. Dobbs-Allsopp, "Tragedy, Tradition, and Theology," 42–43.

Significance of Lamentations for Suffering Individuals and Communities

The book of Lamentations is "the scriptural centerpiece"³ for *Tisha b'Av* (Ninth of Av) in the Jewish liturgical calendar, the day on which the Jewish people commemorates not only the destruction of the first temple, but a series of catastrophes that occurred before and after the destruction in 586 BCE, including God's decree that the people may not enter the Promised Land at the end of the wilderness wandering (Num 14: 20–38), as well as the expulsion of the Jews from England and Spain that happened in the medieval and modern periods.⁴ The book of Lamentations thus becomes the prototypical text that embraces and articulates pain and suffering, not only during the aftermath of the destruction of the first temple, but throughout Jewish history as well. In this way, it functions as a vehicle for suffering communities to deal with pain.

This chapter will first analyze ways the suffering community deals with pain in Lamentations, i.e., Lamentations as a polyphonic text, its insistence on Yhwh as the dialogic partner and the images of God in both Lamentations and *Lamentations Rabbah*; second, this chapter will explore the book's enduring significance, especially its interaction between different perspectives, its emphasis on the human role in the God-human dialogue and its remaining in lament when this is necessary for contemporary suffering individuals and communities.

WAYS THE SUFFERING COMMUNITY DEALS WITH PAIN IN LAMENTATIONS

Lamentations is a unique text that deals with pain. It remains as a polyphonic text and holds onto Yhwh as "you," as Israel's dialogic partner. Various perspectives are expressed, but no one is given the authority to override or eliminate the others; these different perspectives coexist and the book remains as an open text to the very end. God is absent and the absence of God determines the tragic nature of the book; however, God is paradoxically acutely present due to the community's calling upon him and holding onto him.

Lamentations as a Polyphonic Text

A polyphonic text is a literary work that approximates a genuine dialogue according to M. Bakhtin.⁵ G. S. Morson and C. Emerson, the primary trans-

---

3. Stern, "Lamentations in Jewish Liturgy," 88.
4. For more details, see ibid., 88–91.
5. Newsom, "Bakhtin, the Bible, and Dialogic Truth," 295.

lators of Bakhtin, affirm that "polyphony is one of Bakhtin's most intriguing and original concepts."[6] Bakhtin never explicitly defines a polyphonic text, but a number of its distinctive characteristics can be extracted from Bakhtin's works.[7] First, in most literary works, the author's perspective dominates all voices; the characters do not address the reader directly, but "through the author's evaluating perspective."[8] A polyphonic text, however, does not have an authoritative perspective; the author's perspective is simply "one among others, without privilege."[9] Second, a polyphonic text aims at promoting "a dialogic sense of truth" and a dialogic play of ideas is the motive behind the entire literary work.[10] Morson and Emerson put it well: when reading a polyphonic text, "one must not read for the plot, but for the dialogues, and to read for the dialogues is to participate in them."[11] The dialogic sense of truth "requires a plurality of consciousnesses" and these consciousnesses meet as equals and engage in an open dialogue.[12] Finally, since genuine dialogue is by nature open, a polyphonic text is an open one, without a closure. I would argue that the book of Lamentations has the characteristics of a polyphonic text which, as such, helps the suffering community to deal with pain in its various dimensions and at a deeper level.

Lamentations Has No Authoritative Perspective

Different perspectives are woven together in Lamentations and no single one is more privileged than the others. The author(s)' voice is expressed through those of the narrator, Zion, the suffering man and the community, but does not dominate any of these. The book's various voices are expressed freely in an open dialogue and interact with one another. The narrator who approaches Zion first, observes her misery (Lam 1:1–11b) and reasons that her current fate must be Yhwh's just punishment for her sins (Lam 1:8); however, he changes his attitude toward her dramatically (Lam 2:11) after hearing her side of the story (Lam 1:11c–22). The narrator's judgmental attitude turns into sympathy and solidarity with Zion's suffering. Zion, who has never denied the possibility that her misery is God's just punishment of her sins, nonetheless holds onto her integrity by standing against God for

6. Morson and Emerson, *Mikhail Bakhtin*, 231.
7. Newsom, "Bakhtin, the Bible, and Dialogic Truth," 295–96.
8. Ibid., 295.
9. Ibid., 296.
10. Morsen and Emerson, *Mikhail Bakhtin*, 234.
11. Ibid., 249.
12. Ibid., 238.

the sake of her children and her people, by recognizing and proclaiming that God indeed has been acting like an enemy (Lam 2:1-10). She is less concerned with any possible reason for her suffering; rather, her focus is on persuading God and people to look and see her pain. Zion, the sufferer, deserves attention, and the author of the book grants her the attention of the narrator (Lam 2:11-13), who has been previously very critical of her.

After the interchange between the narrator and Zion, the suffering man's attempt to affirm the goodness of Yhwh is heard in Lam 3:21-33. He speaks from out of the wisdom tradition and his words have to be understood on their various levels as a whole. The suffering man affirms traditional wisdom and advocates right responses to suffering: to sit quietly and bear one's suffering in silence (Lam 3:25-30), but his own experience of suffering will not permit him to sit still and be silent; he cries to Yhwh (Lam 3:55) and joins Zion and the narrator with eyes flowing with tears to persuade Yhwh to look and see (Lam 3:48-51).

The narrator in Lamentations 4 describes the deteriorating situation in the city, while the community in Lamentations 5 utters its "why" questions to Yhwh about their being forgotten and forsaken by him, "why"s which have been suppressed so far (Lam 5:19-22). God remains silent and Lamentations ends as an open text. No closure is achieved; no final say from God is heard; no authority is given to any one particular perspective. The dialogue continues on, even beyond the book of Lamentations itself, into Rabbinic literature. Lamentations is thus different from the book of Job where Yhwh affirms that Job is right and his friends are wrong: "My wrath is kindled against you and against your two friends; for you have not spoken of me what is right, as my servant Job has" (Job 42:7).[13] In the book of Job, the author takes the side of Job by having God affirm him. In Lamentations, no affirmation of any particular perspective is given by God. K. O'Connor affirms that God's failure to speak in Lamentations is "a calculated choice, a conscious theological decision," and "an inspired control by the book's composers" since any words from God "would endanger human voices."[14] Given God's silence, all different perspectives and voices in Lamentations have their valid place in the book and deserve attention.

---

13. Newsom ("Book of Job as Polyphonic Text," 107; Newsom, *The Book of Job*, 3-31) points out that even though God's voice silences the voices of Job's friends, the narrative conclusion (Job 42:10-17) actually validates the friends' claims with God's restoring Job's fortunes twice as much as he had before. Newsom holds that the book of Job has an ironic and self-contradictory conclusion, which points to the polyphonic nature of the book.

14. O'Connor, *Lamentations and the Tears of the World*, 85.

Forgotten and Forsaken by God (Lam 5:19-20)

Lamentations Reflects a Dialogic Sense of Truth

The book of Lamentations is meant to be an ongoing dialogue. First of all, different voices in Lamentations engage in a dialogue among themselves. Those voices do not address each other directly most of the time; rather, they focus mainly on God. Still, they do interact to some extent and their attitudes toward one another change. Their experiences and expressions of pain unify them, even though their perspectives differ. The book of Lamentations reflects a plurality of consciousnesses. Different representatives of various communal traditions all find a place in Lamentations. Different questions are asked: did Zion suffer because of her sins? How could Yhwh act like an enemy? Is it possible to sit in silence and trust in God in the face of such vast devastation? Could the leaders of Zion have done differently so that she would be faring better now? How could God forget and forsake for so long, and reject God's chosen people to such an extent? . . . The list of questions could go on and on, with no answers given. All possible explanations are explored, but no one is found adequate enough to claim authority over the others. The author(s) did not try to reconcile the different perspectives in Lamentations. They remain different in the book. No authoritative perspective is given, whether from God or from the author(s).

Second, the dialogue in Lamentations is part of a larger dialogue between Lamentations and deuteronomistic/priestly/prophetic traditions. Lamentations carries on the proceeding biblical dialogue concerning suffering and the relationship between Yhwh and his chosen people, and moves it toward a deeper level, to a level that calls the community to remain faithful when Yhwh seems absent. A new beginning depends on Yhwh, the community affirms; the community is committed to a future with Yhwh, now it is Yhwh's turn to make a like commitment.

In sum, Lamentations aims at a dialogic sense of truth. The book encompasses all possible interpretations of the community's current plight; it is also open to new possibilities from Yhwh's side.

Lamentations Hold Yhwh as "You"

Yhwh is the only אתה, "you" (Lam 1:21; 3:42; 5:19), the ultimate dialogic partner, in Lamentations. Yhwh is the "you" that the community has known for generations, but no longer understands; Yhwh is the "you" whose destructive power the community experiences, but for whose benevolent presence the community yearns; Yhwh is the "you" that has become an enemy, but also the one with whom the community wants to have a future.

Yhwh as "you" in Lamentations can be understood on several levels. First, it is to "your"—Yhwh's ears that the community cries out in agony, complaints, questions, laments and prays spontaneously; "you"—Yhwh is the community's focus, the foundation of everything.

Second, by calling Yhwh—and only Yhwh—"you," the community shows its deepest trust in the absent Yhwh. The community tries to comprehend everything in terms of its relationship with Yhwh, to grasp everything in relation to Yhwh.[15]

Third, the community is telling Yhwh that it does not have a future except with him. The community might be in the wrong and be responsible for Yhwh's absence, but they are not willing to give up on their relationship with Yhwh; indeed, they are willing to start all over again with Yhwh. Now that the dialogue with Yhwh has been severed, it is the faith of the community that keeps the dialogue going, the honest protest of the community that creates an open space. The community tries to persuade Yhwh to walk with them again, to reengage in their unique relationship.

Images of God in Lamentations and Lamentations Rabbah

The images of God in Lamentations are contradictory and irreconcilable.[16] God remains absent in Lamentations; meanwhile God is being talked about and talked to, even though God's voice is not heard. God is the enemy and the destroyer, but also the expected savior. E. Boase points out that "God is identified as the cause of the current suffering, but is also the only hope for the future."[17] Boase's study focuses on three conflicting images of God in Lamentations—God as the violent destroyer, God as absent, and God as a God of steadfast love and hope.[18] She avers that Lamentations is experiential; "God was both problem and solution, violent, absent and longed for future hope"[19] for Israel at this time in its history. Lamentations invites the reader to grapple with these different experiences of God and enter into dialogue with the book and with God. The Rabbinic tradition does engage in such a dialogue, with the images of God in *Lamentations Rabbah* serving as an example of that effort. In this part, I will first analyze the absent and

---

15. See Buber, *I and Thou*, 127.

16. Boase ("Characterization of God in Lamentations," 32) says that the images of God in Lamentations are "varied and at times contradictory."

17. Ibid.

18. Ibid., 34.

19. Ibid., 44.

abusive God in Lamentations, and then the lamenting and repenting God in *Lamentations Rabbah*.

The Absent God in Lamentations

God's absence is underlined by all speakers in Lamentations. Zion sits alone at the beginning of the book (Lam 1:1). It is mentioned five times in Lamentations 1 that there is no comforter for Zion, three times by the narrator (Lam 1:2, 9, 17) and twice by Zion (Lam 1:16, 21). Zion's repeated plea to God to "look" and "see" (Lam 1:9, 11, 20) highlights God's absence and God's failure to look and see.

In Lamentations 2, the narrator describes a series of destructive, violent actions by God against Zion: Judah and Jerusalem were destroyed (Lam 2:2–3), gone are festivals and Sabbath, king and priest (Lam 2:6). Boase notes that these actions suggest that God is no longer dwelling among the people.[20]

The suffering man in Lamentations 3 also underlines God's absence. The man dwells in darkness and pain (3:2); his tears cannot stop until God looks down from heaven and sees (3:49–50). God is described as "not forgiving" (3:42) and as one who "wraps himself with a cloud so that no prayer can pass through" (3:44). God is not only absent, but intentionally hiding himself.

The prayer of the community in Lamentations 5 is situated in the context of an absent God as well. It asks God to "remember," "look, and see" in the beginning (5:1) and ends with the question of why God has forgotten and forsaken them for so long (5:20). The end of the book again mentions God's utter rejection and anger; hence, any hope and a possible future for the people depends on a response from God, on the return of God's presence.

Even though God is painfully absent, the suffering community makes the presence of God acutely felt through its repeated calls upon God. They have no one else to turn to—except to the God they have known for generations. They see God as the source of their suffering, but as the only hope for their future as well.

The Abusive God in Lamentations

Quite a number of scholars note the problem of the image of a violent and abusive God in Lamentations.[21] K. O'Connor points out four approaches

---

20. Ibid., 37.

21. O'Connor, *Lamentations and the Tears of the World*, 110–23; Mandolfo, *Daughter Zion Talks Back*, 103–19.

Significance of Lamentations for Suffering Individuals and Communities

that have been taken by scholars regarding God's abusive character in the book.[22] The first is to ignore divine violence and choose texts that reveal a loving and compassionate God; this approach "ignores Lamentations' ability to mirror tragic experiences of believers" and dissolves God's freedom into "positive thinking."[23] The second is to justify God's violence by emphasizing the people's sin. The third approach is to reject texts (e.g., Lam 2:1–9) that portray an abusive God. The fourth one is to see God as both abusive and loving. O'Connor herself values Lamentations' raw honesty and iconoclastic power, but calls for Lamentations' insistence on God's punishing violence to be critiqued in our time.[24]

I think that the image of a violent and abusive God portrayed in Lamentation holds legitimacy if we are serious and honest about our God-talk. Lamentations reflects one way to portray God in suffering. But this is not the only image of God and it has to be situated within the context of the entire book where God's compassion and mercy are constantly called upon as well. Lamentations hopes that God's anger and rejection would not last forever, that God will return to God's people. It is because of this hope that Lamentations moves from self-absorption to direct appeals to God.

The Lamenting and Repenting God in Lamentations Rabbah

The Midrash on Lamentations (*Lamentations Rabbah*) struggles with the book's conflicting images of God as well. In human terms, it depicts a God who was angry, destroyed his own people, but then shocked by his own actions, laments, weeps and finally repents.[25] There are two "almost incompatible"[26] portraits of God found in two distinct narratives in the twenty-fourth *Petihta* (or proems) of *Lamentations Rabbah*: in the first one, God identifies himself totally with the Jewish people's catastrophe to the extent that God "virtually claims to be its sole victim as well as chief mourner."[27] In the second narrative, God is portrayed as distant and indifferent throughout most of the narrative;

---

22. O'Connor, *Lamentations and the Tears of the World*, 116–19.

23. Ibid., 106.

24. Ibid., 120.

25. Mintz, *Ḥurban*, 57–62; Stern, "*Imitatio Hominis*," 151–74; Kraemer, *Responses to Suffering in Classical Rabbinic Literature*, 140–46; Linafelt, *Surviving Lamentations*, 100–116.

26. Stern, "Two Narratives about God," 47.

27. Ibid., 48.

nonetheless, God finally repents over the destruction, being persuaded to do so by the matriarch Rachel.[28]

In *Lamentations Rabbah*'s first narrative, when God thinks to destroy the temple, he realizes that as long as he dwells in it, no one could touch it, so God detaches himself. After the temple was burned, God realizes that he no longer has a dwelling place, so he withdraws his presence/*Shekinah* from the land and returns to heaven, his former habitation. At that point, God weeps and laments, saying, "Woe to me! What have I done? I caused My *Shekinah* to dwell below for Israel's sake, and now that they have sinned, I have returned to my original place. . . . I would become a laughing stock for the gentiles, a thing of ridicule to human beings!"[29] The archangel then persuades God not to weep, but God replies that if the angels do not leave God alone to weep, then God is going to weep in a place that no one has permission to enter. Next, God summons the ministering angels and inspects the destroyed temple site, where he meets the weeping and lamenting patriarchs. Seeing them, God immediately calls for weeping and lamenting on that day. God and the patriarchs go weeping from one gate to the next. God said: "woe to the king who succeeded in his youth but failed in his old age!" It is obvious that God is the king here. God had to punish Israel for its sin, but now that Israel is gone, God is the one who suffers its loss like an old king who has lost his only son. God is the sole victim, chief mourner and lamenter.

R. Samuel bar Nahman then tells the second narrative. Once the temple is destroyed, Abraham comes weeping before God and the ministering angels also compose lamentations and arrange themselves in rows like mourners. God tells Abraham that Israel had sinned against the whole of Torah which was composed of twenty-two letters. The Torah and the letters then come forward to testify against Israel, but Abraham refutes them one by one.[30] Next

---

28. *Midrash Rabbah* 7:40–49.

29. Translation taken from Stern, "Two Narratives about God," 49.

30. The story goes like this: the Torah came as a witness against Israel. Abraham said to the Torah: "My daughter, are you really going to testify against Israel that they transgressed your commandments? Have you no shame in my presence? Remember the day that the Holy One took you around to every nation and people, but no one wished to accept you—until my children came to Mount Sinai and accepted you and honored you. And now, are you about to testify against them on the day of their misfortune?" Torah stepped aside and did not testify against them. The twenty two letters approached. Abraham said to Alef, "Alef, you, the first of the letters, are about to testify against Israel on the day of their misfortune! Remember the day that the Holy revealed Himself on Mount Sinai and began with you, *Anokhi*, 'I am the Lord your God (Exodus 20:2). No nation or people was willing to accept you—except for my children. And now you are about to testify against them!" Alef stood aside and did not testify. Beth came to testify; Abraham said to Beth, "My daughter, are you going to testify against my children? They are zealous for the five books of the Torah, and you are the Torah's beginning. This is

Significance of Lamentations for Suffering Individuals and Communities

Abraham, Isaac, Jacob, and Moses plead with God one after another, but God is not moved. Moses then goes to the exiles in Babylon and affirms them that even though it is impossible to bring them back right now, God will soon cause them to return. Moses thereupon reports the terrible fate of the exiled Israelites to the patriarchs, who all weep, but again God is not moved. Then Moses accuses God of remaining silent while the Babylonians killed countless mothers with their children, this in violation of the Torah commandment: "No animal from the herd or from the flock shall be slaughtered on the same day with its young" (Lev 22:28). At this moment, Rachel leaps up and speaks before God.[31] As D. Stern points out, Rachel invokes her past deeds like the patriarchs before her; yet she also recounts one of her deeds that was "less famously exemplary."[32] In particular, Rachel tells God how she overcame her jealousy and helped her father Laban in tricking Jacob into believing that Leah was Rachel on their wedding night. Rachel did this so that Leah would not be disgraced or "exposed to shame."[33] Rachel declares: "If I, a creature of flesh and blood, formed of dust and ashes, was not envious of my rival and did not expose her to shame and contempt, why should you, a king who lives eternally and are merciful, be jealous of idolatry in which there is no reality, and exile my children and let them be slain by the sword, and their enemies have done with them as they wished!"[34]

God is moved by Rachel's words and promises to restore Israel to its place for the sake of Rachel. Linafelt notes that it is Rachel's advocacy for her children and her refusal to be comforted in their absence (cf. Jer 31:15) that finally moves God.[35] Mintz points out that it is neither Abraham nor Moses

---

what is written, *Bereshit*, 'in the beginning, God created' (Genesis 1:1)." Beth stood aside and did not testify. Then Gimmel came to testify against Israel, but Abraham said to her, "Gimmel! Are you going to testify against my children perform the commandment of wearing fringes, *tsitsit*—the commandment that begins with you? For this is what is written, '*Gedilim*, tassels, you shall make on the four corners of the garment with which you cover yourself' (Deuteronomy 22:12)." Gimmel stood aside and did not testify. When the other letters saw that Abraham had silenced them, they too were embarrassed, and stood aside, did not testify against Israel. The translation is taken from Stern, "Two Narratives about God," 52–53.

31. Rachel represents all mothers who have lost their children throughout the ages here. The death of a child influences a mother profoundly, usually provoking a religious response from her, and making her into a religious seeker and activist; see Sered, "Mother Love, Child Death and Religious Innovation," 55–74.

32. Stern, "*Imitatio Hominis*," 163.

33. For the details of Rachel's words to God, see *Midrash Rabbah* 7:48–49.

34. Ibid., 49.

35. Stern ("Two Narratives about God," 48) considers God's motives for saving Israel in the second narrative involve shame, and thus are "petty ones, unworthy of God." Linafelt (*Surviving Lamentations*, 115), however, holds that God is motivated by compassion

who effects a reorientation on God's part, but rather the female voice of Mother Rachel; it also reminds the reader the power of children's suffering that breaks through to the narrator in Lamentations 2.[36] Linafelt further points out that it is vitally important to note that the midrash is not content with "just an emotional response from God," but demands that Israel's children should "live again."[37] The second narrative ends with God's promise of the return of the children.

The Rabbinic communities must have wrestled with the images of God in Lamentations and they creatively depict the hidden side of God in the above two narratives. Consequently, the God who is violent and absent in Lamentations meets the God who is weeping, lamenting, and repenting in *Lamentations Rabbah*. It is the same God, the same passionate God who takes human suffering seriously and suffers with the sufferer.

The ways the suffering community in Lamentations deal with pain hold significance for contemporary suffering communities. The way they share their sufferings even with their different perspectives, their ability to hold their differences together as a community, their insistence and deep trust in holding onto Yhwh as their partner for the future after their devastating experiences, the images of God the community in Lamentations and the Rabbinic communities creatively depict—all of these dimensions have significance for a contemporary suffering community.

SIGNIFICANCE OF LAMENTATIONS FOR SUFFERING INDIVIDUALS AND COMMUNITIES

The book of Lamentations has become a liturgical prototype for a suffering community to deal with loss and pain. I will now explore the significance of Lamentations for contemporary suffering individuals and communities in this part. I will focus on four dimensions: the importance of social sharing of emotions since Lamentations is a dialogical text, the importance of the human role in God-human dialogue when God seems absent, the necessity of remaining in lament when needed, and finally the importance of human presence in suffering.

---

for the lost children, rather than by shame as Stern suggests. I agree with Linafelt.

36. Mintz, *Ḥurban*, 62.

37. Linafelt, *Surviving Lamentations*, 115.

Significance of Lamentations for Suffering Individuals and Communities

Importance of Social Sharing of Emotion

Lamentations is a typical dialogical text. The expression of emotions by the book's different speakers evokes sympathy from others and influences the feelings of the listener. This is most obviously shown in Lamentations when Zion's expression of pain in 1:11c-22 affects the narrator to such an extent that he changes his view about Zion and expresses his support for her in 2:11-13. The expression of deeply felt emotions by the speakers, mainly the narrator, Zion, the suffering man, and the community, draws Lamentations' speakers together into a symphony that aims at moving God and the passersby to look and see. The book of Lamentations thus becomes a prototypical text for a suffering community to express pain, a text where different voices engage in a kind of social sharing of pain. There are a number of important findings in empirical psychological research that lend credibility to Lamentations' dialogic expression and social sharing of pain.

Lamentations underlines the importance of social sharing of emotion and the value of lament. Empirical psychological research makes clear that people across age groups and cultures are all inclined to share their emotions, both positive and negative, with family and friends.[38] Generally speaking, "emotion is followed by social sharing of emotion" and "the more intense the emotion felt by the participant, the more he/she talked about the event."[39] There are a number of noteworthy discoveries about such social sharing of emotion by empirical psychological research:

First, the Freudian notion that expression of emotion is "cathartic" and that social sharing of emotion brings emotional relief is flawed.[40] Rimé and his colleagues found out that their survey data failed to support such a notion. They claim that "the cathartic notion is an illusion; the simple fact of socially sharing an emotion does not have the power to change the emotional memory."[41] Talking about an emotional experience with a trusted friend or family member does not contribute to emotional recovery.[42] Since people do nonetheless willingly share their emotional experience with others—"social

---

38. Rimé, "Mental Rumination, Social Sharing, and the Recovery from Emotional Exposure," 271–91; Rimé et al., "Emotion, Verbal Expression, and the Social Sharing of Emotion," 186–87; Rimé et al., "The Social Sharing of Emotion," 27–41.

39. Rimé et al., "Emotion, Verbal Expression, and the Social Sharing of Emotion," 186–87.

40. My view on this point is very much influenced by Bosworth; see his article "Catharsis Canard and the Value of Lament," forthcoming.

41. Rimé et al., "Social Sharing of Emotion," 35.

42. Ibid., 32.

sharing is the rule after an emotion and secrecy is the exception"[43]—the reasons for the value of social sharing of emotion must lie elsewhere.

Second, even though social sharing of emotion does not bring about emotional recovery, people spontaneously engage in social sharing of an emotion and clearly experience it as beneficial.[44] It was also discovered that "although the sharing of emotions does not relieve the *emotional load* of the event, it is associated with *physical health* improvement."[45]

Third, the repetitive aspect of social sharing of emotion on the one hand consolidates a vivid memory of tragic events that caught people by surprise; on the other hand, it helps the participant to come to face reality rather than persist in denial.[46] Moreover, social sharing of emotion helps a person to "work through" the process, to give constructive meaning to the tragic event, and thus preserves a sense of coherence in memory.[47]

Fourth, social sharing of emotion most notably enhances "interpersonal relationships and social integration."[48] Rimé and his colleagues found that specific dynamics take place between the speaker and the listener. The listener often expresses interest and empathy toward the speaker. Moreover, "the more emotional a story is, the more the listener will experience emotion, and will consequently express support and warmth."[49] A third response is the attraction generated by social sharing of emotion: the more interest and empathy a story calls for, the more the listener "likes" the speaker and vice versa. When intense emotions are shared, verbal expressions usually turn to non-verbal gestures of comfort and support, like hugging, kissing, or touching. Thereby, distances between persons are reduced and mutual ties strengthened.

The value of lament is thus not cathartic, but social. Honest expression and sharing of emotions in lament strengthens personal ties and enhances communal solidarity.

---

43. Rimé et al., "Emotion, Verbal Expression, and the Social Sharing of Emotion," 191; they further note that the main factor that prevents people from sharing an emotion is the subjective experience of shame or guilt.
44. Rimé et al., "Social Sharing of Emotion," 36.
45. Ibid. (italics original).
46. Ibid., 37.
47. Ibid.
48. Ibid., 38.
49. Ibid.

Significance of Lamentations for Suffering Individuals and Communities

Importance of the Human Role in God-Human Dialogue

In Lamentations, the tragic hero—the community—remains active, as one who "holds to God against God."[50] W. L. Humphreys points out that suffering is necessarily "at the very core of the human situation in this world" and that the tragic hero does not remain passive in the face of this necessary suffering.[51] The tragic hero "lives at the very edge of human power and potential," takes others to the "limits of the human condition," and defines these limits with "new sharpness," thereby enlarging the vision of all.[52] The community in Lamentations indeed lives at the very edge of existence, physically and spiritually; the people try to survive, to engage God, to explore new possibilities, and to challenge others to leave their comfort zones so as to enter into their world of suffering.

Lamentations, like other lament prayers in the Bible, does not *reflect on* the reality of suffering, nor does it offer a *thoughtful meditation* on suffering; rather, as S. Balentine puts matters, it *expresses* "the reality of suffering."[53] The community is neither docile nor submissive, but rather forceful; it does not accept easily the readymade answer that its suffering is caused by sin. The community explores suffering in its various dimensions and dares to accuse God of actively forgetting and forsaking them: "Why have you forgotten us completely? Why have you forsaken us these many days?" (Lam 5:20).

Lamentations and other lament texts in the Bible affirm the role of the human side in the divine-human dialogue. W. Brueggemann has long pointed out that those traditions that affirm the world, celebrate culture, and highlight human responsibility and capacity in the Hebrew Bible have been largely neglected.[54] Brueggemann further argues that the mainstream of Old Testament theology seeks to legitimate structure, to affirm the order of the world and to interpret pain within this structure; however, the effort to embrace pain remains a crucial, valid countervoice.[55] The tension between these two stances must be maintained. In the embrace of pain, it is no longer assumed that God is the all-powerful covenant partner who must be blindly obeyed and whose will is to be docilely followed; rather, Israel found "the nerve and the faith" to

---

50. Westermann, *Elements of Old Testament Theology*, 172; Balentine, *Prayer in the Hebrew Bible*, 149.

51. Humphreys, *The Tragic Vision and the Hebrew Tradition*, 3.

52. Ibid.

53. Balentine, *Prayer in the Hebrew Bible*, 150.

54. Brueggemann, *In Man We Trust*, 7.

55. Brueggemann, "A Shape for Old Testament Theology, I," 28–46; Brueggemann, "A Shape for Old Testament Theology, II," 395–415.

risk an assault on God with bold protest.[56] Israel engages in a lament that is "a dramatic, rhetorical, liturgical act of speech which is irreversible";[57] it is a protest "against a legitimacy that has grown illegitimate" because it does not take seriously enough the suffering reality of Israel.[58] When the reality of suffering is not dealt with, structures become illegitimate, with the result that "the voice of pain assumes enough authority to be heard."[59] Brueggemann holds that the voice of Israel "in the fray" reaches God "above the fray;" thereby, God is inevitably drawn back "into the fray."[60] It is also worth noting that God takes Israel's speech of pain seriously; the initiative and risk Israel takes permit newness for God and for their relationship. It is in this process that the bond between Israel and God is strengthened.

Balentine notes that the faith community is commissioned to become "a house of prayer."[61] Becoming a house of prayer is a two dimensional process: to keep the community and the world in God and to keep God in the community and the world. To keep the community and the world in God is to shape the future of the people and its institutions in accordance with transcendent reality and its demands. The faith community must also be at work in shaping the future of God, i.e., to keep God in the community and the world. A. Heschel says that to pray means to bring God back into the world and to expand God's presence there; such a task is not only possible, but also necessary.[62] Surely God is always in the world; but in times of crisis and pain when God seems absent, prayer can make a difference, even change God's plans and intentions about punishing. Balentine analyzes a number of relevant texts in the Hebrew Bible (e.g., Gen 18:22–33; Exod 32:7–14; Num 11:4–34; 14:11–23; and Josh 7:7–9) that represent a significant tradition concerning prayer as a standing in loyal opposition to God and God's ways of executing justice.[63] When a crisis occurs between God and humans, divine justice and intentions are called into question, and pray-ers, like Abraham, Moses and Joshua, stand before God challenging, interrogating, petitioning and are taken seriously

---

56 Brueggemann, "A Shape for Old Testament Theology, II," 400.

57. Ibid.

58. Ibid., 401.

59. Ibid.

60. Ibid., 406.

61. Balentine, *Prayer in the Hebrew Bible*, 272.

62. Heschel, *The Insecurity of Freedom,* 258; and Balentine, *Prayer in the Hebrew Bible*, 284–85.

63. For a more detailed analysis of these texts, see Balentine, *Prayer in the Hebrew Bible*, 118–45.

Significance of Lamentations for Suffering Individuals and Communities

by God. "They not only assault God; at times they even prevail."[64] The point here is not to force God to change, but rather to engage in a radical dialogue with God and thus come to a deeper and stronger sense of God's presence in the world. Balentine affirms that the task of keeping God in the world is perhaps nowhere more clearly illustrated than in these bold prayers of questioning and lamenting.[65]

The community in Lamentations brings their pain before God, accuses God of becoming like an enemy, of being absent while Israel is most in need of him; in this instance, however, the community does not prevail with God—God remains absent and silent. The outcome of the situation is not altered, but rather prolonged and worsened. The lament of the community continues; and the community remains in lament at the end of the book. Lament thus painfully and necessarily persists, a topic to which I now turn.

Necessity of Remaining in Lament When Needed

The journey from lament to praise, from disorientation to new orientation can be unpredictably long—or may never occur at all. In situations of prolonged suffering and despair, to remain in lament becomes necessary. In this part, I will look at lament as a human condition, the necessity and risks of lament, the suffering God and the importance of human presence in suffering.

Lament As a Human Condition

P. D. Miller holds that laments are "the voice of the human" and "serve to define our humanness."[66] He notes that human cries toward God never stop; this crying out to God is "indeed the primary mode of conversation between God and the human creature. It begins not in ritual, not in Israel, not in any particularity, but in our being human."[67] Miller affirms that the human cry to God for help is one of the Bible's foundation stones, for both its anthro-

---

64. Ibid., 142.
65. Ibid., 285.
66. Miller, "Heaven's Prisoners," 15; see also Grant, "Hermeneutics of Humanity," 182–202.
67. Ibid., 16. The first Chinese historian Qian Sima (probably born in 145 BCE and died in 86 BCE), who wrote the first Chinese chronicle commented along the same lines; he said that God is the origin of a human person, parents the root of a person; when a person is desperate, s/he goes to the origin and root; thus whenever a person is suffering, exhausted, and in dire need, s/he cries out to God; whenever a person is sick and feels pain, s/he cries out to parents.

pology and theology. Miller further avers that lament is not exceptional, but the rule; it is the voice of pain and prayer at the same time.[68]

The Bible is filled with human cries to God for help, from the blood of Abel crying out to God from the ground (Gen 4:10), that cry never stops. C. Westermann notes that lament, both communal and individual, is pervasive in the entire Hebrew Bible. The people cried out in Egypt because of their oppression (Exod 2:23-25). The cry out of deep anguish accompanies Israel through every stage of her history. It happened over and over again in times of distress, up to the catastrophe of the exile, when the book of Lamentations and many other biblical texts (e.g., Psalm 89 and Isaiah 63-64) were composed. This cry continues up to and including 4 Ezra, bringing before God the distress and suffering of the nation.[69] Individual laments likewise pervade the Hebrew Bible, "Out of the depth I cry to you, O Yhwh" (Ps 130:1). This cry persists.

Miller holds that lament is "utterly human" and "arises out of the reality of human existence";[70] lament assumes that "there is something beyond that reality that can transform human existence without destroying it."[71] Lament is by its nature a prayer that affirms humanness; it gives voice to humanity's questioning spirit, acknowledging questioning as a basic and persistent characteristic of human consciousness. Balentine puts it well: "whenever man and woman are being fully human, the drive to question and probe and explore and wonder about anything and everything—including God—is relentlessly at work."[72] Laments are not only for times of faith crisis; they are also faith opportunities, times for a person and a community to articulate again their expectations of and assumptions about God. Lament clearly shows the dialogical character of biblical faith, in a remarkable combination of honesty and dialogue.

Dorothee Soelle notes that suffering makes people cry out "why"? If this "why" question could be answered, "it would be possible to explain and offer consolation for suffering."[73] Simone Weil, whom Soelle quotes frequently, affirms that there is no reply to the "why" that the soul cries out in affliction;[74] she continues, "if the word 'why' expressed the search for a cause, the reply would appear easily. But it expresses *the search for an end*. This whole universe

---

68. Ibid.
69. Westermann, *Praise and Lament*, 262-64.
70. Miller, "Heaven's Prisoners," 17.
71. Ibid.
72. Balentine, *Prayer in the Hebrew Bible*, 287.
73. Soelle, *Suffering* 155.
74. Weil, *Intimations of Christianity among the Ancient Greeks*, 198.

is empty of finality. The soul which because it is torn by affliction, cries out continually for this finality, *touches the void*.[75] If the soul does not "renounce loving" in the void, it will one day hear "not a reply to the question which it cries, for there is none, but the very silence as something infinitely more full of significance than any response, like God himself speaking."[76] The soul then knows that God's absence here below is "the same thing" as God's secret presence on earth.[77] Soelle agrees with Weil here and holds that if the soul does not stop loving "in the void," in the dark night of despair, then the object of that love can rightly be called "God."[78]

Lament is a human condition; in this condition, we are caught in the tension of the paradox of the absent and present God, of God who can be known, but remains hidden. Lament holds together two truths of this paradox which at first sight may seem logically contradictory, but which need each other and interact with each other.[79] In the dark night of despair in lament where God seems absent, there is nothing to love; for the one who ceases to love, God's absence becomes final; but the one who goes on loving, or at least wanting to love one day meets the silent God whose presence is brighter than daylight.[80]

Necessity and Risks of Lament

It is indispensable and necessary for a faith community to engage in lament. Balentine lists a number of reasons for this necessity,[81] e.g., lament affirms the biblical portrait of both God and humanity; "humanity's relentless drive to question collides most dramatically with the God who is present and available and at the same time hidden and unresponsive."[82] Lament keeps hope alive even in the grips of despair; it keeps the radical divine-human dialogue going on those occasions when God seems absent. More importantly, when the faith community practices lament, it most clearly embodies divine compassion and justice and most effectively engages in the ministry of keeping God in the world.

---

75. Ibid., 198–99 (italics added).
76. Ibid., 199.
77. Ibid.
78. Soelle, *Suffering*, 157.
79. Davidson, *The Courage to Doubt*, xi.
80. Weil, *Waiting for God*, 120–21.
81. Balentine, *Prayer in the Hebrew Bible*, 291–92.
82. Ibid., 291.

Forgotten and Forsaken by God (Lam 5:19–20)

Soelle notes that the language of lament helps the sufferer to get over the initial stage of muteness, to put into words before God the experience of affliction, and to move to the third stage of constructive response when "liberation and help for the unfortunate can be organized."[83]

However, Balentine also points out risks of lament.[84] First, as he puts it, "lament is unmanageable."[85] The Bible, he notes, witnesses that God takes seriously hard and accusing questions; but the biblical record is equally clear that God seldom answers questions, at least not in the way they are asked. God is expected to hear, believed to be receptive, but when questions end, faith must bear the burden of the silence that follows.[86] Or put it another way, the "why" questions driven by despair simply have no answers, which poses an enormous challenge to the practice of lament. Lament poses more questions than answers. Balentine says, "Primal screams rarely bother with orthodoxy, and silence is so quiet and unpredictable. Will it lead to renewed speech and fresh faith, or will it be a step further into the black hole of doubt, despair and cynicism?"[87] Second, questioning alters one's faith. In the curiosity, anxiety, uncertainty and restlessness of lament, "the questioner brings the definition of everything presented to her or him under review: the real, the true, the good, self, and God."[88] The process of questioning leaves neither the questioner nor the questioned the same as before. Questioning is both creative and destructive. Are we ready to rethink faith and even the reality of God?

The preceding question is not rhetorical, and we should honestly admit that we do not know the answer. To engage in such questioning is to risk losing one's faith. W. Brueggemann points out that perhaps the greatest irony of biblical witness and prayer is that when one loses faith in God, it is precisely to God that one returns.[89]

The Suffering God

The lamenting community in Lamentations struggles with an absent God. The affliction of the community is not only its physical suffering, but more

---

83. Soelle, *Suffering*, 73–78.
84. Balentine, *Prayer in the Hebrew Bible*, 292–95.
85. Ibid., 292.
86. Ibid.
87. Ibid., 293.
88. Ibid.
89. Brueggemann, "Costly Loss of Lament," 66.

Significance of Lamentations for Suffering Individuals and Communities

the anguished question about where is God in the midst of suffering.[90] Where is God? is a question that all afflicted persons ask, which leads either to atheism or God's suffering with the afflicted. Soelle holds that in the face of senseless suffering, "faith in a God who embodies both omnipotence and love has to waver or be destroyed."[91] Atheism arises out of human suffering; it is a rejection of an all-powerful and loving God in senseless suffering. Yet, for those who would not give up faith in an even absent God, they meet the God who suffers with the afflicted. The communities that recited Lamentations for generations gave rise to the weeping, lamenting, and repenting God in *Lamentations Rabbah*. Later generations' reflection led them to believe that God went into exile with the people.

Literature on the Shoah often comes to the recognition of a suffering God as well.[92] Elie Wiesel, a survivor of the Shoah and the Nobel Peace Prize-winner in 1986, in a widely quoted passage, recounts an incident in a camp when all the prisoners were forced to watch the hanging of two men and a young boy. The two men die quickly, but the boy holds on because he was still a child, very light, still breathing. Someone behind Wiesel asks: "Where is merciful God? Where is He?" The boy remained for half an hour, lingering between life and death, writhing before their eyes. The same man behind Wiesel asks again, "For God's sake, where is God?" Wiesel heard a voice from within him answer: "Where He is? This is where—hanging here from this gallows."[93] Wiesel's understanding of the suffering God draws on the concept of the *Shekinah*—the indwelling presence of God in the world.[94] D. Bonhoeffer, a Lutheran pastor and theologian who opposed the Nazi regime from the beginning, was imprisoned and eventually executed, evokes a suffering God as well; he holds that "only a suffering God can help."[95] Bonhoeffer believes that God reveals Godself most fully in the crucified Christ, thereby attaining power through weakness. Christians are those who participate in the suffering of God in the life of the world, who see the face of God in the afflicted.[96]

---

90. Weil (*Waiting for God*, 117–19) explains that affliction is "an uprooting of life, a more or less attenuated equivalent of death, made irresistibly present to the soul by the attack or immediate apprehension of physical pain." Weil considers affliction as rooted in physical pain, which also "makes God appear to be absent for a time, more absent than a dead man, more absent than light in the utter darkness of a cell."

91. Soelle, *Suffering*, 142.

92. Ryan, *God and the Mystery of Human Suffering*, 166–91.

93. Wiesel, *Night*, 64–65.

94. Ryan, *God and the Mystery of Human Suffering*, 179; Soelle, *Suffering*, 145–46.

95. Bonhoeffer, *Letters and Papers from Prison*, 361.

96. Ibid., 361–63.

However, Wiesel believes that the suffering God offers neither a solution to the problem of suffering nor real consolation to suffering people. The suffering God "compounds" rather than "alleviates" human suffering.[97] Wiesel further avers that a suffering God cannot justify the reality of human suffering either, since nothing justifies the immense suffering in the Shoah; God is both question and answer, pain and healing, injury and peace.[98]

It is in the context of the suffering God, the paradoxical concept that God is among the weak and becomes weak yet reveals power in weakness that we come to the importance of human presence in suffering. Situations of human suffering require the presence of the other.

Importance of Human Presence in Suffering

While in the book of Lamentations, the community's painful cry of "why" (Lam 5:19–22) falls into the void, with no reply from God, in *Lamentations Rabbah*, when God fails to be moved by the petition of the patriarchs to save the exiled people, Moses takes it upon himself to go to Babylon to comfort the people, without being sent by God. Mandolfo notes that "the potentially provocative image of the patriarchs taking over God's responsibilities represents a powerful rhetoric-theological strategy that emphasizes human responsibility—when God does not seem to be exercising justice, it does not mean that we shouldn't."[99] The seeming absence of God in suffering calls for human response and action.

A key concept in the book of Lamentations is the repeated appeal of Zion, the man and the community to God and other people to "look and see" their pain (Lam 1:9, 11, 12, 18, 20; 3:36, 59, 60; 5:1). The sufferer yearns for recognition and deserves attention. Yet, in reality, just like the suffering Zion, the man, and the community in Lamentations, sufferers are often left in oblivion and isolation. Soelle notes that "one of the fundamental experiences about suffering is precisely the lack of communication, the dissolution of meaningful and productive ties. To stand under the burden of suffering always means to become more and more isolated."[100] It is thus essential for

---

97. These two terms are used by Ryan (*God and the Mystery of Human Suffering*, 179), who thus summarizes Wiesel's words. Elie Wiesel (*All Rivers Run to the Sea*, 104) says that divine suffering does not cancel out the suffering of the human person; rather, the two are added together.

98. Wiesel, *All Rivers Run to the Sea*, 104–5.

99. Mandolfo, *Daughter Zion Talks Back*, 125.

100. Soelle, *Suffering*, 75.

the sufferer to put his/her situation into words and share it with someone, and this requires the presence of others.

However, it is not easy to be a true witness to other people's suffering; it requires patience and courage to be a faithful listener to other people's experiences of horror, especially in a society and at a time where the dominant regime is ruled by lies and the mainstream is intentionally blind. In an interview with C. Rittner, Wiesel states that evil has many faces, and all of these faces have masks, and "beneath the mask there is indifference. That is what all the faces of evil have in common: indifference."[101]

Besides overcoming indifference, one has to avoid two further attitudes in order to be really present in other people's suffering. One is to defend God, as Job's friends did. When crushed, Job started cursing the day of his birth and posing his questions before God, Job's friends "had to choose between taking a stand for their beaten and defeated friend or God. They made the wrong choice, the easiest one."[102] Wiesel states in this connection: "These three self-righteous strangers from afar exaggerated when they tried to explain to Job events whose tragic weight is rested only on his shoulders. *He* suffered, and *they* made speeches on suffering. *He* was crushed by sorrow, and *they* build theories and systems on the subjects of grief, suffering and persecution."[103] A follower of God should never take the position of Job's friends in the face of another's senseless suffering. Wiesel spells this out in more detail in his play, *The Trial of God*.[104] The play takes place in Shamgorod in 1649 on the day of Purim, after a pogrom at the wedding of the innkeeper Berish's daughter, when all the Jewish inhabitants except Berish were killed, and his daughter was brutally gang raped. Berish acts as the prosecutor and stages a trial against God, with three erudite rabbis as judges. No one is willing to act as God's defendant, until a stranger, a neat and almost elegant young man steps in, who defends God and justifies God's ways in a learned, pious, and cool manner. But at the end of the play, when everyone removes their masks, God's capable defendant turns out to be Satan.

The other attitude one should avoid is to try to persuade the sufferer that things are not really that bad. Nicholas Wolterstorff, who lost his son in a climbing accident, feels that in the place of his son, "only a hole remains, a void, a gap, never to be filled."[105] He writes: "Do not say it is not really so bad. Because it is. Death is awful, demonic. If you think your task as comforter

---

101. Elie Wiesel, in Rittner, "An Interview with Elie Wiesel," 400.
102. Wiesel, *Messengers of God*, 199.
103. Ibid. (italics original).
104. Wiesel, *The Trial of God*, 125–61.
105. Wolterstorff, *Lament for a Son*, 33.

is to tell me that really, all things considered, it's not so bad, you do not sit with me in my grief but place yourself off in the distance away from me. Over there you are of no help. What I need to hear from you is that you recognize how painful it is."[106] To recognize how painful another's suffering is, a comforter has to listen, to listen attentively to the lamenter. N. J. Duff notes that when the lamentation makes space for the sufferer to give voice to anguish, anger, and despair, it thereby provides a space for others to listen.[107] S. Hauerwas further states that it is important to realize that we do not have a "solution" to the problems of evil and suffering; rather, our task is to be a community of care that makes it possible "to absorb the destructive terror of evil that constantly threatens to destroy all human relations."[108]

In the face of suffering, we do not need to defend God, nor do we need to assure the sufferer of a better future. What we can do is form a community of care where a lamenter's silence is respected and their words attentively listened to. In this community, a lamenter is accepted and feels free to express pain in honest words, so that our dialogue with God and with one another might continue.

CONCLUSION

The book of Lamentations holds significance for contemporary suffering individuals and communities. Lamentations insists on dialogue and on keeping God as the community's dialogic partner—even though God seems absent and remains silent. The book's community shows strength, honesty and faith when its relationship with God is undergoing crisis. The community refused to give up. Images of God are multi-dimensional in Lamentations, but all stand within the context of the community's faith expression. Lamentations coheres with the findings of psychological-empirical research that the value of lament is not cathartic; rather, social sharing of emotions strengthens personal relationships and consolidates social ties. Lament also values the human side of the exchange in the divine human dialogue.

For faith communities, when we are facing the suffering and lamenting of others, we need not defend God, nor try to comfort the lamenter by downplaying the tragic side of events. Instead, we need to be with the lamenter, to respect their silence and to listen to attentively their words.

So far, I have analyzed the acrostic in Lamentations, studied its text closely, compared Lamentations with other selected communal laments

---

106. Ibid., 34.
107. Duff, "Recovering Lamentation as a Practice in the Church," 12.
108. Hauerwas, *God, Medicine, and Suffering*, 53.

Significance of Lamentations for Suffering Individuals and Communities

regarding mood change and admission of guilt, and explored the significance of Lamentations for contemporary suffering individuals and communities; in the next and final chapter, I will conclude the book, synthesize its findings, and note possibilities for further study.

7

Review of Findings and Possibilities for Further Study

This work intends to contribute to Lamentations scholarship by providing a more holistic approach to the book. It examines the extent to which an intrinsic connection exists between the acrostic structure and the content of the book; it reads the book as a whole from the angle of the mini-acrostic in Lam 5:19–20 and explores whether this mini-acrostic underlines the main themes running through the book. It also explores the dialogic interaction among the voices within Lamentations and between Lamentations and other related communal laments in the Hebrew Bible regarding mood change and admission of guilt. Finally, the book examines the significance of Lamentations for contemporary suffering individuals and communities. I will synthesize the most salient findings of the book in my perspective and explore possibilities for further study in this conclusion.

REVIEW OF FINDINGS

Lamentations as a Literary Unity of Form and Content

Lamentations is a literary unity of form and content. The meaning and intention of the book is intrinsically connected with the alphabetic acrostics found in Lamentations 1–4 and the mini-acrostic in Lamentations 5. Moreover, different voices in Lamentations interact with one another, and the shifting of voices and changing perspectives are connected with the structure of each acrostic and all five poems.

Lamentations 5 forms an integral part of the book as a unity of both structure and content; the voice of the community in Lamentations 5 echoes, combines, and highlights the voices of the narrator, Zion, and the suffering man in the previous chapters.

Lamentations 5 as the Climax of the Book

Lamentations 3 forms the structural center of the book with its triple alphabetic acrostic, while Lamentations 5 serves as the book's climax with its carefully designed structure—a structure that is even more carefully developed than the previous four chapters. The lack of an alphabetic acrostic in Lamentations 5 is intentional; it does not diminish the chapter's poetic beauty and literary power, but rather enhances them. Lamentations 5's seeming loosening of the alphabetic acrostic structure along with a more careful overall design that results in a more complicated structure is expressed in the following ways: first, the lack of the alphabetic acrostic in Lamentations 5 calls attention to the mini-acrostic in Lam 5:19-20 which itself underlines the main themes running throughout the book; second, it highlights the significance of the position of letter ע by repeating it twice in Lam 5:17-18, with the first ע pointing to the פ-ע sequence found in Lamentations 2-4 and the second ע followed by an acrostic in Lam 5:19-22 that reads אלהך, "your God," which underlines the dialogic nature of the book with its focus on God once more; third, Lamentations 5 contains a hidden message by combining the techniques of acrostic-mesotic (first letters of half verses)-telestic (last letter of a verse) found at the beginning (vv. 1-3) and ending of the chapter (vv. 19-22) which reads "Zechariah the prophet proclaims that your God will be greatly exalted," thus injecting a concealed voice of hope into a book dominated by devastation and despair. All this evidence points then to the importance of chapter 5 which can rightly be considered as the climax of the book.

Lamentations 5 is thus a well-designed and highly complex chapter; it is an alphabetic poem even though it does not follow an alphabetic order. The significance of Lamentations 5 as the end of the book without an end affirms B. H. Smith's claim that a poem's closure or non-closure is crucial for the understanding of the whole poem.

Forgotten and Forsaken by God (Lam 5:19–20)

Significance of Remaining in Lament in Lamentations

Lamentations occupies a unique place within the biblical communal lament genre since the book remains in lament without moving into praise; it thus challenges the commonly held scholarly view that lament is invariably a transitional form leading to praise. In comparing Lamentations and a selected number of lament psalms (Psalms 12, 44, 88) regarding mood change, I have shown that mood change is not simply a one way street from lament to praise: the shift can also move from praise to lament or alternate between the two. Moreover, the so-called "sudden change of mood" that usually occurs in individual laments is not as evident in communal laments, and the book of Lamentations serves as a good example of remaining in lament without obvious change of mood. Thus, lament is not simply a transitional form that moves toward praise as the purported goal of prayer; rather, lament itself is an authentic form of prayer and has value in itself.

Remaining in lament does not exclude the presence of hope in Lamentations. Scholars often connect hope in Lamentations with admission of guilt based on Deuteronomistic theology according to which once the people admit their sin, God will forgive them and consequently bring about a better future. Hope in Lamentations, however, is not based on a cause and effect view of the God-human relationship, neither is hope limited to the words of hope found in Lam 3:24–31; rather, it is rooted in the courage and faithfulness of the community which continues to choose God when God seems absent and silent.

By comparing Lamentations with a selected number of communal laments (Isa 63:7—64:12; Jer 14:1—15:9; and Psalm 79) regarding admission of guilt, I have shown that biblical lamenting communities usually are not primarily concerned with possible reason for their suffering; rather, they are preoccupied with the question of when their suffering will come to an end. They are not searching for a rationale for their suffering, but its termination. The "why" questions in communal laments then are not really "why did this happen to us?," but are rather to be seen as "why has our suffering been so long?" The laments' admission of guilt is also to be seen in this context. Afflicted communities are willing to do anything to end their suffering. Even though they question justice behind their suffering and do not accept the readymade answer that their suffering is caused by sin, they admit their guilt before God in order to regain their unique love relationship with God, to persuade God to return to them, thus ending their affliction. The admission of guilt in Lamentations is one voice among a number of others that protest against God.

A Dialogic Sense of Truth in Lamentations

Lamentations holds onto God as its ultimate dialogic partner and features a dialogic sense of truth. The suffering community in Lamentations recognizes the validity of different perspectives and various interpretations of current events; all voices are presented, evaluated by others and listened to. The book of Lamentations thus affirms findings in psychological empirical research that the importance of lament is not cathartic, but rather social. Sharing deeply felt emotions does not alleviate one's emotional burden; rather, it strengthens personal and social bonds. By keeping the voice of God silent in the book, Lamentations also affirms the importance of the human partner in the relationship with God: when God seems silent and absent, it is the fidelity of the human individual and community that keeps the dialogue with God going and prevents the relationship with God from falling apart. This feature is also related to the presence of hope in Lamentations; the book's hope lies in its insisting on God as its dialogic partner even though God remains silent and in refusing to let God off the hook, in choosing to be faithful to a God who seems to have betrayed them.

POSSIBILITIES FOR FURTHER STUDY

This volume tackles various issues connected with Lamentations; the focus is mainly on Lamentations, i.e. a limited corpus for discussion. At the same time, this study also raises a number of possibilities for further research that extend beyond the book of Lamentations itself.

Significance and Meaning of Partial and Broken Acrostics

Contrary to a number of scholars' view that Lamentations 5 is less poetically beautiful and literally meaningful than the previous four chapters, this dissertation has shown that the lack of alphabetic acrostic in Lamentations 5 actually points to its more sophisticated poetic structure. The superficial "looseness" of the chapter directs attention to its hidden messages waiting to be discovered.

More broadly, the significance and meaning of the broken and partial acrostics in the Hebrew Bible would be worth exploring further, especially in their literary context and in connection with the overall message of the literary unit within which they are found. Scholarly efforts to emend these broken and partial acrostics (e.g., Nahum 1) have not yielded consensus; it may be better to consider their disruption and non-adherence to the order of the alphabet as intentional and to search for possible meanings behind this feature. Besides Nahum 1, there is another possible partial acrostic in Prov 29:22–27; there are also other poems that contain twenty-two lines but do not follow the order of the alphabet (e.g., Proverbs 2, 24; Psalms 33, 103) as well as those that follow the alphabetic order but with missing letters or change of patterns (e.g., Psalms 9/10, 25, 34). In these texts, the disruption of alphabetic order often seems to serve as a signpost for hidden meanings. It would be worthwhile then to explore the intentions behind the disruption of order, change of pattern, or partial "alphabetizing" in these poems, and their bearing on the meaning of their larger literary context. A study on this type might indeed expand our understanding of biblical acrostics.

Imagery and Iconography of Lament in the Ancient Near East

Lamentations is unfathomable suffering expressed in poetry—a form of art. There are images of suffering, lamenting and mourning in Lamentations conveyed in poetic words. This dissertation mainly focuses on the significance and value of lament in words. For the afflicted individuals and communities, words are essential for survival and moving forward toward a possible future. However, words are often inadequate, especially when used to express deeply felt emotions; words can be deceptive, when experiences are hard to put into words. Therefore, in the expression of suffering and lament, paintings and photographs may be more intuitive, direct and powerful. Consequently, studies on the imagery and iconography of suffering, mourning, and lament in the ancient Near East might greatly enhance our understanding of lament and its social effects.

The ancient world in general provided more space for mourning and lamenting than does the modern world; people in the ancient world also relied more on each other in times of trouble when fewer technologies were available. Studies on the ancient Near Eastern imagery and iconography of suffering and lamenting may provide a further angle on the social dimension of lament, and how ancient comforters interacted with the mourners and lamenters.

The Value of Lament and the Definition of Hope

Lament is a form of prayer that one utters in times of crisis and despair, often from situations of seeming hopelessness. The book of Lamentations is the darkest book in the Hebrew Bible, but not a book without hope. Lamenting and hoping do not contradict or negate each other. Words of hope are found in Lam 3:24–31, but hope in Lamentations is deeper than these words can express; rather, hope in Lamentations is rooted in the community's fidelity in times of crisis, in its authentic faith in an absent God.

The question of how hope should be defined has been constantly in my mind in the process of writing this book. Lament has often been misunderstood by both nonbiblicists as a mere complaint against God, and biblicists who view it as a (mere) transitional form leading into praise. Lament, however, is rooted in solid faith in God, which may not move toward praise, but lingers. Lament expresses situations of hopelessness, but lament is not without hope since the lamenter refuses to terminate the relationship with God. I find hope in Lamentations because the community chooses loyalty and fidelity to God when there are no apparent signs of God's favor or God's returning to them. Further work needs, however, be done in defining hope in connection with the intrinsic value of lament itself.

Since it is part of human nature to lament, lament serves as an open forum for people from various backgrounds, faith traditions, and cultures. Sharing experiences of suffering may forge solidarity among people with different ethnic and religious identities, and so be a source of hope for the human family. Research concerning these possibilities might profitably be undertaken in theology, spirituality and pastoral care, with biblical lament serving as a bridge among these disciplines.

Bibliography

PRIMARY SOURCES AND TRANSLATIONS

Alexander, Philip S., translator. *The Targum of Lamentations: Translated, with a Critical Introduction, Apparatus, and Notes*. ArBib 17B. Collegeville: Liturgical, 2007.
Baillet, M. et al. *Les "petites grottes" de Qumran*. 2 vols. DJD 3. Oxford: Clarendon, 1962.
Freedman, H., and Maurice Simon, editors. *Midrash Rabbah*. Vol. 7, *Deuteronmy*, translated by J. Rabbinowicz; *Lamentations*, translated by A. Cohen. London: Soncino, 1951.
Levine, Étan, editor. *The Aramaic Version of Lamentations*. New York: Hermon, 1976.
Neusner, Jacob, translator. *Lamentations Rabbah: An Analytical Translation*. Brown Judaic Studies 193. Atlanta: Scholars, 1989.
Schäfer, R., editor. *Biblia Hebraica Quinta 18 Megilloth: Lamentations*. Stuttgart: Deutsche Bibelgesellschaft, 2004.
Sperber, Alexander, editor. *The Bible in Aramaic*. Vol. 4A, *Targum to Lamentations*. Leiden: Brill, 1992.
Ulrich, Eugene et al. *Qumran Cave 4*. Vol. 11, *Psalms to Chronicles*. DJD 16. Oxford: Clarendon, 2000.
Ziegler, Joseph, editor. *Jeremias, Baruch, Threni, Epistula Jeremiae*. Septuaginta: Novum Testamentum Graecum 15. Göttingen: Vanderhoeck & Ruprecht, 1976.

SECONDARY SOURCES

Achenbach, Reinhard. "Zum Sitz im Leben mesopotamischer und altisraelitischer Klagegebete." *ZAW* 116 (2004) 364–78, 581–94.
Achtemeier, Elizabeth. *The Community and Message of Isaiah 56–66*. Minneapolis: Augsburg, 1982.
———. "Righteousness in the Old Testament." In *IDB* 4:80.
Aejmelaeus, Anneli. "Der Prophet als Klageliedsänger: Zur Funktion des Psalms Jes 63,7–64,11 in Tritojesaja." *ZAW* 107 (1995) 31–64.

Albertz, Rainer. *Israel in Exile: The History and Literature of the Sixth Century BCE*. Translated by David Green. SBLStBl 3. Leiden: Brill, 2004.

Albrektson, B. *Studies in the Text and Theology of the Book of Lamentations: With a Critical Edition of the Peshitta Text*. Studia Theologica Lundensia 21. Lund: Gleerup, 1963.

Allen, Leslie C. *Jeremiah: A Commentary*. OTL. Louisville: Westminster John Knox, 2008.

———. *A Liturgy of Grief: A Pastoral Commentary on Lamentations*. Grand Rapids: Baker Academic, 2011.

Alter, Robert. *The Book of Psalms: A Translation with Commentary*. New York: W. W. Norton, 2007.

Anderson, G. W. "נצח." In *TDOT* 9:529–33.

Assis, Elie. "The Alphabetic Acrostic in the Book of Lamentations." *CBQ* 69 (2007) 710–24.

———. "The Unity of the Book of Lamentations." *CBQ* 71 (2009) 306–29.

Babinowitz, Isaac. "The Qumran Hebrew Original of Ben Sira's Concluding Acrostic on Wisdom." *HUCA* 42 (1971) 173–84.

Bakhtin, M. M. *The Dialogic Imagination: Four Essays*. Edited by Michael Holquist. Translated by Caryl Emerson and Michael Holquist. University of Texas Press Slavic Series 1. Austin: University of Texas Press, 1981.

Balentine, Samuel E. "'I Was Ready to Be Sought Out by Those Who Did Not Ask.'" In *The Origins of Penitential Prayer in Second Temple Judaism*, edited by Mark J. Boda et al., 1–20. Seeking the Favor of God 1. SBLEJL 21. Atlanta: Society of Biblical Literature, 2006.

———. *Prayer in the Hebrew Bible: The Drama of Divine-Human Dialogue*. OBT. Minneapolis: Fortress, 1993.

Baloian, Bruce Edward. *Anger in the Old Testament*. American University Studies Series 7. Theology and Religion 99. New York: Lang, 1992.

Batto, Bernard F. "The Sleeping God: An Ancient Near Eastern Motif of Divine Sovereignty." *Bib* 68 (1987) 153–77.

Baumgartner, Walter. *Jeremiah's Poems of Lament*. HTIBS. Translated by David E. Orton. Sheffield: Almond, 1988.

Bautch, Richard. *Developments in Genre between Post-exilic Penitential Prayers and the Psalms of Communal Lament*. SBLABib 7. Atlanta: Society of Biblical Literature, 2003.

Begrich, Joachim. "Das Priesterliche Heilsorakel." *ZAW* 52 (1934) 81–92.

Bellinger, W. H. *Psalmody and Prophecy*. JSOTSup 27. Sheffield: JSOT Press, 1984.

Benun, Ronald. "Evil and the Disruption of Order: A Structural Analysis of the Acrostics in the First Book of Psalms." *JHS* 6 (2006) 2–30.

Bergant, Dianne. *Lamentations*. AOTC. Nashville: Abingdon, 2003.

Berges, Ulrich. "'Ich bin der Mann, der Elend sah' (Klgl 3, 1). Zionstheologie als Weg aus der Krise." *BZ* 44 (2000) 5–20.

———. *Klagelieder: Übersetzt und Ausgelegt*. HTKAT. Herder: Freiburg, 2002.

Bergler, Siegfried. "Threni V—Nur ein Alphabetisierendes Lied? Versuch einer Deutung." *VT* 27 (1977) 304–20.

———. "Review of Books—*Weep, O Daughter of Zion: A Study of the City-Lament Genre in the Hebrew Bible* by F. W. Dobbs-Allsopp." *JAOS* (1995) 319.

Berlin, Adele. *Lamentations: A Commentary*. OTL. Louisville: Westminster John Knox, 2002.

Bibliography

Berlin, Adele, and Marc Zvi Brettler, editors. *The Jewish Study Bible*. Oxford: Oxford University Press, 2004.

Beuken, Willem A. M., and Harm W. M. van Grol. "Jeremiah 14:1—15:9: A Situation of Distress and Its Hermeneutics, Unity and Diversity of Form—Dramatic Development." In *Le livre de Jérémie: Le Prophète et son milieu, les oracles et leur transmission*, edited by Pierre M. Bogaert, 297-342. BETL 54. Leuven: Peeters, 1981.

Bezzel, Hannes. "'Man of Constant Sorrow'—Rereading Jeremiah in Lamentations 3." In *Jeremiah (Dis)placed: New Directions in Writing/Reading Jeremiah*, edited by A. R. Pete Diamond and Louis Stulman, 253-65. LHBOTS 529. London: T. & T. Clark, 2011.

Blenkinsopp, Joseph. *Isaiah 56-66: A New Translation with Introduction and Commentary*. AB 19B. New York: Doubleday, 2003.

Boase, Elizabeth. "The Characterisation of God in Lamentations." *ABR* 56 (2008) 32-44.

———. *The Fulfillment of Doom? The Dialogic Interaction between the Book of Lamentations and the Pre-Exilic/Early Exilic Prophetic Literature*. LHBOTS 437. New York: T. & T. Clark, 2006.

Boda, Mark J. "From Complaint to Contrition: Peering through the Liturgical Window of Jer 14:1—15:4." *ZAW* 113 (2001) 186-97.

———. *Praying the Tradition: The Origin and Use of Tradition in Nehemiah 9*. BZAW 277. Berlin: de Gruyter, 1999.

———. "The Priceless Gain of Penitence: From Communal Lament to Penitential Prayer in the 'Exilic' Liturgy of Israel." *HBT* 25 (2003) 51-75.

Boda, Mark J., Daniel K. Falk, and Rodney A. Werline, editors. *Seeking the Favor of God, 1: The Origins of Penitential Prayer in Second Temple Judaism*. SBLEJL 21. Atlanta: Society of Biblical Literature, 2006.

Bonhoeffer, Dietrich. *Letters and Papers from Prison*. Edited by Eberhard Bethge. New York: Simon & Schuster, 1997.

Bosworth, David. "The Catharsis Canard and the Value of Lament." *CBQ* forthcoming.

Bouzard, Walter C. *We Have Heard with Our Ears, O God: Sources of the Communal Laments in the Psalms*. SBLDS 159. Atlanta: Scholars, 1997.

Brady, Christian M. M. "Lamentations." In *Theological Interpretation of the Old Testament: A Book-by-Book Survey*, edited Kevin J. Vanhoozer, 221-25. Grand Rapids: Baker Academic, 2008.

Brandscheidt, Renate. *Gotteszorn und Menschenleid: Die Gerichtsklage des leidenden Gerechten in Klgl 3*. TThSt 41. Trier: Paulinus, 1983.

Bright, John. *Jeremiah*. AB 21. New York: Doubleday, 1965.

Broyles, Craig C. *The Conflict of Faith and Experience in the Psalms: A Form-Critical and Theological Study*. JSOTSup 52. Sheffield: JSOT Press, 1989.

———. *Psalms*. NIBCOTS 11. Peabody, MA: Hendrickson, 1999.

Brueggemann, Walter. "Bounded by Obedience and Praise: The Psalms as Canon." *JSOT* 50 (1991) 63-92.

———. "A Convergence in Recent Old Testament Theology." *JSOT* 18 (1980) 2-18.

———. "The Costly Loss of Lament." *JSOT* 36 (1986) 57-71.

———. "The Formfulness of Grief." *Int* 33 (1977) 263-75.

———. "From Hurt to Joy, From Death to Life." *Int* 28 (1974) 3-19.

———. *In Man We Trust: The Neglected Side of Biblical Faith*. Atlanta: John Knox, 1972.

———. *The Message of the Psalms*. Minneapolis: Augsburg, 1984.

———. "Psalms and the Life of Faith: A Suggested Typology of Function." *JSOT* 17 (1980) 3–32.

———. *The Psalms and the Life of Faith*. Minneapolis: Fortress, 1995.

———. "Response to John Goldingay's 'The Dynamic Cycle of Praise and Prayer.'" *JSOT* 20 (1981) 141–42.

———. "A Shape for Old Testament Theology, I: Structural Legitimation." *CBQ* 47 (1985) 28–46.

———. "A Shape for Old Testament Theology, II: Embrace of Pain." *CBQ* 47 (1985) 395–415.

Brug, John F. "Biblical Acrostics and Their Relationship to Other Ancient Near Eastern Acrostics." In *The Bible in Light of Cuneiform Literature*, edited by William W. Hallo, et al., 283–304. Scripture in Context 3. Lewiston, NY: Mellen, 1990.

Buber, Martin. *I and Thou: A New Translation with a Prologue "I and You" and Notes by Walter Kaufmann*. New York: Schribner, 1970.

Castellino, G. R. "Observations on the Literary Structure of Some Passages in Jeremiah." *VT* 30 (1980) 398–408.

Childs, Brevard. *Introduction to the Old Testament as Scripture*. London: SCM, 1979.

Clements, R. E. *Jeremiah*. Interpretation. Atlanta: John Knox, 1988.

Clifford, Richard J. "Narrative and Lament in Isaiah 63:7–64:11." In *To Touch the Text: Biblical and Related Studies in Honor of Joseph A. Fitzmyer*, edited by Maurya P. Horgan and Paul J. Kobelski, 93–102. New York: Crossroad, 1989.

———. "Psalm 89: A Lament over the Davidic Ruler's Continued Failure." *HTR* 73 (1980) 35–47.

———. *Psalms 1–72*. AOTC. Nashville: Abingdon, 2002.

———. *Psalms 73–150*. AOTC. Nashville: Abingdon, 2003.

Cohn, Robert L. "Biblical Responses to Catastrophe." *Judaism* 35 (1986) 263–76.

Cooper, Alan. "The Message of Lamentations." *JANES* 28 (2001) 1–18.

Craigie, Peter C. *Psalms 1–50*. WBC 19. Waco, TX: Word, 1983.

Crow, Loren D. "The Rhetoric of Psalm 44." *ZAW* 104 (1992) 394–401.

Culley, Robert C. "Psalm 88 among the Complaints." In *Ascribe to the Lord: Biblical & Other Studies in Memory of Peter C. Craigie*, edited Lyle Eslinger & Glen Taylor, 289–302. JSOTSup 67. Sheffield: JSOT Press, 1988.

Dahood, M. *Psalms*. Vol. 1, *1–50*. AB 16. Garden City, NY: Doubleday, 1966.

Day, John. *Psalms*. OTG 14. Sheffield: JSOT Press, 1990.

Davidson, Robert. *The Courage to Doubt: Exploring an Old Testament Theme*. Philadelphia: Trinity, 1989.

DeClaissé-Walford, Nancy L. "Psalm 44: O God, Why Do You Hide Your Face?" *RevExp* 104 (2007) 745–59.

Dearman, Andrew. "Daughter Zion and Her Place in God's Household." *HBT* 31 (2009) 144–59.

Des Pres, Terrence. *The Survivor: An Anatomy of Life in the Death Camps*. New York: Oxford University Press, 1976.

De Vries, Simon J. "The Acrostic of Nahum in the Jerusalem Liturgy." *VT* 16 (1966) 476–81.

Dobbs-Allsopp, F. W. *Lamentations*. Interpretation. Louisville: John Knox, 2002.

———. "Tragedy, Tradition, and Theology in the Book of Lamentations." *JSOT* 74 (1997) 29–60.

———. *Weep, O Daughter of Zion: A Study of the City-Lament Genre in the Hebrew Bible*. BibOr 44. Rome: Editrice Pontificio Istituto Biblico, 1993.

Bibliography

Dobbs-Allsopp, F. W., and Tod Linafelt, "The Rape of Zion in Thr 1,10." *ZAW* 113 (2001) 77–81.

Dorsey, David A. "Lamentations: Communicating Meaning through Structure." *EvJ* 6 (1988) 83–90.

Duff, Nancy J. "Recovering Lamentation as a Practice in the Church." In *Lament: Reclaiming Practices in Pulpit, Pew, and Public Square*, edited by Sally A. Brown and Patrick D. Miller, 3–14. Louisville: Westminster John Knox, 2005.

Erbele-Küster, Dorothea. *Lesen als Akt des Betens: Eine Rezeptionsästhetik der Psalmen*. WMANT 87. Neukirchen-Vluyn: Neukirchener, 2001.

Exum, J. Cheryl. *Tragedy and Biblical Narrative: Arrows of the Almighty*. Cambridge: Cambridge University Press, 1992.

Farley, Wendy. *Tragic Vision and Divine Compassion: A Contemporary Theodicy*. Louisville: Westminster John Knox, 1990.

Ferris, Paul Wayne. *The Genre of Communal Lament in the Bible and the Ancient Near East*. SBLDS 127. Atlanta: Scholars, 1992.

Fischer, Irmtraud. *Wo ist Yahwe? Das Volksklagelied Jes 63,7–64,11 als Ausdruck des Ringens um eine gebrochene Beziehung*. SBB 19. Stuttgart: Katholisches Bibelwerk, 1989.

Floyd, Michael H. "Welcome Back, Daughter of Zion!" *CBQ* 70 (2008) 484–504.

Freedman, David Noel. "Acrostic and Metrics in Hebrew Poetry." *HTR* 65 (1972) 367–92.

———. "Acrostic Poems in the Hebrew Bible: Alphabetic and Otherwise." *CBQ* 48 (1986) 408–31.

Fretheim, Terence E. *The Suffering of God: An Old Testament Perspective*. OBT. Philadelphia: Fortress, 1984.

Frost, S. B. "Asseveration by Thanksgiving." *VT* 8 (1958) 380–90.

Gadd, C. J. "The Second Lamentation for Ur." In *Hebrew and Semitic Studies. Presented to Godfrey Rolles Driver*, edited by D. Winton Thomas and W. D. McHardy, 59–71. Oxford: Clarendon, 1963.

Gärtner, Judith. "'. . . Why Do You Let Us Stray from Your Paths . . .' (Isa 63:17): the Concept of Guilt in the Communal Lament Isa 63:7–64:11." In *The Origins of Penitential Prayer in Second Temple Judaism*, edited by Mark J. Boda et al., 145–63. Seeking the Favor of God 1. SBLEJL 21. Atlanta: Society of Biblical Literature, 2006.

Gerstenberger, Erhard S. *Psalms Part 2 and Lamentations*. FOTL 15. Grand Rapids: Eerdmans, 2001.

Goldenstein, Johannes. *Das Gebet der Gottesknechte: Jesaja 63,7–64,11 im Jesajabuch*. WMANT 92. Neukirchen-Vluyn: Neukirchner, 2001.

Goldingay, John. "The Dynamic Cycle of Praise and Prayer in the Psalms." *JSOT* 20 (1981) 85–90.

———. *Psalms*. Vol. 1, *1–41*. Grand Rapids: Baker Academic, 2006.

———. *Psalms*. Vol. 2, *42–89*. Grand Rapids: Baker Academic, 2007.

Gordis, Robert. "The Conclusion of the Book of Lamentations." *JBL* 93 (1974) 289–93.

———. *The Song of Songs and Lamentations: A Study, Modern Translation and Commentary*. New York: KTAV, 1974.

Gottwald, Norman K. "The Book of Lamentations Reconsidered." In *The Hebrew Bible in Its Social World and in Ours*, 165–73. SemSt 25. Atlanta: Scholars, 1993.

———. "Social Class and Ideology in Isaiah 40–55: An Eagletonian Reading." *Semeia* 59 (1992) 43–56.

———. *Studies in the Book of Lamentations*. SBT 14. London: SCM, 1962.

Gous, I. G. P. "A Survey of Research on the Book of Lamentations." *OTE* 5 (1992) 184–205.

Grant, Jamie A. "The Hermeneutics of Humanity: Reflections on the Human Origin of the Laments." In *A God of Faithfulness: Essays in Honour of J. Gordon McConville on His 60th Birthday*, edited by Jamie A. Grant et al., 182–202. LHBOTS 538. New York: T. & T. Clark, 2011.

Greenstein, Edward L. "The Book of Lamentations: Response to Destruction or Ritual of Rebuilding?" In *Religious Responses to Political Crisis in Jewish and Christian Tradition*, edited by Henning Graf Reventlow and Yair Hoffman, 52–71. LHBOTS 444. New York: T & T Clark, 2008.

Grossberg, Daniel. *Centripetal and Centrifugal Structures in Biblical Poetry*. SBLMS 39. Atlanta: Scholars, 1989.

———. "Form and Content and Their Correspondence." *HS* 41 (2000) 47–52.

Guest, Deryn. "Hiding behind the Naked Women in Lamentations: A Recriminative Response." *BibInt* 7 (1999) 413–48.

Guillaume, Philippe. "Lamentations 5: The Seventh Acrostic." *JHS* 9 (2009) 2–6.

Gwaltney W. C. "The Biblical Book of Lamentations in the Context of Near Eastern Lament Literature." In *More Essays on the Comparative Method*, edited by William W. Hallo et al., 191–211. Scripture in Context 2. Winona Lake, IN: Eisenbrauns, 1983.

Hanson, Paul D. *The Dawn of Apocalyptic: The Historical and Sociological Roots of Jewish Apocalyptic Eschatology*. Philadelphia: Fortress, 1979.

Hasan-Rokem, Galit. *Web of Life: Folklore and Midrash in Rabbinic Literature*. Stanford: Stanford University Press, 2000.

Hauerwas, Stanley. *God, Medicine, and Suffering*. Grand Rapids: Eerdmans, 1990.

Heater, Homer. "Structure and Meaning in Lamentations." *BSac* 149 (1992) 304–15.

Heim, Knut M. "The Personification of Jerusalem and the Drama of Her Bereavement in Lamentations." In *Zion, City of Our God*, edited by Richard S. Hess and Gordon J. Wenham, 129–69. Grand Rapids: Eerdmans, 1999.

Helberg, Jacob L. "Land in the Book of Lamentations." *ZAW* 102 (1990)372–85.

Heschel, Abraham Joshua. *The Insecurity of Freedom: Essays on Human Existence*. New York: Farrar, Straus & Giroux, 1966.

Heskett, Randall. *Reading the Book of Isaiah: Destruction and Lament in the Holy Cities*. New York: Palgrave Macmillan, 2011.

Hillers, Delbert R. *Lamentations: A New Translation with Introduction and Commentary*. AB /A. 2nd ed. Garden City, NY. Doubleday, 1992.

Hoppe, Leslie. "Vengeance and Forgiveness: The Two Faces of Psalm 79." In *Imagery and Imagination in Biblical Literature: Essays in Honor of Aloysius Fitzgerald, FSC*, edited by Lawrence Boadt and Mark S. Smith, 1–22. CBQMS 32. Washington, DC: Catholic Biblical Association of America, 2001.

Houk, Cornelius. "Multiple Poets in Lamentations." *JSOT* 30 (2005) 111–25.

House, Paul R. *Song of Songs. Lamentations*. WBC 23B. Nashville: Nelson, 2004.

Hossfeld, Frank-Lothar, and Erich Zenger. *Psalms 2: A Commentary on Psalms 51–100*. Translated by Linda M. Maloney. Hermeneia. Minneapolis: Fortress, 2005.

Humphreys, W. Lee. *The Tragic Vision and the Hebrew Tradition*. OBT 18. Philadelphia: Fortress, 1985.

Hunter, Jannie. *Faces of a Lamenting City: The Development and Coherence of the Book of Lamentations*. BEATAJ 39. Frankfurt: Lang, 1996.

Bibliography

Janowski, Bernd. *Konfliktgespräche mit Gott: Eine Anthropologie der Psalmen*. Neukirchen-Vluyn: Neukirchener, 2003.
Johnson, A. R. "The Psalms." In *The Old Testament and Modern Study*, edited by H. H. Rowley, 162–209. Oxford: Clarendon, 1952.
Johnson, Bo. "Form and Message in Lamentations." *ZAW* 97 (1985) 58–73.
Joüon, Paul. *A Grammar of Biblical Hebrew*. Translated by T. Muraoka. SubBi 27. Rome: Pontifical Biblical Institute, 2006.
Joyce, Paul M. "Lamentations and the Grief Process." *BibInt* 1 (1993) 304–20.
———. "Sitting Loose to History: Reading the Book of Lamentations without Primary Reference to Its Original Historical Setting." In *In Search of True Wisdom: Essays in Old Testament Interpretation in Honor of Ronald E. Clements*, edited by Edward Ball, 246–78. JSOTSup 300. Sheffield: Sheffield Academic, 1999.
Kaiser, Barbara B. "Poet as 'Female Impersonator': The Image of Daughter Zion as Speaker in Biblical Poems of Suffering." *JR* 67 (1987) 164–82.
Kalmanofsky, Amy. "Women of God: Maternal Grief and Religious Response in 1 Kings 17 and 2 Kings 4." *JSOT* 36 (2011) 55–74.
Kepnes, Steven. *The Text as Thou: Martin Buber's Dialogical Hermeneutics and Narrative Theology*. Bloomington: Indiana University Press, 1992.
Kim, Ee Kon. *The Rapid Change of Mood in the Lament Psalms: A Matrix for the Establishment of a Psalm Theology*. Seoul: Korea Theological Seminary, 1985.
Kitamori, Kazoh. *Theology of the Pain of God*. Richmond: John Knox, 1965.
Koch, Klaus. "חטא." In *TDOT* 4:309–19.
Kotze, G. R. "LXX Lamentations 4:7 and 4:14: Reflections on the Greek Renderings of the Difficult Hebrew Wordings of These Verses." *JSem* 20 (2011) 250–70.
Kramer, Samuel Noah. "Lamentation over the Destruction of Nippur." *ErIsr* 9 (1969) 89–93.
———. "The Weeping Goddess: Sumerian Prototypes of the *Mater Dolorosa*." *BA* 46 (1983) 69–80.
Krašovec, Jože. "The Source of Hope in the Book of Lamentations." *VT* 42 (1992) 223–33.
Labahn, Antje. "Fire from Above: Metaphors and Images of God's Actions in Lamentations 2:1–9." *JSOT* 31 (2006) 239–56.
———. "Metaphor and Intertexuality: 'Daughter of Zion' as a Test Case." *SJOT* 17 (2003) 49–67.
Lanahan, William F. "The Speaking Voice in the Book of Lamentations." *JBL* 93 (1974) 41–49.
Lee, Nancy C. *The Singers of Lamentations: Cities under Siege, from Ur to Jerusalem to Sarajevo*. BIS 60. Leiden: Brill, 2002.
———, and Carleen Mandolfo, editors. *Lamentations in Ancient and Contemporary Cultural Context*. Symposium Series 43. Atlanta: Society of Biblical Literature, 2008.
Lee, Sung-Hun. "Lament and the Joy of Salvation in the Lament Psalms." In *The Book of Psalms: Composition and Reception*, edited by Peter W. Flint and Patrick D. Miller, 224–47. VTSup 99. Formation and Interpretation of Old Testament Literature 4 Leiden: Brill, 2005.
Landy, Francis. "Lamentations." In *The Literary Guide to the Bible*, edited by Robert Alter and Frank Kermode, 329–34. Cambridge, MA: Belknap, 1987.
Linafelt, Tod. "Margins of Lamentations, Or, The Unbearable Whiteness of Reading." In *Reading Bibles, Writing Bodies: Identity and the Book*, edited by Timothy K. Beal and David M. Gunn, 219–31. Biblical Limits. London: Routledge, 1997.

———. "The Refusal of a Conclusion in the Book of Lamentations." *JBL* 120 (2001) 340–43.

———. *Surviving Lamentations: Catastrophe, Lament, and Protest in the Afterlife of a Biblical Book*. Chicago: University of Chicago Press, 2000.

———. "Surviving Lamentations (One More Time)." In *Lamentations in Ancient and Contemporary Cultural Contexts*, edited by Nancy C. Lee and Carleen Mandolfo, 57–63. SBLSymS 43. Atlanta: Society of Biblical Literature, 2008.

Lohfink, N. "Enthielten die im Alten Testament bezeugten Klageriten eine Phase des Schweigens?" *VT* 12 (1962) 260–77.

Löhr, Max. "Der Sprachgebrauch des Buches der Klagelieder." *ZAW* 14 (1894) 31–50.

Maier, Christl M. *Daughter Zion, Mother Zion: Gender, Space, and the Sacred in Ancient Israel*. Minneapolis: Fortress, 2008.

Maloney, Les D. "Intertextual Links: Part of the Poetic Artistry within the Book I Acrostic Psalms." *ResQ* 49 (2007) 11–21.

Mandolfo, Carleen R. *Daughter Zion Talks Back to the Prophets: A Dialogic Theology of the Book of Lamentations*. SemeiaSt 58. Atlanta: SBL, 2007.

———. "Psalm 88 and the Holocaust: Lament in Search of a Divine Response." *BibInt* 15 (2007) 151–70.

Marcus, David. "Non-Recurring Doublets in the Book of Lamentations." *HAR* 10 (1986) 177–95.

Markschies, Christoph. "Ich aber vertraue auf dich!—Vertrauenäußerungen als Grundmotiv in den Klageliedern des einzelnen." *ZAW* 103 (1991) 386-98.

Mays, James Luther. *Psalms*. Interpretation. Louisville: John Knox, 1994.

McCann, J. Clinton. *Psalms*. In *The New Interpreter's Bible*, edited by Leander E. Keck et al., 4:641–1280. Nashville: Abingdon, 1996.

McDaniel, Thomas F. "The Alleged Sumerian Influence upon Lamentations." *VT* 18 (1968) 198–209.

———. "Philological Studies in Lamentations, I." *Bib* 49 (1968) 27–53.

———. "Philological Studies in Lamentations, II." *Bib* 49 (1968) 199–220.

Michalowski, Piotr. *The Lamentation over the Destruction of Sumer and Ur*. Mesopotamean Civilizations 1. Winona Lake, IN: Eisenbrauns, 1989.

Middlemas, Jill. "Did Second Isaiah Write Lamentations III?" *VT* 56 (2006) 505–25.

———. *The Templeless Age: An Introduction to the History, Literature, and Theology of the "Exile."* Louisville: Westminster John Knox, 2007.

———. *The Troubles of Templeless Judah*. Oxford Theological Monographs. New York: Oxford University Press, 2005.

———. "The Violent Storm in Lamentations." *JSOT* 29 (2004) 81–97.

Miller, Charles William. "The Book of Lamentations in Recent Research." *CBR* 1 (2002) 9–29.

———. "Reading Voices: Personification, Dialogism, and the Reader of Lamentations 1." *BibInt* 9 (2001) 393–408.

Miller, Patrick D. "Heaven's Prisoners: The Lament as Christian Prayer." In *Lament: Reclaiming Practices in Pulpit, Pew, and Public Square*, edited by Sally A. Brown and Patrick D. Miller, 15–26. Louisville: Westminster John Knox, 2005.

Mintz, Alan. *Ḥurban: Responses to Catastrophe in Hebrew Literature*. New York: Columbia University Press, 1984.

———. "The Rhetoric of Lamentations and the Representation of Catastrophe." *Prooftexts* 2 (1982) 1–17.

Miskotte, Kornelis H. *When the Gods Are Silent*. Translated by John W. Doberstein. New York: Harper & Row, 1967.
Moore, Michael B. "Human Suffering in Lamentations." *RB* 90 (1983) 535-55.
Morse, Benjamin. "The Lamentations Project: Biblical Mourning through Modern Montage." *JSOT* 28 (2003) 113-27.
Morson, C. S., and C. Emerson. *Mikhail Bakhtin: Creation of a Prosaics*. Stanford: Stanford University Press, 1990.
Mowinckel, Sigmund. *The Psalms in Israel's Worship*. Translated by D. R. Ap-Thomas. 1962. Reprinted, Biblical Resource Series. Grand Rapids: Eerdmans, 2004.
Mrozek, Andrzej, and Silvano Votto. "The Motif of the Sleeping Divinity." *Bib* 80 (1999) 415-19.
Murphy. Roland E. *The Psalms Are Yours*. New York: Paulist, 1993.
Neusner, Jacob. *Israel after Calamity: The Book of Lamentations*. The Bible of Judaism Library. Valley Forge, PA: Trinity, 1995.
Newsom, Carol A. "Bakhtin, the Bible, and Dialogic Truth." *JR* 76 (1996) 290-306.
―――. *The Book of Job: A Context of Moral Imagination*. Oxford: Oxford University Press, 2003.
―――. "The Book of Job as Polyphonic Text." *JSOT* 97 (2002) 87-108.
―――. "Response to Norman K. Gottwald, 'Social Class and Ideology in Isaiah 40-55.'" *Semeia* 59 (1992) 73-78.
Nguyen, Kim Lan T. "Lady Zion and the Man: The Use of Personae in the Book of Lamentations." PhD diss., University of Wisconsin-Madison, 2010.
Niskanen, Paul. "Yhwh as Father, Redeemer, and Potter in Isaiah 63:7—64:11." *CBQ* 68 (2006) 397-407.
Nowell, Irene. "Psalm 88: A Lesson in Lament." In *Imagery and Imagination in Biblical Literature: Essays in Honor of Aloysius Fitzgerald, FSC*, edited by Lawrence Boadt and Mark S. Smith, 105-18. CBQMS 32. Washington, DC: Catholic Biblical Association of America, 2001.
O'Connor, Kathleen M. "The Book of Lamentations: Introduction, Commentary, and Reflections." In *The New Interpreter's Bible*, edited by Leander E. Keck et al., 6:1013-72. Nashville: Abingdon, 1994.
―――. *Lamentations and the Tears of the World*. Maryknoll, NY: Orbis, 2006.
―――. "Speak Tenderly to Jerusalem: Second Isaiah's Reception and Use of Daughter Zion." *PSB* 20 (1999) 281-94.
Parry, Robin A. *Lamentations*. Two Horizons Old Testament Commentary. Grand Rapids: Eerdmans, 2010.
Pham, Xuan Huong Thi. *Mourning in the Ancient Near East and the Hebrew Bible*. JSOTSup 302. Sheffield: Sheffield Academic, 1999.
Plöger, Otto. "Die Klagelieder." In *Die Fünf Megilloth*, 127-64. HAT 18. Tübingen: Mohr/Siebeck, 1969.
Preuss, H. D. "שׁוּב." In *TDOT* 14:671-77.
Prouser, Joseph H. "Darkness on the Face of the Deep: Lamentations as Midrash on Creation." *Conservative Judaism* 56 (2004) 37-42.
Provan, Iain W. *Lamentations*. NCBC. Grand Rapids: Eerdmans, 1991.
―――. "Past, Present and Future in Lamentations III 52-66: The Case for a Precative Perfect Re-examined." *VT* 41 (1991) 164-75.
Reimer, David J. "Good Grief?: A Psychological Reading of Lamentations." *ZAW* 114 (2002) 542-59.

Renkema, Johan. *Lamentations*. Historical Commentary on the Old Testament. Leuven: Peeters, 1998.

———. "The Literary Structure of Lamentations." In *The Structural Analysis of Biblical and Canaanite Poetry*, edited by W. van der Meer and J. C. de Moor, 294–396. JSOTSup 74. Sheffield: JSOT Press, 1988.

———. "The Meaning of the Parallel Acrostics in Lamentations." *VT* 45 (1995) 379–83.

———. "Theodicy in Lamentations?" In *Theodicy in the World of the Bible*, edited by Atti Laato and Johannes C. de Moor, 410–28. Leiden: Brill, 2003.

Renz, Thomas. "A Perfectly Broken Acrostic in Nahum 1?" *JHS* (2009) 1–26.

Rimé, Bernard. "Mental Rumination, Social Sharing, and the Recovery from Emotional Exposure." In *Emotion, Disclosure & Health*, edited by James W. Pennebaker, 271–91. Washington, DC: American Psychological Association, 1995.

———, et al. "Emotion, Verbal Expression, and the Social Sharing of Emotion." In *The Verbal Communication of Emotions: Interdisciplinary Perspectives*, edited by Susan R. Fussell, 185–208. Mahwah, NJ: Erlbaum, 2002.

——— et al. "The Social Sharing of Emotion: Illusory and Real Benefits of Talking about Emotional Experiences." In *Emotional Expression and Health: Advances in Theory, Assessment, and Clinical Applications*, edited by Ivan Nykliček et al., 27–41.Hove, East Sussex UK: Brunner-Routledge, 2004.

Rittner, Carol. "An Interview with Elie Wiesel." *America* 159 (1988) 397–401.

Rom-Shiloni, Dalit. "Psalm 44: The Powers of Protest." *CBQ* 70 (2008) 683–98.

Rosenfeld, Azriel. "Aqrostikon be-ʾekhah pereq 5." *Sinai* 110 (1992) יג.

Rudolph, Wilhelm. *Das Buch Ruth. Das Hohe Lied. Die Klagelieder*. 187–263. KAT. Gütersloh: Gütersloher, 1962.

Ryan, Robin. *God and the Mystery of Human Suffering: A Theological Conversation across the Ages*. New York: Paulist, 2011.

Saebø, Magne. "Who is 'the Man' in Lamentations? A Fresh Approach to the Interpretation of the Book of Lamentations." In *Understanding Poets and Prophets: Essays in Honour of George Wishart Anderson*, edited by A. Graeme Auld, 294–306. JSOTSup 152. Sheffield: JSOT Press, 1993.

Salters, Robert B. *A Critical and Exegetical Commentary on Lamentations*. ICC. London: T. & T. Clark, 2010.

———. "Searching for Pattern in Lamentations." *OTE* 11 (1998) 93–104.

———. "Structure and Implication in Lamentations 1." *SJOT* 14 (2000) 293–300.

———. "The Text of Lam. II 9A." *VT* 54 (2004) 273–76.

——— "The Unity of Lamentations." *IBS* 23 (2001) 102–10.

———. "Using Rashi, Ibn Ezra and Joseph Kara on Lamentations." *JNSL* 25 (1999) 201–13.

Schramm, Gene M. "Poetic Patterning in Biblical Hebrew." In *Michigan Oriental Studies in Honor of G. G. Cameron*, edited by L. Orlin et al., 167–91. Ann Arbor: University of Michigan Department of Near Eastern Studies, 1976.

Seebass, H. "פשע." In *TDOT* 12:133–51.

Seidman, Naomi. "Burning the Book of Lamentations." In *Out of the Garden: Women Writers on the Bible*, edited by Christina Buchmann and Celina Spiegel, 278–88. New York: Fawcett Columbine, 1992.

Seow, C. L. "A Textual Note on Lamentations 1:20." *CBQ* 47 (1985) 416–19.

Sered, Susan Starr. "Mother Love, Child Death and Religious Innovation: A Feminist Perspective." *JFSR* 12 (1996) 5–23.

Bibliography

Shea, William H. "The *qinah* Structure of the Book of Lamentations." *Bib* 60 (1979) 103-7.
Slavitt, David R. *The Book of Lamentations: A Meditation and Translation*. Baltimore: Johns Hopkins University Press, 2001.
Smith, Barbara Herrnstein. *Poetic Closure: A Study of How Poems End*. Chicago: University of Chicago Press, 1968.
Soelle, Dorothee. *Suffering*. Translated by Everett R. Kalin. Phiadelphia: Fortress, 1975.
Soll, William Michael. "Acrostic." In *ABD* 1:58-60.
———. "Babylonian and Biblical Acrostics." *Bib* 69 (1988) 305-22.
Sommer, Benjamin D. *A Prophet Reads Scripture: Allusions in Isaiah 40-66*. Contraversions: Jews and Other Differences. Stanford: Stanford University Press, 1998.
Spronk, Klaas. "Acrostics in the Book of Nahum." *ZAW* 110 (1998) 209-22.
Stern, David. "*Imitatio Hominis*: Anthropomorphism and the Character(s) of God in Rab-binic Literature." *Prooftexts* 12 (1992) 151-74.
———. "Two Narratives about God." In *Rabbinic Fantasies: Imaginative Narratives from Classical Hebrew Literature*, edited by David Stern and Mark Jay Mirsky, 47-57. Philadelphia: Jewish Publication Society, 1990.
Stern, Elsie R. "Lamentations in Jewish Liturgy." In *Great Is Thy Faithfulness? Reading Lamentations as Sacred Scripture*, edited by Robin A. Parry and Heath A. Thomas, 88-91. Eugene, OR: Pickwick Publications, 2011.
Stinespring, W. F. "No Daughter of Zion: A Study of the Appositional Genitive in Hebrew Grammar." *Encounter* 26 (1965) 133-41.
Stokes, Ryan E. "I, Yhwh, Have Not Changed? Reconsidering the Translation of Malachi 3:6; Lamentations 4:1; and Proverbs 24:21-22." *CBQ* 70 (2008) 264-76.
Strugnell, John, and Hanan Eshel. "Psalms 9 and 10 and the Order of the Alphabet." *BibRev* 17 (2001) 41-44.
Tate, Marvin E. *Psalms 51-100*. WBC 20. Dallas: Word, 1990.
Terrien, Samuel. *The Psalms: Strophic Structure and Theological Commentary*. Eerdmans Critical Commentary. Grand Rapids: Eerdmans, 2003.
Thomas, Heath. "'I Will Hope in Him': Theology and Hope in Lamentations." In *A God of Faithfulness: Essays in Honour of J. Gordon McConville on His 60th Birthday*, ed. Jamie A. Grant et al., 203-21. LHBOTS 538. London: T. & T. Clark, 2011.
Thompson, J. A. "Israel's 'Lovers.'" *VT* 27 (1977) 475-81.
Treves, Marco. "Two Acrostic Psalms." *VT* 15 (1965) 81-90.
Tull, Patricia K. *Remember the Former Things: The Recollection of Previous Texts in Second Isaiah*. SBLDS 161. Atlanta: Scholars, 1997.
Van Hecke, Pierre J. P. "Lamentations 3,1-6: An Anti-Psalm 23." *SJOT* 16 (2002) 264-82.
Villanueva, Federico G. *The "Uncertainty of a Hearing": A Study of the Sudden Change of Mood in the Psalms of Lament*. VTSup 121. Leiden: Brill, 2008.
Waltke, Bruce K., and Michael O'Connor. *An Introduction to Biblical Hebrew Syntax*. Winona Lake, IN: Eisenbrauns, 1982.
Walton, John H. *Ancient Israelite Literature in Its Cultural Context: A Survey of Parallels between Biblical and Ancient Near Eastern Texts*. Grand Rapids: Zondervan, 1989.
Watson, Wilfred G. E. *Classical Hebrew Poetry: A Guide to Its Techniques*. JSOTSup 26. Sheffield: JSOT Press, 1984.
Weil, Simone. *Intimations of Christianity among the Ancient Greeks*. Collected and Translated from the French by Elisabeth Chase Geissbuhler. Boston: Beacon, 1957.
———. *Waiting for God*. Translated by Emma Craufurd. New York: Putnam, 1951.

Weiser, Artur. *The Psalms: A Commentary*. Translated by Herbert Hartwell. OTL. London: SCM, 1962.

Werline, Rodney Alan. *Penitential Prayer in Second Temple Judaism: The Development of a Religious Institution*. SBLEJL 13. Atlanta: Scholars, 1998.

Westermann, Claus. *Elements of Old Testament Theology*. Translated by Douglas W. Stott. Atlanta: John Knox, 1982.

———. *Lamentations: Issues and Interpretation*. Translated by Charles Muenchow. Minneapolis: Fortress, 1994.

———. *Praise and Lament in the Psalms*. Translated by Keith R. Crim and Richard N. Soulen. Atlanta: John Knox, 1981.

———. "The Role of Lament in the Theology of the Old Testament." *Int* 28 (1974) 20–38.

Wevers, J. W. "A Study in the Form Criticism of Individual Complaint Psalms." *VT* 6 (1956) 80–96.

Whybray, R. N. *Isaiah 40–66*. NCBC. Grand Rapids: Eerdmans, 1975.

Wiesel, Elie. *All Rivers Run to the Sea: Memoirs*. New York: Knopf, 1996.

———. *Messengers of God: Biblical Portraits and Legends*. Translated by Marion Wiesel. New York: Random House, 1976.

———. *Night*. Translated by Stella Rodway. New York: Bantam, 1982.

———. *The Trial of God (As It Was Held on February 25, 1649, in Shamgorod)*. Translated by Marion Wiesel. New York: Schocken, 1979.

Wiesmann, Hermann. *Die Klagelieder: übersetzt und erklärt*. Frankfurt: Philosophisch-theologische Hochschule Sankt Georgen, 1954.

Wilkins, Lauress L. *The Book of Lamentations and the Social World of Judah in the Neo-Babylonina Era*. Biblical Intersections 6. Piscatawy, NJ: Gorgias, 2010.

Williamson, H. G. M. "Isaiah 63:7–64:11: Exilic Lament or Post-Exilic Protest?" *ZAW* 102 (1990) 48–58.

———. "Reading Lament Psalms Backwards." In *A God So Near: Essays on Old Testament Theology in Honor of Patrick D. Miller*, edited by Brent A. Strawn and Nancy R. Bowen, 3–15. Winona Lake, IN: Eisenbrauns, 2003.

Willey, Patricia Tull. "The Servant of YHWH and Daughter of Zion: Alternating Visions of YHWH's Community." In *Society of Biblical Literature 1995 Seminar Papers*, edited by E. H. Lovering, 267–303. SBLSP. Atlanta: Scholars, 1995.

Wolterstorff, Nicholas. *Lament for a Son*. Grand Rapids: Eerdmans, 1987.

Zenger, Erich. *A God of Vengeance?: Understanding the Psalms of Divine Wrath*. Translated by Linda M. Maloncy. Louisville. Westminster John Knox, 1996.

www.ingramcontent.com/pod-product-compliance
Lightning Source LLC
Chambersburg PA
CBHW070317230426
43663CB00011B/2162